GIUSEPPE DE SANTIS AND POSTWAR ITALIAN CINEMA

One of the founding fathers of the Neorealist movement and a communist dedicated to populist filmmaking, Giuseppe De Santis (b. 1917) has been a significant force in Italian cinema. In spite of his crucial contribution De Santis has received little critical recognition and his work has been largely excluded from the canon of traditional cinematic teaching. In this first book-length study of De Santis, Antonio Vitti explores the filmmaker's life and work, and addresses why he has been marginalized as a result of the politics of critical reception in Italian cinema and within the academy.

Through critical analysis of such films as *Riso amaro* (Bitter Rice), *Non c'è pace tra gli ulivi* (No Peace among the Olives), and *Cesta Duga Godinu Dana* (The One-Year-Long Road), Vitti offers an informative profile of a director who refused to compromise what were often unpopular political and aesthetic principles. De Santis emerged as a strong opponent of government censorship in Fascist Italy and strove throughout his career to remain faithful to his political objectives: to create a genuine popular narrative voice, and to offer, through filmmaking, a form of entertainment for the masses and a means of promoting social and political change. At the same time, possessed of considerable technical abilities and a passion for formalized beauty and sensuality, De Santis resisted the rigid rules for socio-realistic representation dictated by the Soviet Union. He conformed neither to the mainstream nor to the leftist critical expectations of his day. He anticipated, in his own critical approach, the direction of contemporary film theory, and focused on the role of the medium itself as a means of mass communication and a repository of collective imagination.

Vitti draws on his extensive personal interviews with De Santis as well as on the latter's previously unpublished writings. This volume captures the intelligence, passion, aesthetic flair, and occasionally fiery temperament of this important filmmaker.

A foreword by Ben Lawton provides additional context for the appreciation of De Santis's life and work.

(Toronto Italian Studies)

ANTONIO VITTI is an associate professor in the Department of Romance Languages at Wake Forest University.

BEN LAWTON is chair of Italian Studies in the Department of Foreign Languages and Literatures at Purdue University.

ANTONIO VITTI

Giuseppe De Santis and Postwar Italian Cinema

UNIVERSITY OF TORONTO PRESS
Toronto Buffalo London

© University of Toronto Press Incorporated 1996
Toronto Buffalo London
Printed in Canada

ISBN 0-8020-0775-9 (cloth)
ISBN 0-8020-7141-4 (paper)

Printed on acid-free paper

Toronto Italian Studies

Canadian Cataloguing in Publication Data

Vitti, Antonio
Giuseppe De Santis and postwar Italian cinema

(Toronto Italian studies)
Includes bibliographical references and index.
ISBN 0-8020-0775-9 (bound) ISBN 0-8020-7141-4 (pbk.)

I. De Santis, Giuseppe, 1917– . 2. Motion
pictures – Italy – History. 3. Realism in
motion pictures. 4. Motion picture producers
and directors – Italy – Biography. I. Title.
II. Series.

PN1998.3.D47V5 1996 791.43'0233'092 C95-932249-3

All photographs are courtesy of Giuseppe De Santis.

University of Toronto Press acknowledges the financial
assistance to its publishing program of the Canada
Council and the Ontario Arts Council.

To my parents,
Magno and Maria Luisa Vitti

Contents

Part III: The Working Classes Declassed

Foreword

Giuseppe De Santis: An Introduction

Sometime in spring 1989 I received a call from Antonio Vitti, the author of this volume. He told me he had met Giuseppe De Santis and wanted to arrange the Italian film director's first North American tour, and asked if I would be interested in participating. More specifically, he wanted to know if Purdue University would be interested in co-sponsoring the trip. My answer, qualified by the usual fiscal constraints, was immediate and enthusiastic. De Santis is the director of *Riso amaro* (1948; Bitter Rice), a film which, during my childhood in Italy, had conjured up powerful and tantalizing erotic images, even though (or perhaps precisely because) I had never been allowed to see it. Much later, in the early 1970s, when I began teaching Italian cinema at UCLA, I eventually saw the film and discovered a work which, under the patina of seeming commercial eroticism, and contrary to the general critical consensus, was subversive, both on the level of the narrative and in its very filmic structure. Needless to say, I very much wanted to meet De Santis and hear what he had to say about a film which I thought had been completely misunderstood by critics on both sides of the Atlantic. Thanks to Vitti's persistence, De Santis's tour became a reality. The filmmaker agreed to include in his heavy lecture schedule the keynote address at the first Purdue University Conference on Romance Languages, Literatures, and Film (PURL) in October 1989. Thus it was that, on a freezing, stormy October night, my wife, Lorraine, and I were at the Purdue University airport, awaiting – with somewhat mixed feelings – the arrival of Giuseppe De Santis and his wife, Gordana, on the first stop of their first American tour. My feelings were mixed because, while I was very interested in what De Santis might have to say, I had had rather frustrating experiences with other filmmakers. Almost invariably

I had found that they were reluctant to discuss their own works in anything beyond the most superficial terms. I was also concerned because, as a result of a last-minute change of plans, the De Santises were arriving one day early, and there was, quite literally, no room at any local inn. Finally, I was somewhat uneasy because, while I had seen photographs of De Santis taken in 1948 as he directed *Riso amaro*, I had no idea what he looked like in 1989. And so we waited. When they did not arrive on the scheduled flight, we decided to stay until the next and last flight of that evening arrived. As the hours slowly passed, I began to reflect on what the participants in our conference might know about De Santis and his oeuvre.

From past experience, I had a fairly strong feeling that, if I approached faculty members at the most prestigious film schools in North America and asked them who Giuseppe De Santis was, I would receive blank stares in response. At best, I surmised, someone might remember that he was the director of *Riso amaro*, the film that had introduced to American cinema screens the so-called *maggiorate fisiche*, those preternaturally endowed actresses who contributed significantly to the international financial success of 'Hollywood on the Tiber.' In fact, I had a sneaking suspicion that, outside of those participating in the sessions on Italian film, I would not have found much better responses, even among the Italianists who would be attending our conference. I asked myself how many of his films anyone could name, how many knew how or why at the young age of thirty-two he had been given the opportunity to direct a relatively big-budget film such as *Riso amaro*, how many knew why he had not been able to (he would say, why he had not been allowed to) make any films since *Un apprezzato professionista di sicuro avvenire* (A Respected Professional with a Bright Future) in 1972.[1] In short, given that, unlike the canonical Neorealist directors (Roberto Rossellini, Vittorio De Sica and Cesare Zavattini, Luchino Visconti, etc.), he is hardly a household name in North America, I asked myself: how could they possibly know who Giuseppe De Santis is, and what he did that warranted a college lecture tour and this book?

The information available on De Santis is limited and contradictory, particularly that published in English. We do know that he was born in Fondi, a small town in the rural area south of Rome known as Ciociaria, on 11 February 1917. According to one official history, he received a degree in jurisprudence.[2] De Santis himself states that he studied humanities and then went to the Italian film school Centro Sperimentale di Cinematografia to study directing. He became an important contributor to the most important pre–Second World War Italian film journal, *Cinema*, along with, among others, Michelangelo Antonioni, Luchino Visconti, Umberto Barbaro, Gianni Puccini, and Cesare Zavattini, most of whom would become far more famous than De Santis as directors or critics. His role as writer, critic, and theoretician of Neorealism is mentioned only very much *en passant* in the major English-language histories of Italian cinema.[3] Millicent Marcus does dedicate three pages to this aspect of his career in her important reappraisal of Neorealism,[4] but that's the extent of what is available in English. As for De Santis the filmmaker, while everyone interested in Italian film is acquainted with Luchino Visconti's *Ossessione* (1942; Obsession), not many know that De Santis's first important film-production experiences were his collaboration on the script of this film and his work as its second-unit director. Very few people in North America have seen De Santis's first film, *Caccia tragica* (1947; Tragic Pursuit). And yet this film was very well received, critically and commercially. The film won, among others, first prize for the best Italian film at the 1947 Venice International Film Festival and a 'special mention' at the Karlovy Vary Festival. To my knowledge, this film was never released in the United States. Although I have been teaching Italian film for twenty years, I saw it for the first time when De Santis brought a print to this country during his 1989 tour. *Riso amaro*, De Santis's most famous work, did receive wide international distribution. It was the fifth most profitable film released in Italy in 1949 and was nominated for an Oscar for best original story in 1950. And yet the film was roundly panned by critics on the Right and the Left for its alleged heterodoxical approach to Neorealism, which juxtaposed committed political subject-matter, flamboyant eroticism, and a baroque, Hollywood-inspired style. These and analogous critiques plagued his subsequent works, and eventually, notwithstanding the general continuing profitability of his films, De Santis, who had come to be known as a 'difficult director' because of his unwillingness to compromise his vision, was no longer able to find backers for his projects.

Why did this happen to a major theoretician of Neorealism, to a filmmaker who had directed commercially successful, award-winning films? The search for answers to these questions began in earnest when Antonio Vitti met De Santis in 1985. As Vitti's research progressed, he began to pursue passionately a question which a few others had begun to ask in Italy: why the long silence? However, as my wife and I waited for the De Santises at the Purdue airport, the answers to this question were far in the future.

Finally, the De Santises arrived. We had no trouble identifying them. The distinguished-looking gentleman and the lovely woman, both dressed in elegant Italian clothes, stood out immediately among the blue jean– and parka-clad passengers crawling out of the small commuter airplane. We were delighted that they had arrived safely, but somewhat apprehensive. How would the allegedly 'difficult' filmmaker and his movie-star wife react to the news that, because of their last-minute change in plans, we had not been able to secure a hotel room for them for this extra night? Even more to the point, how would they feel about our alternative plan, that they spend one night at our home? We need not have worried. By the following morning, not only were we on first-name basis, but 'Peppe' announced that he and Gordana liked our hospitality so much that they had decided to spend their week's stay in Lafayette at our house. At first the prospect seemed a bit daunting. It was mid-semester, and we were trying to run our first major conference. How were we going to also entertain a couple of 'big shots' from the world of the cinema? The reality turned out to be absolutely delightful. The De Santises were cordial, cheerful, undemanding, unobtrusive, helpful – Gordana even prepared dinner on a couple of occasions when the rest of us were tied up with the conference.[5] Most important, from our perspective, however, they were endless sources of information.[6]

From the moment we met, it was clear that De Santis is an exceptionally intelligent, charming, cultured, creative person. He is an organic intellectual of sorts.[7] He is also a person who, unlike so many other filmmakers, not only has obviously thought about his work and his craft at length, but is willing and delighted to share his views, his experiences, and his projects and dreams with anyone who will listen. This, in any case, was the impression I had of De Santis in person. I had, of course, already 'met' De Santis through his work, at least to a limited degree. As I stated above, my first experience of *Riso amaro* was a complete surprise. Given what I had read about it, in 1972 I decided to screen it in a course on Italian Neorealism as an example of the decadence of that 'movement.' As a result I experienced the film before the publication of *Il neorealismo cinematografico italiano* (1975), the important re-evaluation of Neorealism edited by Lino Miccichè, and well before the publication of the various books by Alberto Farassino (*Giuseppe De Santis*, 1978), Stefano Masi (*De Santis*, 1981), and Antonio Parisi (*Il cinema di Giuseppe De Santis: Tra passione e ideologia*, 1983), among others. As a result, in 1972 I had begun to say, teach, and write things about *Riso amaro* which were totally at odds with everything I had read prior to that time.[8] And so, I was, as I think anyone would be, looking forward, albeit with some trepidation, to the prospect of testing my almost fifteen-year-old theses on the director himself.

Much to my surprise, unlike so many directors who refuse to discuss their work or who scoff at academic criticism, De Santis not only brought up the subject of my essay almost immediately but actually had a copy of it in his possession. Honesty compels me to admit that he had copies of virtually everything ever written about him in his various suitcases. Certainly, he had all the major books and essays, and everything was meticulously underlined, annotated, and corrected. He also had the script of *Riso amaro*. With a generosity which is typical of him, he gave me free access to everything he had, and he discussed everything with complete frankness. By and large, with few exceptions (my essay being one of them – or at least so he stated at that time, but what else could he say since he was a guest in my house?), he was far from thrilled with what had been written about him. His annotations corrected names, dates, and other assorted facts. More important, he seemed to feel that most critics simply did not understand what he had meant to do and what he had actually accomplished: making films from a working-class perspective, that is, films which reflected what he defined as the true spirit of Neorealism. But, what is the 'true spirit' of Neorealism? Critics on both sides of the Atlantic have struggled for the past fifty years trying to define Neorealism, but we have had little success in finding characteristics which are exclusively or primarily found in Neorealism. Everyone agrees that it is far easier to identify a film as Neorealistic than to identify those qualities which make it such. Everyone has sought its antecedents, and everyone is still looking for one aspect or another of its descendants. For De Santis, the issue is quite simple. Neorealism, he has stated repeatedly, has no fathers. It does, however, have 'one great mother: the Resistance.'[9] This simple formula, he argued, cuts through the Gordian knot of antecedents and descendants of Neorealism to focus on those films which are truly Neorealist.

Neorealism, in his definition, dealt with a historical phenomenon: 'it was the first time that the working classes armed themselves. The people took up arms and became the protagonist of their own destiny. They fought against the dictatorship to win their freedom and to demand their right to their own aspirations. The face of Italian cinema suddenly changed: no longer was it the petty or middle bourgeoisie, but the people in all their layerings. These people had now become protagonists, they wanted to matter.'[10] At first blush, one might argue that this definition of Neorealism is not only simple, but simplistic. This, in any case, would appear to be the general response of most critics in Italy and elsewhere to De Santis's repeated and insistent claims that his works were misconstrued and to his demand that he be taken seriously. This was, as recently as 1989, the response of Ernest Callenbach, then editor of *Film Quarterly*, when my wife and I sent him a translation of De Santis's keynote address delivered at the 1989 Purdue Romance Languages conference. 'De Santis,' Callenbach wrote, 'is a charming man on paper as he is in person ... but there just isn't enough of solid substance or novelty here.'[11] And yet, De Santis's simple formula is sufficient, as I said earlier, to put in question not only Neorealism's antecedents, from *Cenere* (Ashes) to *Ossessione*, but also some of those which have come to be considered the canonical Neorealist films. It also serves to identity those which might be described as the legitimate heirs to Neorealism.

I will skip a discussion of *Cenere*. While the film has been highly praised for its realism, according to Centro Sperimentale di Cinematografia, there is no print of the film to discuss. As for *Ossessione*, many consider it to be the first Neorealist film. And yet, De Santis, who had been Visconti's assistant director on the film, states quite explicitly that it cannot be considered properly Neorealist.[12] Granted, the film may have been found wanting by the Fascist establishment because it failed to present the usual bombastic and rhetorical glorification of all things Italian. Certainly, as De Santis contends, it may well have been the greatest act of transgression possible against the Fascist regime, but this, again according to De Santis, did not make it a Neorealist work.[13] The protagonist may well have been laid off from the British-owned dockyards of Trieste because of the war, but who, even in the Italy of the time, would or could have picked up on this critical allusion to the negative impact of the regime? How could the protagonist be construed to represent a populace in arms, a people that has become the protagonist of their destiny, in conflict with the dictatorship. Here, at best, we have a sort of proto-Resistance predicated on a mindless rejection of all aspects of society. So much for the antecedents.

For De Santis, 'Neorealism was born with the birth of the Resistance and the fall of Fascism.'[14] Under Fascism, it was not possible, he argued, for films such as Rossellini's *Roma città aperta* (1945; Rome, Open City) and *Paisà* (1946), De Sica and Zavattini's *Ladri di biciclette* (1948; Bicycle Thieves), and *Riso amaro*, to be made. With these films, according to De Santis, for the first time in the history of Italian cinema the poor, subordinate classes appear: the workers, the peasants, the partisans, the fishermen, people hungry for homes and land to cultivate.[15] *Roma città aperta* and *Paisà* clearly and explicitly deal with the Resistance and its effects. But what about *Ladri di biciclette* and *Riso amaro*? What about Visconti's *La terra trema* (1948; The Earth Trembles) and De Sica's *Umberto D* (1951), for that matter? In fact, if we really want to test De Santis's theory, what about De Sica and Zavattini's *Miracolo a Milano* (1950; Miracle in Milan) and Rossellini's *La macchina ammazza cattivi* (1948; The Machine to Kill Bad People)? Suffice it to say that none of these films would have been possible under Fascism. All of them feature the poor subordinate classes. All of the canonical Neorealist films, with the possible exception of *Ladri di biciclette*, deal explicitly, as De Santis stated, with the common people's conflict with the power structure, with their battle to become the protagonist of their own destiny, to win their liberty, and to demand their right to their own aspirations.

De Santis's definition of Neorealism did not spring, full-grown, into being. As one of the regular contributors to *Cinema*, De Santis was actively engaged in the frequently polemical debate over the nature and function of Italian cinema. His own position shifted between the extremes represented eventually by Cesare Zavattini's obsessive realism[16] and Italo Calvino's focus on form. Calvino, in the 1967 preface to his *I sentieri dei nidi di ragno* (The Path to the Nest of Spiders; p. 8), was to state that, while the content of Neorealism was important, Neorealist authors were more concerned with the form of the stories to be told than with the stories themselves. De Santis's earliest position on Neorealism, in an essay written with Alicata in 1941, would appear to foreshadow Calvino's: 'Realism not as a passive obeisance to a static, objective truth, but as a creative force, in fantasy, of a history of events and of persons, is the true and eternal measure of every narrative expression.'[17] When they were attacked for abandoning realism, De Santis and Alicata responded, in another 1941 essay, with words that are reminiscent of Zavattini's roughly contemporary, and far more famous, theory of *pedinamento*: 'we too, more than anyone else, want to take our camera into the streets, into the fields, into the ports, into the factories of our country. We too are convinced that one day we will make our best cinema following the slow tired steps of the worker who is returning home, telling the essential poetry of a new and pure life, which closes within itself the secret of its aristocratic beauty.'[18]

But, this seeming surrender to the Zavattinian *pedinamento* is only temporary. In 1947, De Santis writes: 'My position on realism implies a transfiguration of reality. Art is not the reproduction of simple documents. If we are satisfied with placing our cameras in the street or between real walls, we can achieve only a completely external realism. In my opinion realism does not in any way exclude fiction, nor all of the classic cinematic devices.'[9] In short, for De Santis Neorealism rests ultimately on two pillars: one, the empowerment of the people as a result of the Resistance; the other, absolute artistic freedom of expression in conveying the reality of this empowerment. For De Santis, therefore, Neorealism is under no obligation to conform to those clichés which leftist critics in particular tried to impose on it *ex post facto*: real people, real events, real locations (conditions which, in any case, cannot be found in any film ever described as Neorealist). In fact, his theory undermines the entire notion of the primacy of the representation of reality in Neorealism.

What is the impact of De Santis's theories on the Neorealist canon? Let us consider briefly De Sica and Zavattini's *Miracolo a Milano*, a work which, to my knowledge, has never been included in the Neorealist canon. The film, based on Zavattini's novel *Totò il buono* (Totò the Good) and dedicated to him, presents, quite programmatically, the exploitation of the poor by capitalists aided and abetted by the local police, fire department, and army; the at-first-successful rebellion of the people against these forces; the people's co-optation by materialism; and finally, their flight from this materialism. This is the film's plot, an almost doctrinaire Marxist / Resistance text. The film's politics, however, are carefully concealed under the film's presentation as fable. Totò is born under a cabbage; he has a fairy godmother; angelic, airborne military policemen flit about; miracles occur; and, in the happy ending, all the good people fly away on brooms above the Milan cathedral. The result is that the film has been considered an aberration and generally has been overlooked as a potentially Neorealist work. Conversely, De Sica and Zavattini's *Ladri di biciclette* historically has been considered one of the corner-stones of the Neorealist movement. While it employs all the expressive devices available in De Sica's considerable arsenal, in order to become what Bazin called 'the perfect illusion of reality,'[20] with the significant exception of the child, Bruno, who repeatedly manifests his willingness to challenge the status quo, it reveals no more of the spirit of the resistance than did *Ossessione*, nor can one see in it any trace of the effects of the resistance.[21] While the film may discuss, albeit indirectly, the impact of the war on Italy, and while the film does roundly criticize the postwar Italian government, there is no sense of an empowerment of the working classes. At best, what unitary effort we see operates at the level of the family, friends, mob, and pre-Christian superstition. In short, I find it ironic, to say the very least, that, from De Santis's perspective, *Miracolo a Milano* has to be considered far more Neorealistic than *Ladri di biciclette*.

De Santis's criteria offer us the possibility of a programmatic re-interpretation of all the films of the period, from the much maligned 'neorealismo rosa'[22] works, such as Luigi Zampa's *Vivere in pace* (To Live in Peace), to de Santis's own melodramatic epic, *Riso amaro*. In the latter, De Santis's intent is clear. While the 'class enemy' is not identified explicitly (it is difficult to attack capitalism openly when capitalists are financing the film you are shooting in Agnelli's rice paddies),[23] I don't think there can be any question as to De Santis's position. The entire structure of capitalist society is condemned, from the exploitation of workers by the bosses to the destruction of solidarity among workers effected by the conflict between labour unions and scabs. And, while De Santis does not identify Italian capitalism by name, given the constraints under which he was labouring, his explicit barbs directed at the United States as the source of all things electric, including the chair, make an explicit identification superfluous. What little hope there is, if any, is to be found in a sort of mystical faith in the intrinsic goodness of the working classes, and in their joining forces to fight for their collective good.

Following his own prescription, De Santis uses every expressive device available to him. He had already begun this process in his earlier *Caccia tragica* (1947), which could and should be compared favourably with the great classics of neorealism. In fact, incredibly, it goes well beyond them in its explicit rejection of naturalistic realism. I think what struck me most forcefully was how clearly this work foreshadows, among others, De Sica (in the accretion of images of bicycles in the final scenes of *Ladri di biciclette*), Fellini (in the use of masks and curtains to depict the tenuous and arbitrary separation between reality and representation), and Bernardo Bertolucci (in the use of circular camera work). With *Riso amaro*, De Santis goes farther along this path. The film is, arguably, the most self-consciously artistic Neorealist film. While dealing with sociopolitical issues, as we have seen, it also focuses on the medium through continual intertextual references to pop culture and to cinematic and literary sources. The film is also one of the most impressive examples of deconstructive criticism in film. By foregrounding the undermining of texts as sources of authority, the film reveals the fundamental unreliability of all media, print and broadcast. By extension, the film invites us to question what we see and challenges us to penetrate beneath the surface patina of the narrative.

One final observation: It is impossible to discuss *Riso amaro* without addressing De Santis's representation of women in general, and of Silvana Mangano in particular. The pervasive eroticization of these representations was greeted, from the film's first appearance, with two distinct reactions: (1) it helped ensure the financial success of the film and (2) it elicited generally negative critical reactions.[24] Even today, when accused of exploiting the women in *Riso amaro*, De Santis reacts angrily, stating that it was his intent to present a new, modern, liberated woman. He adds that he was then and is now a feminist, that the film was intended as an indictment of American-style materialism, of capitalism, and of questionable values.[25] And yet, as has been observed repeatedly, his exposure of Silvana Mangano's ample cleavage and of her long legs not only ensured the financial success of the film; it also helped transform Silvana Mangano into precisely the kind of sex object he had allegedly been condemning.

Is this a valid criticism? Of course it is. At the same time there are at least two mitigating factors which must be considered: (1) De Santis came from Fondi, a small, rural southern Italian town; (2) he was raised and educated under Fascism. I realize that it is currently fashionable to condemn past texts and behaviour, completely ignoring the fact that we have increasingly come to realize that behaviour and gender roles are largely constructed. Over time, certain modes of behaviour have become no longer acceptable. As a consequence, in a thousand different ways, society is constructing new roles and behavioural models. Thus I find it odd that, when reconsidering texts and behaviour which at one time may well have been progressive and even revolutionary, we now presume to attack, condemn, revile, and proscribe them for their failure to meet standards which would not be set for decades and, at times, centuries to come.[26]

What I am saying is that we have to consider the time and culture which produced De Santis. By definition, according to our politically correct standards, he had two strikes against him *a priori*: (1) as I stated above, he was raised in a town and region in which the oppression/veneration of women was still very much the norm. The roles of men and women were very rigidly constructed, down to the most minute detail. Deviation from socially accepted behaviour, particularly by women, was punishable by death; (2) he was raised under Fascism, a system which was phallocratic, chauvinistic, misogynist; a regime which promulgated the crime of honour laws; a state which rewarded families with cash and honours for generating more soldiers for the reborn Roman empire. De Santis was, in other words, raised in a cultural world virtually inconceivable today in the Western world. When he arrived in the north of Italy and for the first time witnessed the masses of *mondine* (women labourers) as they returned home from their six weeks in the rice paddies, he must have felt as if he had landed on another planet. Here were hundreds of young, handsome, loud, boisterous, vigorous, sensual, unchaperoned women who verbally gave as good as they got. And later, when he observed them working in the rice paddies, they must have seemed more than half-naked to him. As I said, we must remember his frame of reference.[27]

Regardless of how we perceive *Riso amaro* today, I contend that De Santis wanted to celebrate the sense of liberation he had observed in these working-class, unionized, independent, autonomously sexual women, while at the same time condemning the exploitation to which they were subject. He also attempted to show the destruction of traditional values when liberation, affected by foreign materialistic values and by the absence of proper new values, becomes licence. There is a second mitigating factor which inevitably should affect our reading of the film. As I have stated, for De Santis what the media show is not necessarily reality. As he demonstrates repeatedly in *Riso amaro*, both print and broadcast media are inaccurate when they aren't actually lying. People who, like Silvana Mangano, naïvely believe what they hear and what they read inevitably are deceived, make wrong choices, and suffer as a consequence. De Santis seems to be saying that any text, print or audio-visual – including *Riso amaro* – must be taken with a grain of salt. After all, *Riso amaro* is a movie which uses all the expressive devices available to the medium to tell a story. These devices may include a specially constructed wooden dolly, a crane, and Silvana Mangano's body. But none of what we see is necessarily the 'truth' or 'reality.' What we see are constructions which we, the viewers, must read and decode. This is a constant refrain in all the better Neorealist films, forty years before the term 'deconstruction' began to appear in academic journals.

While there has been as much debate concerning the demise of Neorealism as to its genesis, the critical consensus is that De Sica and Zavattini's *Umberto D* (1953) marks the end of Neorealism proper.[28] De

Santis, however, once again, offers a different perspective. He asks: 'Why did it die? Did it die a natural death? Did it simply become extinct, as the majority of film historians, at least in Italy, contend? NO! It was murdered by the enemies of democracy, by the enemies of a full-fledged democracy ... A thousand different devices were implemented to halt the neorealist wave: negative press campaigns, censorship, financial boycotts.'[29] As a result, films which dealt with the struggle of the working classes ceased to be made, while films which dealt with psychological and metaphysical problems elicited favourable critical and popular responses. He cites as the definitive turning-point the contrasting fate of two films that appeared in 1960: Luchino Visconti's *Rocco e i suoi fratelli* (Rocco and His Brothers) and Federico Fellini's *La dolce vita*. The former deals with the destruction of a southern Italian peasant family which has emigrated to the north in search of work. The latter concerns the destruction of the soul of a bourgeois intellectual. While both films are generally considered to be masterpieces, 'Father Fellini [gave] birth to his children, [Marco] Bellocchio, Bertolucci, etc., who only tell stories about the bourgeoisie' while 'Visconti [was] unable to create children of his own.'[30] The result, according to De Santis, is so dismal that ten years must pass before blue-collar workers reappear on Italian screens (Elio Petri's *La classe operaia va in paradiso* [1971; The Working Class Goes to Heaven]), and almost another decade before we see peasants again (Ermanno Olmi's *L'albero degli zoccoli* [1978; The Tree of the Wooden Clogs]). While these are not the only films that might be said to fall within the parameters of Neorealism as defined by De Santis (suffice it to think of Bertolucci's *1900* [1975–6] and Wertmüller's *Mimi metallurgico ferito nell'onore* [1971; Seduction of Mimi], to name only two), he is essentially correct when he argues that 'the neorealist project has failed'[31] and that, at most, one finds scattered traces of Neorealism in Italian films of the last four decades. This notwithstanding, and notwithstanding his own long-enforced silence, De Santis continues to preach the virtues of Neorealism, and he continues to work feverishly on dozens of film projects, scripts, and books.

In closing, I will return to my original questions: why the college lecture tour? And why a book on De Santis? Because he, more than others whose names are far better known that his, pointed Italian cinema away from the trap of an obsession with a pseudo-objective reality. Because, he contributed significantly to one of the more important periods in the history of world cinema. Because, while his theories may not encompass all aspects of Neorealism – no map can be the land it represents – his writings can lead us to a better understanding of some of the forgotten masterpieces of that period. Why the long silence? I would suggest, tentatively, that his problem was that he was perhaps too bold, too committed, and too stubborn to compromise. The result is that, while others kept on working, he was not allowed to do so. But it may be of some consolation to him that, while we have forgotten about – in fact, we have never known about – most of the directors who worked during his long silence, we are still talking and writing about him.

In the final analysis, however, mine are only tentative answers. If anyone can answer these questions more definitively, it is the author of this book: Antonio Vitti. Born in Ciociaria, like De Santis, Vitti feels the same burning anger against the injustices perpetrated against the inhabitants of the rural south of Italy. As a consequence, he brings to the study of Italian cinema in general, and of De Santis in particular, a perspective that is uncluttered by fashionable critical trends on either side of the Atlantic. Rather than rely on secondary sources and critical theory, Vitti has gone back to the original historical, political, and cinematic documents to validate his theses. He has also had the privilege of spending far more time with his subject than is usually accorded an academician, particularly when the subject is a filmmaker, and he has had, as I understand it, complete access to De Santis's unpublished creative, theoretical, and polemical writings. Needless to say, he has also spent considerable time studying De Santis's films, including those works which can be viewed only with De Santis's special permission. Most recently he has written this, the most important book on a filmmaker and theoretician who, far from being difficult, is a friend and mentor to anyone interested in Italian Neorealism, past and future.

Ben Lawton
Purdue University

Preface

Il neorealismo, come lo concepivo io, era un modo di dare espressione alle classi subalterne: operai, contadini, piccoli impiegati ... Dedicarsi al mondo degli emarginati, dei poveri, delle vittime della società: ecco qual era, per me, il vero obiettivo del cinema neorealista.

Neorealism, the way I conceived of it, was a means to give voice to the lower classes: workers, peasants, humble clerks ... To commit myself to the world of the marginal people, the poor, the victims of society: this was, for me, the real goal of Neorealist cinema.[1]

Giuseppe De Santis

Why write a book about Giuseppe De Santis? Many of my colleagues, friends, and students have repeatedly posed that question to me over the years. For many, De Santis's name meant and means little, if anything at all. Yet, when I began this investigation, his name aroused in me conflicting thoughts and mixed feelings as well as jumbled memories of that vivid, stark, and sometimes lyrical imagery that characterizes many of his scenes filmed in Ciociaria.[2] I also felt an immense admiration for the director who, as a young critic in Fascist Italy, had fought many battles against bureaucracy and government censorship to gain ground for the rebirth of Italian cinema and a curiosity about the man whom I first glimpsed from a distance at the Centro Sperimentale di Cinematografia in Rome.

My intention in undertaking this study was never to spark a revival of interest in a filmmaker who has not made a film since 1972, or to prove that De Santis is a Neorealist director, although he is, of course, one of the founding fathers[3] of that movement, along with Roberto Rossellini, Luchino Visconti, and Vittorio De Sica. I started out with the desire to find out why De Santis's name was not, and is not, fashionable, and why his films were not, and are not now, part of the traditional canon in academic teaching about cinema. I wanted to find out why the same critical clichés about him are repeated when his name is mentioned in texts on Neorealism and Italian national cinema.[4] I also hoped to discover what had happened to Giuseppe De Santis after the great international box-office success of *Riso amaro* (Bitter Rice), which in Italy alone earned more than 400 million lire, and *Non c'è pace tra gli ulivi* (No Peace under the Olives), which earned close to 500 million lire, and why a film like *La strada lunga un anno* (The One-Year-Long Road), shot in 1958 in Yugoslavia and awarded the Golden Globe in the United States, received little popular or academic attention in Italy. My desire to study De Santis's career had nothing to do with the revival and favourable reviews of his films at the Tenth Mostra Internaziale del Nuovo Cinema at Pesaro in 1974,[5] which was followed in 1978 by the publication of the first monograph on the director.[6] Rather, my research was spurred on by a strong antagonism that I felt towards the language often used by the political Left in denouncing De Santis's films for their alleged 'eroticism,' 'formalism,' and 'indebtedness to Hollywood.' I was struck by the evidence that a critical double standard was being applied. The same analyses which somehow always interpreted the work of De Santis's contemporaries such as Visconti within the framework of a pure Neorealist aesthetic dismissed De Santis's films as well-intentioned but unsuccessful attempts to translate preconceived ideological and political ideas into artistic discourse.

In the 1950s, during the years of political restoration, Italian film critics showed themselves to be unprepared to deal openly and objectively with a young, talented director who displayed an impressive ability to use the camera, a passion for formalized beauty and sensuality, and, if all these were not enough, an Italian Communist Party membership card. What made De Santis a more complex and problematic figure was the fact that he never hesitated to transgress the rigid rules dictated by the Soviet Union on sociorealistic representation, Marxist typification, characterization, and prudishness. All such guidelines for filmmaking were strictly followed in the Italian intellectual sphere by the critics Carlo Salinari and Emilio Sereni, and by Guido Aristarco, who, with the help of the newly founded Fronte Nuovo delle Arti, made sure that

Zhdanovism[7] was observed and put into practice by the leftist Italian artists. De Santis was never interested in adhering to political doctrines. He saw himself as a committed filmmaker devoted to freedom of expression and to the use of film as an instrument both to entertain the masses and to promote social and political reforms.

De Santis has often been described as 'una persona scomoda' (a troublesome individual). My research has led me, instead, to a peaceful man, driven by a strong and sincere democratic compassion for the underprivileged and the peasant culture, and by dedication to his art form.

Besides anticipating critical reflection on cinema as a medium, De Santis was one of the first Italian directors to analyse cinema theoretically as a means of mass communication and as the repository of the collective imagination. For him, film became, by means of its power of seduction and the tendency of its viewers to identify with the events and characters on the screen, a medium whereby popular taste meets with the symbolic products of industrial society. For De Santis, cinema became a circuit of exchange between a new society of consumers and producers of cultural artefacts. From his first film reviews, written for *Cinema*, and his articles, to his collaboration as story writer and scriptwriter, to his participation in pre-Neorealist and Neorealist films, De Santis has always played a prominent role. The history of Italian cinema could not be written without including his name.

Acknowledgments

De Santis always says that all films, and his in particular, are collective and collaborative efforts. In his candid and humble way, he recalls the important and invaluable role played by those who collaborated with him on his films, including Gianni Puccini, Otello Martelli, Anna Gobbi, Goffredo Petrassi, Piero Portalupi, and Elio Petri. In a similar manner, I offer my gratitude to those who helped in the realization of this project.

First, thanks go to Alicia for her criticism, help, and unstinting support of my project throughout its various phases.

I am also very grateful to Wake Forest University for the Reynolds Grant, which made possible my research in Italy, and for the grant from the Research and Publication Fund in support of the book.

I would like to express my appreciation as well to former provost Edwin Wilson and my departmental chairman, Byron R. Wells, for their endorsement and help in bringing Giuseppe De Santis and his wife, Gordana Miletic, to Wake Forest University.

In preparing the manuscript I received assistance from my colleague and friend Miki Margitic, who helped in revising the text.

I am also grateful to Cathy Harris for her patience and expert typing. My Italian friends Rita Pignatelli, Michele Mercuri, Alessandro Coricelli, and Professor Davy Carozza made informative comments about the manuscript.

My final thanks and gratitude go to Giuseppe De Santis and Gordana Miletic, whose great help, together with their hospitality and cordiality, cannot be measured.

A.V.
Winston-Salem

De Santis among the Ciociari peasants, who will later appear in *Non c'è pace tra gli ulivi* (No Peace under the Olives), shot near Fondi.

Medieval castle in Fondi, near the De Santis family residence.

De Santis during a summer vacation in Fondi.

De Santis and his best friend, Mario Puccini, strolling around Rome during their carefree days at the film school, Centro Sperimentale.

De Santis with director Aldo Vergano in Milan, at the premier of *Il sole sorge ancora* (The Sun Rises Again).

De Santis's legendary crane used for the shooting of *Caccia tragica* (Tragic Pursuit).

Daniela, known as Lilì Marlene (Vivi Gioi), in a Dietrich pose in *Caccia tragica*.

The graceful and seductive Silvana Mangano, captured during a break in the filming of *Riso amaro* (Bitter Rice).

One of the *mondine* (rice planters), reminiscent of Mary in many Italian paintings of Christ's crucifixion, laments Maria Grazia's miscarriage in *Riso amaro*.

Real peasants demonstrating *la tarantella* to the actors in *Non c'è pace tra gli ulivi*.

Maria Grazia Francia waits for the next take in the historic centre of Sperlonga in *Non c'è pace tra gli ulivi*.

De Santis discusses the last details with the director of photography for *Roma, Ore 11* (Rome, 11 O'clock).

Simona (Lucia Bose) awaits the return of her lover Carlo (Raf Vallone) in *Roma, Ore 11*.

The barrier between Andrea (Massimo Girotti) and Anna Zaccheo (Silvana Pampanini) that results from his double standard is visually reinforced by the fence in *Un marito per Anna Zaccheo* (A Husband for Anna Zaccheo).

Anna Zaccheo (Silvana Pampanini) tolerates harassment to keep her job.

Pasquale (Marcello Mastroianni) and Angela (Marina Vlady) choose their rings in *Giorni d'amore* (Days of Love).

The colourful and folkloristic hut envisioned by painter Domenico Purificato in *Giorni d'amore*.

De Santis and Yves Montand, who plays Ricuccio in the film, overlooking the desolate village where parts of *Uomini e lupi* (Men and Wolves) were filmed.

No longer 'the Italian version of the atomic bomb,' as she was seen to be in *Riso amaro*, actress Silvana Mangano is transformed by De Santis into a lonely, grief-stricken widow in *Uomini e lupi*.

Massimo Girotti, as Chiacchiera, poses for the crew's amusement during the shooting of *Cesta Duga Godinu Dana*/*La strada lunga un anno* (The One-Year-Long Road).

Gordana Miletic (who would later marry De Santis) and Antun Vrdoliak in Yugoslavia during the shooting of *Cesta Duga Godinu Dana*.

The seductive Susanna (Eleonora Rossi Drago) surveys the construction in *Cesta Duga Godinu Dana*.

Peasants celebrating the construction of the road that will end their isolation in *Cesta Duga Godinu Dana*.

Davide (Milivoje Zivanovic) testing his bridge's reliability, on which his future and reputation depend, in *Cesta Duga Godinu Dana*.

Italian Fascist 'Squadristi' pillage a Russian village in *Italiani brava gente* (Italians, Good People).

An early scene in *Italiani brava gente* juxtaposes the Italian invasion with the Russian abandonment of the wheat crops.

Mussolini's easy victory has turned into a major retreat, in this scene from *Italiani brava gente.*

A German and an Italian soldier go to give themselves up to the Red Army as they whistle 'The International,' in *Italiani brava gente*. At this moment, they do not know that their hopes will end in tragedy.

The frozen body of the last survivor, from the closing scene of *Italiani brava gente*, symbolizes the futility of war.

Italian soldier Giuseppe Sanna (Riccardo Cucciolla) shares his bread with a Russian prisoner in *Italiani brava gente*.

De Santis closely observes Nicola Parella (Riccardo Cucciolla) as curious bystanders look on in *Un apprezzato professionista di sicuro avvenire* (An Esteemed Professional with a Secure Future), the director's last film.

Lucietta Arduni (Fermi Benussi) in *Un apprezzato professionista di sicuro avvenire*. The blasphemous contrast of the cross around the nude actress's neck reveals De Santis's views on modern Italian life.

Village streets in Pulia, where 'Pettotondo' would have been filmed (1959).

The local custom of drawing water with ancient copper amphoras, a detail that the director wanted to include in 'Pettotondo' (1959).

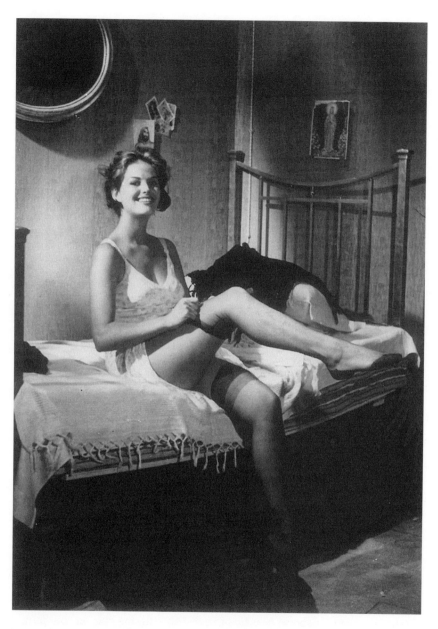

The then young and inexperienced actress Claudia Cardinale posing for test shots for 'Pettotondo.'

Poverty-stricken Calabrese peasants in a test shot for the epic on southern poverty and peasantry, 'Noi che facciamo crescere il grano' (We Who Grow Grain).

Children awaiting the return of their parents from the fields in a desolate Calabrese village. De Santis said that the girl in the foreground took care of the house and her siblings, instead of attending school.

Turin, summer 1989: De Santis with ex-terrorists Benedetti, Tosi, and Ronconi and the journalist Nino Ferrero during an interview for the making of 'Il Permesso' (The Leave).

PART I
A BIOGRAPHICAL PROFILE

1

De Santis's Early Years: From Fondi to Rome

Figlio di quei ciociari della costa i cui antenati tempo addietro avevano abbandonato le loro donne in pasto alle voglie dei predoni turchi, arabi e saraceni.

Son of those coastline Ciociari whose ancestors long ago left their women to satisfy the lust of the Turkish, Arabic, and Saracen plunderers.

Giuseppe De Santis

Giuseppe De Santis, son of Oreste De Santis and Teresa Goduti, was born in Fondi, a small town ten kilometres from the Tyrrhenian Sea, on 11 February 1917. The future movie director spent his adolescence basking indolently in the sun, like a lizard, feeding on prickly pears which grew in bunches along the ditches and falling in love with peasants' and workers' daughters, as he recalls in an article published in 1969.[1] During De Santis's youth, Fondi had about ten thousand inhabitants but was an important crossing on the route between Rome and Naples, the two largest cities of southern Italy. At the age of thirteen, De Santis was sent away to a Roman Catholic boarding-school, San Leone Magno, administered by an order of French Marists. Every weekend of the year, and during summer vacations, De Santis would return to his native Fondi, a custom that was to continue even after the entire De Santis family moved to Rome as part of his father's quest for better employment as a civil engineer. In the young De Santis's mind, the distance from Fondi and from those carefree summer days mythologized his homeland, which he continually sought to re-create through different forms of artistic expression. As a college student in Rome, where he frequently contemplated Renato Guttuso's paintings, he wrote:

Guttuso's paintings, which spoke of Sicily, were full of my town in Ciociaria. That plain of Fondi made of olive trees, prickly pears, orange trees, lemon trees, crossed by ancient dusty roads, canal networks; crossed by carts, donkeys, human feet almost always bare; by peasants and fishermen, going and coming to work or following endless processions, illuminated by the sun and by the reflections off the sea which had once aided Circe in enchanting the Greek Ulysses ... : those were the places of my childhood, my adolescence, and my everyday life during my frequent visits to my home town.[2]

During the long summer vacations, De Santis came in contact with a group of prominent intellectuals from Fondi and other parts of Ciociaria, one of whom was the poet Libero De Libero,[3] who, like De Santis, lived in Rome and spent the summer months in Fondi. It was De Libero who induced the young De Santis to read the dialectal poetry of Ciociaria.

After finishing boarding-school, De Santis entered the Liceo Giulio Cesare, where he met Massimo Serato and Massimo Girotti, both of whom were to become famous actors. In 1937, De Santis enrolled at the Facoltà di Lettere (College of Liberal Arts) of the University of Rome, after passing the school-leaving examination (*esame di maturità*) as an external candidate. He never graduated from college, finding more personal satisfaction in writing poetry, short stories, and novels than in pursuing his formal studies. His early short stories won a first and a second prize, in 1938 and 1939, at the annual Littoriali organized by the Fascist regime.[4] As a college student, De Santis preferred reading popular writers such as Francesco Mastriani, Jack London, Emile Zola, and Victor Hugo, rather than the texts and materials required for his college exams. It was during this period that De Santis came into contact with many young intellectuals who would shape his life and play a very important role in his future activities. One of these, the critic Gianni Puccini,[5] the oldest of the Puccini brothers, offered De Santis the opportunity to write for the journal *Cinema*,[6] which in the late 1930s was the most widely read publication of its kind. With the help of his new acquaintances, De Santis gained entry to the circle associated with the journal *Meridiano di Roma*[7] and was thus able to meet some of the most important writers and artists of his time. De Santis was also a habitué of Libero De Libero's art gallery, Cometa, located in a wing of the Pecci-Blunt Palace near the Campidoglio. There, many promising young painters, such as Cagli, Mirko, Mafai, and Purificato, later referred to as 'the Roman school,' were having their first exhibitions.

Recalling those days, De Santis wrote:

It was then that I started to realize that the word, the means of expression of the narrator, was not enough to give form to my world ... I used to write, and I felt the desire to paint. I used to imagine a written dialogue, and I felt a strong desire to recite it or to mime it. I used to describe nature, its silences and its sudden ruptures, and I was overcome by a desire to feel them transformed into music ... and it was for this reason, I believe, that I discovered cinema: that medium which, by including the characteristics of music, miming, painting, could have given me the opportunity, whatever it was, to tell stories dear to my heart.[8]

De Santis decided to attend the Centro Sperimentale di Cinematografia, the state film school founded by Mussolini, in 1935, with the objective of teaching the theory and practice of cinematography. At the Centro Sperimentale, De Santis studied the works of Pudovkin translated by Umberto Barbaro. Barbaro, together with Luigi Chiarini, taught him to appreciate the films of the Russian Formalist school, Eisenstein, American director King Vidor, the German Expressionists, as well as French films by Marcel Carné and Jean Renoir.[9] This rich cultural experience, along with the friendship of Gianni Puccini, helped De Santis in his job as a critic for the journal *Cinema*. The young De Santis had already made a name for himself as a promising writer, having published short stories in some of the most well-known journals of the time, including *L'Italia letteraria, Il selvaggio*, and *La ruota*.[10] However, his experience as a film critic for *Cinema* shaped De Santis's artistic aspirations and introduced him to the intricacies of politics and European culture. Although De Santis is primarily known as a director, his writings as a film critic are important as well, and are in fact essential to the study and understanding of the rebirth of Italian cinema before Neorealism. As the writer of *Cinema*'s column 'Film di questi giorni' (Today's Films), which he started in 1942, De Santis became the driving force in the promotion and development of a new type of cinema, which he defined at the time as: 'a cinema that seeks things and facts inside a definite time and within a realistic space in order to redeem itself from the facile conventions of stultifying bourgeois taste.'[11]

His experience as a writer for *Cinema* changed De Santis's life completely. His encounter with Gianni Puccini and with his circle – young men such as Mario Alicata and Pietro Ingrao – slowly drew the aspiring artist into the world of politics and the dangerous underground movement against the Fascist state. As De Santis confessed during one of our conversations, he was spurred on to become an anti-Fascist by the brave example and dedication of his friends who worked for *Cinema*.

2

A Member of the *Cinema* Circle

Tutto quanto io venivo scrivendo con le mie critiche era prima ancora che dentro di me, al di fuori di me; era nell'aria, nel clima che a mano a mano, come una macchia d'olio, aveva cominciato ad allargarsi conquistando l'animo e la coscienza del cinema italiano più insofferente.

Everything I was writing about in my reviews existed outside of myself even before it dawned inside of me; it was in the air and in the cultural climate, which, little by little, like an oil stain, had started to expand, conquering the mind and the conscience of the most impatient faction of Italian cinema.

Giuseppe De Santis

In the early 1940s, the *Cinema* circle included Michelangelo Antonioni; Domenico Purificato; Dario, Gianni, and Massimo Puccini; Carlo Lizzani; Pietro Ingrao; Francesco Pasinetti; Antonio Pietrangeli; Giuseppe De Santis; Mario Alicata; as well as Luchino Visconti, who in 1941 published the famous article 'Cadaveri' which immediately became a sort of manifesto for the younger members of the group. That same year Luchino Visconti had also written, for another journal, 'Tradizione ed invenzione' (Tradition and Invention), an article accompanied by beautiful illustrations by the painter Renato Guttuso. In it, Visconti expressed his desire to make a film based on Giovanni Verga's novel *I malavoglia* (The House by the Medlar Tree; 1881), a wish that he was to fulfil seven years later with the film *La terra trema* (The Earth Quakes; 1948). It was during those years that Giuseppe De Santis began an intense intellectual collaboration with Mario Alicata, from which would originate the most noted and important essays on the development of realism in Italian cinema, including 'Verità e poesia: Verga e il cinema italiano' (Truth and Poetry: Verga and Italian Cinema) and 'Ancora di Verga e del cinema italiano' (More about Verga and Italian Cinema).[1]

An examination of the association between De Santis and Alicata reveals much about the origins of the battle for realism in cinema. In a study by Sebastiano Martelli, *Il crepuscolo dell'identità*, Mario Alicata is identified as the principal architect of the Communist party's policy towards the South (Mezzogiorno) during the 1950s – a policy that led to the birth of realistic narrative and cinematography pertaining to southern culture, developed as models. Martelli explains:

The role of Alicata in the development of the Communist party's cultural policy in the South of the 1950s was ... definitive and hegemonic. Alicata influenced, in a comprehensive way, the entire spectrum of PCI [Parito Comunista Italiano] policy in relation to the Mezzogiorno, furnishing even the critical parameters for the interpretation and analysis of that culture and its traditions.[2]

Martelli is correct in his assertions about Alicata's influence in the 1950s, but the latter's impact on the PCI's cultural policy can be traced back even farther, to the 1940s, and more specifically to the years when the *Cinema* circle comprised those mentioned at the beginning of this chapter.[3] From this platform, Alicata, armed with a formidable cultural and intellectual arsenal, was able to impose his judgments and political orientation. The other members of the circle acknowledged his incisiveness and his ability to calculate the impact of his cultural proposals. This observation is not gratuitous if one takes into consideration that, in June 1940, Alicata had become the assistant of Professor Natalino Sapegno in the department of Italian literature at the University of Rome and had already started to write for *Primato*, the magazine under the stewardship of then minister of national education, Giuseppe Bottai. *Primato* represented one of the most unusual attempts made by the Fascist regime to enlist as collaborators the best intellectuals of the time. *Primato* was known for printing the poetry of such writers as Cesare Pavese, Giuseppe Ungaretti, and Eugenio Montale.

By the beginning of the 1940s, the creation of a more 'realistic' cinema was a concern shared by many in the movie business, even though 'realism' had various meanings, and only a few of the young men writing for *Cinema* understood it as a political ideology veiled against Fascist censorship.[4] For example, one of Alicata's articles published in the 10 February 1942 issue of *Cinema* reads:

Almost all the characters in our films are lacking a history. They are animated by clichés, by the most conventional and melodramatic leftovers of sentiments and passions, living out their shallow existences in places equally mute and stale, without colour. Those who have, as we do, a penchant for wandering the streets of their own city to glean the inexhaustible poetry of those things which exist naturally, and also have imposed upon themselves the simple but meaningful principle that each person whom one meets is a character, are often shocked by the incapacity of our scriptwriters to adapt themselves to the human reality of the environments from which they choose to spin their tales.[5]

In another article, co-authors De Santis and Alicata say:

Faith in the truth and in the poetry of truth, faith in man and in the poetry of man, is what we want from Italian cinema. It is a simple request and a modest program. We feel more and more committed to this simple modesty since, each time we look at the story of our cinema, we see its development trapped among the rhetorical and archaeological D'Annunzianism of 'Cabiria' and the flight to the non-existent middle-class paradises of Via Nazionale's nightclubs, where the most daring housewives of our sentimental comedies give vent to their frustrations.[6]

In yet another article they say:

But how would it otherwise be possible to understand and interpret man if he is isolated from the elements in which he lives each day and with which he communicates each day – whether they be the walls of his house, which should in an unequivocal way bear the mark of his hands, his taste, his nature, or the streets of the city where he meets with other men.[7]

These passages are more than sufficient evidence that *Cinema*'s purpose was twofold: first, the promotion of cinema as an art form and, second, the expression of a general dissatisfaction with the actual state of that art. Alicata's writings were dialectical and theoretical in nature, while those of De Santis, with which the group as a whole identified itself, were more aggressive, heartfelt, and personal. In 1969, De Santis, reminiscing about how the *Cinema* circle started to develop a political consciousness, wrote:

little by little, like an oil stain, [it] started to expand, conquering the mind and the conscience of that faction of Italian cinema which was most impatient with the circumstances in which everybody lived. Don't ask me how this could happen in the midst of the Fascist regime or how I managed each time to slip through the net of the censors. I can only answer that nothing would have stopped me from doing what I did. I wanted it and that's all.[8]

In order to fully understand De Santis's statement, it is necessary to remember what the magazine was and what it represented for all the intellectuals of the group. *Cinema* was born on 10 July 1936, conceived in the image of *Sapere*, the best-selling magazine of the early 1940s. The film magazine had been founded by the editor Ulrico Hoepli to offer general coverage of technical and artistic aspects of filmmaking. The editorial board comprised the famous German theoretician Rudolf Arnheim and Corrado Pavolini, assisted by Domenico Meccoli, Francesco Pasinetti, and Gianni Puccini. A year later, Luciano De Feo left the Hoepli publishing house for Rizzoli, and the direction of the magazine fell into the hands of the cinema-enthusiast Vittorio Mussolini, son of the *duce*.[9] This turned out to be a fortunate sequence of events in that it guaranteed the funds and publicity needed to maintain a clandestinely political operation. With the editorial change came a shift in approach. The magazine charted a new and more aggressive course, a trend which would become most marked when Giuseppe De Santis became the man in charge of the film-review column. The first column appearing under the signature of the Ciociaro director, 'L'ispirazione sensibile,' was published in the 1940 Christmas issue. Its tone cautious, it examines the merits of sound and silent cinema, a subject somewhat out of style for the early 1940s. This article was very different from those that would later make De Santis the foremost personality of the group. In his more mature articles, he demonstrated his acumen in judging spectacle and sculptural imagery and offered as well the first suggestions and stimulus for a more realistic national cinematography. In order to better grasp the importance and the achievement of the entire group, and of De Santis in particular, it must be understood how and why the regime allowed these young men, all avowed anti-Fascists,[10] to run the only Italian film magazine with a significant circulation (De Santis states that *Cinema* had attained a circulation of 12,000 copies). The only other film magazine of those years, *Bianco e nero*, edited by Professor Luigi Chiarini, was an instrument of the Centro Sperimentale, and thus had a technical and specialized format. *Cinema*, on the other hand, aimed at making certain cinematographic problems known to the general public.

Under the wing of Vittorio Mussolini, the magazine benefited from a degree of political tolerance which permitted the writers to distance themselves from the directives of the regime and to undertake an un-biased and more critical investigation of the issues. The relatively relaxed surveillance led to opportunities and concessions which were increasing-ly denied to other fields of artistic and cultural activity, and allowed the cinematographic movement of those years to become a true avant-garde force. According to De Santis, this margin of tolerance was attributable to several factors, one of which was the disorganization and inefficiency of the regime. Other factors were the high level of illiteracy in Fascist Italy and the government's failure to recognize the film medium's potential as an instrument for forming political consciousness in the masses. De Santis's opinions on this matter are in agreement with those of critic Gian Piero Brunetta, who credits Fascism for having recognized the pronounced popular and social nature of film art, but who, at the same time, acknowledges that the regime underestimated the medium's potential impact on social structures – an impact which, according to Brunetta, was overemphasized by the Neorealists and the Italian left-wing intellectuals of the postwar years. De Santis also maintains that the great merit or fault of the regime was precisely that of having antici-pated the techniques of 'repressive tolerance.' Furthermore, says De Santis, it was this very policy which led the regime to focus on 'white telephone movies'[11] rather than on big propaganda productions. His ex-planation is shared by Brunetta, who writes:

The standard Fascist production prefers to settle on an average level of inter-classist nature with no unifying style, mixing various themes and stylistic narrative models. Above all, these productions attempt to follow the path of indirect propaganda rather than the explicit direct approach of a message transmitted by characters specifically designated for just that very purpose. Any heroic treatment is carefully avoided; 'rhetoric' is dreaded – it's an inferiority complex that springs from a fear of being judged by the intellectuals who are still considered to be somewhat free from subordination to party directives.[12]

The concessions and opportunities given to *Cinema* permitted De Santis to vent his artistic dissatisfactions in reviewing the films of that period, and to stimulate a search for something new, more representative of Italian historical reality. A general analysis of an assortment of these reviews, according to genre, would uphold the significance of De Santis's contribution to the spread of a realistic and artistic cinema. In 1942 the Italian market was dominated by national products which were protected against international competition by law. The then minister of popular culture, Alessandro Pavolini, had set the annual production quota at 140 films, a figure which would not be reached.[13] The governmental production initiative had given space to many new directors, and the average level of technical and artistic expertise had risen, but, generally, with a few exceptions, Italian films remained mediocre, tending to follow old technical and narrative schemes; none the less, the public supported them in the absence of an alternative. These films also satisfied the people's growing need for entertainment in the face of imminent military defeat. De Santis says that Italian cinema during those years could be divided into unique genres: the sentimental comedy, the witty comedy, the 'tout-court' comedy, the musical, the historical adventure story, the rare films of explicit propaganda,[14] and those of the formalist trend. Among those identified with the latter group, Mario Soldati and Renato Castellani were the most important directors; according to De Santis, their films were nothing more than Italian-style traditional costume films intended to reaffirm Italy's image as the cradle of medieval and Renaissance culture.[15] For De Santis, the 'comic-sentimental' was synonymous with the 'white telephone' movie, to which he attributes a falsely constructed language and the lack of a true dramatic centre. He contrasts the Italian comic-sentimental films with those of René Clair. The Italian films, he points out, lack the social truth to demonstrate current issues and the ideology to sustain a point of view. Since creative energy and imagination are absent, the comic arises only from mechanical situations. De Santis can be credited with having saved two films of this genre, De Sica's *Un garibaldino al convento* (1942; Garibaldian in a Monastery), and *Quattro passi fra le nuvole* (1943; Four Steps in the Clouds), by Alessandro Blasetti, from lambasting by the critics. Of De Sica's film, De Santis wrote:

Finally one must take note of the fact that this film is, till now, and we do not know who could dispute us, the only example in Italy of a 'choral' cinema, and with this statement we want to reproach a widespread tendency in our cinema that shows the inability to ever create a world larger than the abstract egocentrism of a few actors, of a few characters, inevitably closed within four walls or irremediably lost inside luxurious ducal living-rooms.[16]

In Blasetti's film, based on a storyline and screenplay by Cesare Zavattini and Piero Tellini, De Santis appreciates a great ability to develop themes rich in hidden meanings and authenticity:

The film narrates the day of an ordinary man – a travelling salesman. The character is depicted with perfect psychological subtlety. He brings to the role a coherence and consistency in his gestures and behaviour that leave no doubt as to his social rank ... We wish that our national cinema were able to avail itself of such situations more frequently. Keep in mind that this is not a question of a preference for certain types of content but rather for a linearity and simplicity in the telling of a story. That calm and unobtrusive anonymous being presents itself without the slightest affectation, but rather in a natural fashion, just as it occurs in real life. This is an aspect of the aesthetic ideology that we have desired for so long.[7]

The young critic seized every opportunity to promote his ideas for a new cinema rooted in social realities. For example, in his negative review[18] of Carmine Gallone's *Harlem* (1943), a film on American gangsters, De Santis deplores the way the Italian film industry co-opted 'America' for financial gain, relying on stereotype to captivate the public imagination. The American myth was always part of Italian life. However, De Santis thought that Italian directors, instead of using banal, stereotyped scripts, such as the one written by Emilio Cecchi and Sergio Amidei for *Harlem*, should have looked back at Faulkner's novels, which revealed the multifaceted realities of America. De Santis also objected to the unrealistic description of the dance halls and to the conventional way in which Black Americans were depicted. This observation, perhaps related to the article 'Il jazz e le sue danze'[19] (Jazz and Its Dances), also written in 1943, confirms De Santis's role in the promotion of a more realistic type of cinema. In his article on jazz and dancing, the future movie director praised King Vidor for having grasped the deep importance jazz and spirituals have for Blacks. De Santis cites the dance sequence in Vidor's *Hallelujah* (1929) where Zebe's (the Black protagonist's) younger brothers tap-dance to a spiritual. In De Santis's judgment, King Vidor, more than any other filmmaker, understood that dancing alleviated Black Americans' misery, frustration, and sense of social oppression – an important precedent ignored by the Italian directors of the 1940s. De Santis's criticisms always attempt to stimulate the search for a cinema more representative of social and cultural realities.

Of the propaganda films, De Santis praises *Vecchia guardia* (1935; Old Guard) by Alessandro Blasetti, recognizing the strong emotional input of this director and his unabashed sincerity in representing the undertakings of the Fascist squads, which the regime itself had no intention of resuscitating.[20]

De Santis's harshest criticism of the formalist[21] school appears in a review of Renato Castellani's film *Un colpo di pistola* (1942; A Pistol Shot):

Those ivory columns and those dignified snow-white candelabras are nothing more than another projection on a gigantic scale of the white telephones with which the middle-class ambience of our film industry has sympathized for so long. The opinion of our readers is now at last solidifying itself against this avowed aspiration of our cinematographers.[22]

De Santis, like the entire *Cinema* group, attacked the trend towards formalism because he considered it the principal obstacle to the achievement of a realist cinema in which the Italian countryside figured as an integral part, along with country dwellers and workers. This new vision of cinema led De Santis to write:

We, too, more than the others, want to take our movie cameras into the streets, the fields, the ports, the factories of our country. We, too, are convinced that one day we will create our most beautiful movie following the slow, fatigued step of the worker as he returns home, narrating the essential poetry of a new and pure life that holds within itself the secret of its own aristocratic beauty.[23]

Through his weekly articles in *Cinema*, De Santis developed a coherent and continuous dialogue whose goal was the promotion of a new type of cinema that would supersede the dominant, confining aesthetic of 1940s Italy, a cinema with a well-defined political and social goal. In those years, De Santis and the entire *Cinema* circle were in the vanguard of such a search. The postwar period, as well as the encounter with a different historical moment, and the role of the new government in sidelining certain types of film production, would dissipate the group's cohesive creative impulse, but the efforts of these young anti-Fascists left a lasting imprint on the Italian national cinema.

3

A Dream Comes True:
From *Cinema* to *Ossessione*

Scrivevo e avevo voglia di dipingere quadri; immaginavo un dialogo di personaggi sulla carta e mi veniva voglia di recitarlo o di realizzarlo mimicamente. E fu per questa ragione, io credo, che scoprii il cinema: quel mezzo cioè che, assommando in sè i modi e gli atteggiamenti della pittura, della musica, della rappresentazione mimica e insieme della parola avrebbe potuto darmi la possibilità, qualunque essa fosse, di narrare le storie che mi stavano a cuore.

I used to write and I felt the desire to paint; I used to imagine a written dialogue and I felt a strong desire to recite it or to mime it. And it was for this reason, I believe, that I discovered cinema: that medium which by including the characteristics of music, miming, painting, and wording could have given me the opportunity to tell stories dear to my heart.

Giuseppe De Santis

De Santis aspired to become a fiction writer. Without going as far as the critic Alberto Farassino, who reads the future movie director's earlier writings as a preparation for filmmaking, one can identify an attraction for visualization in De Santis's essays and reviews published in *Cinema*. In 'Sogni del cineasta' (Dreams of a Filmmaker), which appeared in 1941, De Santis writes about his dream of making films.[1] In another early article, 'Stampe'[2] (Prints), the effort to communicate through images is evident. The article uses reproductions of eighteenth-century prints to discuss children's fashion and costumes, and the captions contain only a few words. These two articles are only small steps in the long process that will lead De Santis to directing. At the Centro Sperimentale, De Santis made a short film titled *La gatta* (The Cat) with Vittorio Duse. The print has been lost or was taken by the withdrawing German troops, along with many others missing from the film library; however, De Santis recalls[3] that the film was a Verghian story of passion and vendetta.[4] A very jealous peasant returns home and, overtaken by rage, kills his wife, whom he has surprised in the act of adultery. The script was based on a story written by De Santis, a circumstance that highlights one of the characteristics that distinguishes him from the rest of the postwar filmmakers, who seldom wrote their own scripts.

The road to filmmaking in the 1940s was very long and extremely difficult. Young, aspiring directors had to undergo a long apprenticeship consisting of small jobs or appointments as assistant director, first-unit or second-unit assistant, and other assignments. All the young intellectuals of the time who aspired to be filmmakers tried to gain entry to one of the various groups working at Cinecittà. Since one of the prerequisites for directing was to have made a documentary, the LUCE Institute (L'Unione Cinematografica Educativa, which produced documentaries and newsreels, and screened and censored foreign newsreels) was the school for almost everyone coming up in the ranks.[5] De Santis, too, proposed to LUCE two documentaries, which, judging from the titles, were indicative of the country–city dichotomy that would characterize his later work. One, entitled 'Fiera di paese' (Country Fair), described the fair in his native Fondi; the other, 'Cortile' (Courtyard), described a courtyard made of old French staircases in the Roman district of San Lorenzo.[6] Neither script was ever filmed, a fate awaiting many other scripts written by De Santis in his career.

Making and promoting documentaries was a common practice of the time, as even a rapid glance through the essays and reviews published in the film magazines confirms. De Santis's writings, though, specifically promote the documentary form for the renewal of national cinema. In reviewing Guido Paolucci's *Portofino* (1942), De Santis identified the documentary as the model that the Italian cinema of the 1940s had to imitate in order to create a more authentic and innovative style:

We have always pointed to the documentary as the most secure road to follow in conducting a search and discovering the authentic Italian cinematographic style. We also declare that it is the only opportunity offered to the new generation, in whom we have great faith, to gain their own experience and their own faith in cinematography.[7]

A similar concept is affirmed in a better-known essay, 'Per un paesaggio italiano'[8] (For an Italian Landscape), in which De Santis proclaimed that only through a fusion between the documentary and the feature film could the formula for an authentic Italian national cinema be found. The young critic rebuked contemporaneous Italian filmmakers for not using the national landscape. Invoking the examples of the great national painters who used the landscape, whether to emphasize the sentimental aspect of a portrait or to dramatize its composition, De Santis called for a cinema in which the film protagonist would bear and reflect the elements of the landscape. He concluded by saying: 'The landscape will have no meaning if man is not included and vice versa.' This essay was accompanied by four illustrations: the first from *The Knights of Texas* by King Vidor; the second from *Piccolo mondo antico* (Ancient Little World) by Mario Soldati; the third from *Tabù* by Friedrich Wilhelm Murnau and Robert Flaherty; and the fourth from *Ganja,* a Latvian documentary. This heterogeneous selection of films and documentaries, as Stefano Masi[9] affirms, was representative of the cinematic tastes of the young intellectuals working for *Cinema*, which encompassed admiration for King Vidor, for the appeal of a real landscape of Soldati, and for the documentary and naturalistic style of Robert Flaherty. The cinematic preferences of the group are reaffirmed by De Santis in two articles written in collaboration with Mario Alicata, 'Verità e poesia: Verga e il cinema italiano' (Truth and Poetry: Verga and Italian Cinema) and 'Ancora di Verga e del cinema italiano' (More about Verga and Italian Cinema). These two essays express the nucleus of some essential components of De Santis's future films and cultural projects – namely, a return to realist literary models as the source of cinematic inspiration, supported by the understanding that realism is not passive obedience to a static, objective truth but a creative force. As Millicent Marcus affirmed, this concept of realism can be read as a 'rejection of a passive, literal-minded transcription of the phenomenal world in favor of a dynamic interpretation of its underlying forces.'[10] De Santis reaffirmed this understanding of realism in 1981 in 'Cinema, sud e memoria'

Neorealism is not only a camera carried in the streets to make contact with the real world, nor actors chosen from among people who have never heard of reciting, nor scenes of an ordinary day as it presents itself. No, these are some secondary, accessory attributes of Neorealism. Nothing, in fact, is served by immersing the camera in the real world if it then does not know itself how to seize the most complex substance of life, life's rich problematics, its hidden poetry, the lucidities of its deepest obscurity. After all, even the most stubborn and faithful belief in pursuing the daily life of this or that character comes to naught if the director is not able to know himself; to choose and select, to give a particular look and sense to the most representative moments of his human condition, or to give substance to the humblest and most apparently useless gestures and acts. It is not true, and it will never be true, that all of daily life, shown in confusion, without organization, can contain a penetrating insight and a significant emotional shift. A poetry of banality and obviousness does not exist, and will never exist, because in the moment in which the banal and the obvious become poetry each ceases to be banal or obvious.[11]

This statement appears to contradict what Alicata and De Santis wrote in 1941 in 'Ancora di Verga e del cinema italiano': 'We also ... want to bring our movie camera into the streets, fields, ports, factories of our country. We also are convinced that one day we will create our most beautiful film following the slow and tired steps of a worker returning home.'[12]

That declaration for unmediated naturalistic reportage was also part of the broad program of the *Cinema* group. This somewhat contradictory assertion can be tied to their admiration for the lyrical approach of King Vidor and the factual documentaries of Robert Flaherty. The various members of the group, including De Santis, have stated on different occasions that, in the early 1940s, although they did not have a well-defined critical awareness of what future developments might be, they were nevertheless well aware of the stylistic breakthrough that they wanted to achieve and, to that end, were studying various models and alternatives without being sure of how to reconcile them.

In 1942, after the review of Rossellini's *Un pilota ritorna*[13] (A Pilot Returns), a film that De Santis found mediocre because of its overt demagoguery and rhetoric, the young critic left the journal *Cinema* for six months to join Visconti as assistant director in the making of the mythological *Ossessione*. The film was the result of a long and painful process, and, as some critics report,[14] a casual encounter on the ship bound for Capri. De Santis had first met Visconti during a visit with Carl Roch, who was in Rome as Jean Renoir's assistant for the production of Puccini's *Tosca*. De Santis and Visconti had already worked together on a screenplay based on Verga's *L'amante di Gramigna* (Gramigna's Lover).[15] The script, written by Puccini and De Santis, was later presented to the then minister of popular culture, Pavolini, who, unwilling to approve a film about banditry, rejected the project. Visconti and De Santis had also worked on the cinematographic treatment of Alain Fournier's *Le grand Meaulnes* before work began on *Ossessione*.[16]

The script for *Ossessione*, first titled 'Palude,' was written by Mario Alicata, Giuseppe De Santis, Gianni Puccini, and Luchino Visconti. The film, which bears the indelible style of Visconti, embodies the ideals of the *Cinema* group. Lino Micciché, who worked extensively on *Ossessione*, states:

'Ossessione' marks Visconti's cinematographic discourse but is at the same time the high point of a group battle and the end of a general itinerary which started in a confused and contradictory fashion at the end of the 1930s, and became more defined between the end of the Spanish Civil War and the outbreak of the Second World War, when an entire generation was forced to evaluate the recent past to deal with the present and to propose a different future for themselves, and for the society in which they lived. This itinerary had acquired clear and defined outlines by 1941, when the polemic promoted by the journal *Cinema*, even if still written in cipher, had attained a notable unity and a common goal.[17]

The film was considered the culmination of their efforts and their artistic manifesto. The start of *Ossessione* is also remembered by the group as the beginning of the political police crackdown on the entire circle. The *Cinema* group fell under the close scrutiny of the Fascist secret police, OVRA. The 'Cineguf' in Rome (Film Organization for university students during the Fascist regime), where the group used to meet, was closed. During the shooting of the film, at the end of 1942, Dario and Gianni Puccini were arrested, along with Marco Cesarini. A week later, Mario Alicata was also arrested, and Pietro Ingrao barely escaped arrest, alerted by a telephone call from De Santis, who, following a prearranged plan, warned him as soon as it was known that Alicata had been arrested.[18]

De Santis, like almost everyone in the *Cinema* circle, has written or spoken in public about the genesis and the making of *Ossessione*.[19] The director of *Caccia tragica* (Tragic Pursuit), in an article published in 1984 by *Cinema nuovo*,[20] relived the experience as first-unit assistant in charge of the background details. In a very personal lecture given at the first Purdue University Conference on Romance Languages, Literatures, and Film, on 7 October 1989, De Santis, recalling the film, said:

Ossessione, however, was not Neorealism, but it was the extreme act of transgression against Fascism. We could go no further. I tried to. As first-unit
director, I constantly tried to tell several additional stories in the background of
the scenes I was shooting. I wanted to show the war cripples, but Visconti, not
illogically, given the political situation, had to stop me. As a result, I put even
more details than necessary into my first film, *Caccia tragica*.

During the collaboration on *Ossessione*, De Santis met Giovanna Vale-
ri, his future wife, who was working as production secretary. Around
that period, De Santis was also working on a book on the pre-war
French cinema, with a special emphasis on Renoir, Clair, and Duvivier.[21]
The book was part of a series of twelve volumes to be published by
Cinema, but that project never materialized because of the historical
events which precipitated the downfall of Fascism and the surrender of
Italy. In spring 1943, De Santis left his job as film critic to join Roberto
Rossellini, on whom *Ossessione* had made a great impact, to work as
assistant director for a film to be called 'Scalo merci' (Freight Station).
Filming was to take place at the Tiburtina Station in Rome, among the
railway workers. According to De Santis, Rossellini gave him much
more freedom than Visconti had allowed him during the making of
Ossessione. De Santis also claims responsibility for the fifteen minutes of
film shot before the July 1943 bombardment of the San Lorenzo district
in Rome interrupted work on the film.[22] After the air raids, Rossellini
moved the cast to the mountains of Tagliacozzo in Abruzzo. De Santis,
who was involved in the urban resistance against the Germans, chose to
remain in Rome. The title of the film was then changed to 'Rinuncia,'
but Rossellini never finished it, abandoning the project when surrender
was announced on 8 September 1943 by the new Italian government of
Badoglio. Two years later, Marcello Pagliero finished the film, using
what Rossellini had already shot, and gave the film its final title,
Desiderio (Desire).

More than an answer to *Ossessione*, as some critics have stated, the
film is a reflection of the cultural climate and the temperament of the
men who worked on the script. 'Scalo merci' (Freight Station) is the
story of a woman who returns to her native place in search of peace
after a great disappointment in love. Instead of finding peace, she
discovers that she is the constant victim of her own sensuality. The
irrepressible sexuality of the film is similar to the heavy erotic atmosphere of *Ossessione*.

On 10 September 1943, Rome was occupied by the Germans. Before its liberation, De Santis, Gianni Puccini, Mario Socrate, Aldo Scagnetti, Franco Calamandrei, and Antonello Trombadori, working secretly in the studio of the producer Alfredo Guarini on Via del Traforo in Rome,[23] wrote a script on the activities of the Gruppo d'Azione Partigiana (GAP), urban partisans, in Rome. The project had been promoted by Trombadori, who had firsthand experience in urban guerrilla warfare. The project must be recorded as one of the first attempts to film the partisans' activities in Rome, predating Rossellini's *Roma città aperta* (Rome, Open City). Incorporated into the script was one of the current news events of the time, the incident of an Italian woman shot down by the Germans in Giulio Cesare Street. The reconstruction of the event was later included in *Roma città aperta* and interpreted by Anna Magnani.

In 1944, after the liberation of Rome, Italian filmmaking could no longer be suppressed, and people from all the underground political movements who were involved with film united in the newly founded Sindacato Lavoratori del Cinema (Union of Film Technicians) to start a new Italian film industry. The Allies, however, were of a different opinion. In a directive delivered by U.S. rear admiral Emery W. Stone, they declared that the new Italy had no need of a film industry. They went on to state that the existing film industry, a creation of Fascism, should be suppressed. In spite of the Allies' plans, almost everyone who had ever been involved in directing or scriptwriting was eager to make films or to write scripts about the dramatic events just witnessed. As De Sica later wrote remembering those days: 'The war experience was crucial for all of us. We were bursting with an overwhelming desire to throw the old stories of Italian cinema out of the window, to place the camera into the mainstream of real life, of everything that stuck our horrified eyes.'[24]

Giorni di gloria (Days of Glory) and *La nostra guerra* (Our War) are the first documentary films on the Resistance and on the anti-Fascist struggle. The former is the product of a collaboration among Giuseppe De Santis, Marcello Pagliero, Luchino Visconti, and Mario Serandrei, who served as editor and general supervisor. This episodic film is a celebration of the end of Fascism, of new-found freedom, and an open invitation to join in the common effort to build a better future. The film combines newsreel footage, documentary materials shot during the war, and reconstructed episodes of the partisans' struggle. The commentary was written by Umberto Barbaro, who is also the narrator for one of the film's episodes. The documentary material and the reconstructed partisans' sequences use a cinematic language very similar to that employed by filmmakers under Fascism. The similarity is evident in the rhythm, the starting approaches, the cuts, and the stylistic solutions. The partisans in action or taking position are presented in heroic postures, while the sense of their valour and commitment is reinforced by the rhetorical statements of the narrator. The sequences that celebrate the liberation of the northern cities are also shot in the style of the LUCE documentaries. The marching partisans are filmed from below, in low-angle shots, while the camera often cuts rapidly to the cheering crowd, filmed from a slightly higher angle to exaggerate its numbers and to emphasize its solidarity. Alfonso Canziani, writing about *Giorni di gloria*,[25] said that it perhaps marks the beginning of the rhetorical celebration of the Resistance. He added that, in some sections of Visconti's, Pagliero's, and De Santis's episodes, the film shows a break with the cinematic language of previous war films. Visconti had the good fortune to record the trial of Pietro Caruso,[26] police chief of Rome during the German occupation, and his subsequent execution, along with his collaborator, Pietro Roch. The filming of the court proceedings demonstrates Visconti's masterful ability to elaborate a news item into an arresting narrative episode. The tension of the moment is conveyed by alternating close-ups of the accused and their lawyers and long-shots of the crowd's, the witnesses', and the victims' relatives' reactions. In order to exploit the moment's dramatic possibilities to the utmost, Visconti employs two cameras. This enables him to play up even the smallest details, such as an angry hand gesture or the wrinkles on the face of a screaming woman.

De Santis, in charge of filming the sequences on the exhumation of the bodies, was overcome by nausea upon entering the catacombs, and the task was taken over by Marcello Serandrei. Instead, De Santis filmed the third episode, on the nation's rebuilding. The tone of this section is very optimistic and shows what the new forces are doing to reconstruct Italy from the war ruins. The influence of Russian realist cinema is very strong. The approach used in showing the urban rebuilding and the ways in which the workers involved are presented bring to mind Sergei Eisenstein and Dziga Vertov. The train crossing a newly rebuilt bridge in the closing shot is the forerunner of the footage of the train in *Caccia tragica*, De Santis's first film, that will cross the plains of Emilia–Romagna, carrying the veterans of war.

Another of the early films on the Resistance made immediately after the end of the war and the national liberation is *Il sole sorge ancora* (The

Sun Rises Again). As the title attests, the film continues the discourse on the anti-Fascist struggle and the national reconstruction started in *Giorni di gloria* by the former *Cinema* circle. Both the storyline and the filmscript were written by Giuseppe De Santis; Guido Aristarco, who provided firsthand information on the Milanese Resistance; and Carlo Lizzani, who also played the major role of Don Camillo, the priest. Before the start of the film, De Santis, together with Lizzani and Massimo Mida Puccini, had moved to Milan to take over the journal *Film* from Mino Doletti. Under new management, the journal, renamed *Film d'oggi*, was completely transformed. The first issue, published on 1 June 1945, was full of pictures, cinematic inquiries, and interviews, a genre still new in those days.[27]

De Santis, whose role was mainly advisory, continued to publish occasional articles, one of which, 'La giusta via,' announced *Il sole sorge ancora*, which De Santis considered a landmark project: 'This film shows Italian cinema the path to follow: the path of realism.'[28]

The project started among myriad problems and delays but was finally completed by the organizational skill and mediation of Libero Salaroli, who had been called in by De Santis. The film was financed by the Associazione Nationale Partigiani d'Italia (ANPI; the National Association of Italian Partisans) and produced by the former partisan commander Giorgio Agliani, who also served as adviser to Aldo Vergano, the director. Vergano had been chosen over Goffredo Alessandrini because the former had been an anti-Fascist and the latter had collaborated and been involved with the Fascist film industry.[29] De Santis served as the first-unit assistant director and, according to Lizzani, played a very significant role in setting the stylistic modes of the film. The future director of *Riso amaro* (Bitter Rice) has repeatedly downplayed his role, but, as Alberto Farassino wrote: 'if the film shows any mark of an authentic "auteur" in its great technical heterogeneity, it must be attributed to De Santis.'[30] Upon its release, the film was criticized for stylistic excess, the use of heterodox elements in the film idiom, and reduction of the world to a manichean struggle between rigid social classes. These objections were similar to the ones aimed at later films that bear De Santis's signature.

This is not to say that De Santis bears full responsibility for either the artistic merits or the flaws in the film. However, its style and attention to composition are strongly De Santis's. The attention focuses on certain elements like the radio (the new symbol of the emerging mass media). That, and the pre-eminence given the musical score and the soundtrack will later distinguish De Santis's cinematic discourse on the mass media from that of his filmmaking contemporaries.

Many sequences foreshadow De Santis's comprehensive style. The influence of American Westerns, for example, is evident in the final scenes of the film. Here, on the Lombard plains, the partisans stage the last charge against the Germans. Descending from the hills on horseback, or hidden, Indian-style, in the midst of the galloping herd, they heroically aid the peasants in revolt. The shooting style is also reminiscent of that used in many Westerns, with a series of rapid cuts between close-ups of peasants shooting from windows and German soldiers below in the courtyard.

Another scene that bears De Santis's mark is the execution of Don Camillo. Here the priest inspires all to recite litanies as he is led before the firing-squad. The choral response of the crowd creates a crescendo of dramatic tension. The effect is riveting, both for its suspense and for its inspirational message. Similar dramatic devices will appear in De Santis's later films, as will the love of the narrative mode that is apparent in this early effort. Here, the love triangle between the main characters is conceived as the source of conflicts which serve to integrate the plot.

PART II
THE FILMMAKER AND HIS FILM STORIES

4

De Santis behind the Camera

Che significa opporsi a ogni forma di violenza se non combattiamo con il nostro linguaggio di uomini del cinema quelle strutture sociali, quegli ambienti, quei caratteri che rendono possibile il perpetuarsi della violenza ... No, è troppo facile, e tanto più disonesto, suscitare miti, quando questi miti non ci costano che qualche centinaio di inquadrature montate in un certo modo. Ma è anche necessario, indispensabile, che ciascuno si renda conto, sottraendosi alla passività cui soggiace nel buio della sala cinematografica, di quale è questo 'certo modo' ...

What does it mean to oppose any form of violence if we filmmakers do not contest with our artistic means the social structures, the milieu, the temperaments that render possible the perpetuation of violence ... No, it is too easy, and even more dishonest, to create myths, when these myths cost us but a few hundred frames taken in a certain way. It is necessary, indispensable, that everyone realize, by overcoming the passivity to which the spectator is subjected in the darkness of the movie house, how this 'certain way' is achieved.

Giuseppe De Santis

At the time of his cinematic debut in 1947, De Santis had not yet fully formulated the definition of theoretical Neorealism that he was to write in the 1950s,[1] but from his first film it is evident that he was moving towards a realism of content rather than a rigid notion of forms or fictional documentary. In making *Caccia tragica* (Tragic Pursuit), he was conscious that his cinematic approach was different from the one seen in the early films of Rossellini and De Sica.[2] His personal and cultural background was different from theirs, and his political commitments led him to place the lower classes at the centre of his world.

De Santis's career started as a project that goes beyond the mere representation of events. He wanted to go to the roots of social problems in order to reveal their causes and to unmask the people responsible for them. In pursuing an interpretative approach, he hoped to broaden the naturalistic investigation of reality. *Caccia tragica* takes a look, not only at the private dilemmas of the individual, but also at the capacity of people to act together as members of a social class. De Santis set out to portray the psychological characteristics of a social group faced with the adversities of a specific historical moment. In his insatiable desire to expose and to expound on problems, and on their causes, De Santis often packed his films with excess detail, restating and reformulating premises in an obsessive fashion. His goal was to promote a cinema with something for everyone that could be appreciated on many different levels, but his primary concern was communicating with the masses. The public that he had targeted needed to be involved, stimulated, and challenged. One of the ways in which he sought to achieve this goal was through a mediation between melodrama and documentary, resulting in a reflection on social engagement elaborated by those classic cinema genres. The director was also engaged in an ongoing self-reflective meditation on the nature of cinema itself. Starting with *Caccia tragica*, De Santis's filmography includes many instances of his reminding his audiences that cinema is a show and a fiction constructed by means of artistic conventions. He is always conscious of the *mise en scène*, and his films are replete with references to a cinematic tradition which is much more than a mere photographic representation of reality. For the director, hyperbole and fiction are not at odds with the concept of a committed cinema. He recognizes that, in the collective imagination of the people, the fantastic and the extraordinary prevail over the ordinary and the mundane. In its earliest days, cinema enthralled the masses by the simple virtue of its new and mysterious techniques. It successfully exploited the archetypes of the melodrama and the popular novel (*romanzo d'appendice*), from which it derived its stories. Mystery, love, and adventure are magic formulas, well codified by traditional American cinema, and have permitted people all over the world to dream, cry, and escape their immediate reality. De Santis was always aware that cinema could represent only an approximation of reality, that, by its very nature, cinema creates its own form of reality. For this reason, De Santis chose the classical conventional language of film and its codified genres to tell stories about social reality that officialdom wanted to suppress. His originality lies in the stylistic solutions adopted to create a popular cinema that could also stimulate the critical awareness of the public. He observed closely the effects of progress, mechanization, mass media, and the new era of electronics that brought telephones, record players, and televisions into common usage. His analysis of mass communication as the repository of collective imagination is evident in the frequent highlighting of these phenomena in his films. His first two films (particularly the second, *Riso amaro* (Bitter Rice), appeared in a period when, for the first time in Italy, the effects of mass culture and consumerism were felt, even though they were still absent from theoretical discussion by the intellectual élite. His first two films promote this examination by making a constant reference to mass media. The same investigation will be present in all of De Santis's films, with the exception of *Non c'è pace tra gli ulivi* (No Peace under the Olives).[3]

In the following analyses of each of De Santis's films, emphasis is placed on the role of mass media, on the influence of classic cinematic genres, on the stylistic solutions adopted, and on the role played by narrative structures and modes. It should be pointed out that all of these elements are present in varying degrees in each of De Santis's films. Although variations in these structural and modal elements may be attributed, in part, to the theoretical, critical, and historical discourses present during the period of each filming, they are mostly the result of De Santis's artistic sensibility in relation to his medium.

In 1946, after his long apprenticeship, De Santis was eager to direct his own film. With his collaboration in the making of *Il sole sorge ancora* (The Sun Rises Again), he had proven (to the producers) his artistic maturity and organizational ability.[4] In spring 1946, at the age of thirty, with a group of collaborators consisting, for the most part, of old friends, former members of the *Cinema* circle, former schoolmates, and fellow party members, De Santis started his adventure in filmmaking. The shooting of his first film, *Caccia tragica*, started in the Bassa Padana (Lower Po Valley), near Ravenna and not far from the site where, four years earlier, he had assisted Visconti in the making of *Ossessione*. This location was chosen for a variety of political, artistic, and even sentimental reasons. The Italian Left had given this area of the Po Valley a special political significance by designating it as the land from which the 'North Wind' would blow its regenerating ideals of solidarity, equality, and democracy to all of Italy.[5] From an artistic and sentimental standpoint, the beauty of the valley, with its rich vegetation, canals, and typical peasant life, reminded De Santis of the plain surrounding his native Fondi. Fondi, an agricultural town made up of merchants and small landowners, was not considered a suitable location. It had never developed peasant cooperatives and, in the postwar period, was not going through a movement for land reforms. De Santis and his collaborators found in the dense population and vast fields of Emilia–Romagna an ideal backdrop to lend authenticity to their production. Here, in a countryside still marked by the atrocities of war, the dramatic events of the postwar peasant movement were actually unfolding.

Caccia tragica,[6] based on a real-life event reported by the journalist Lamberto Rem-Picci, concerns a peasant cooperative which is robbed by a band of masked gangsters of the funds it has accumulated to lease land and livestock. De Santis, with the help of Carlo Lizzani, Corrado Alvaro, Michelangelo Antonioni, Ennio De Concini, Umberto Barbaro, and Cesare Zavattini, developed an elaborate script from this news item, thereby setting a precedent for the group collaboration on screenplays inspired by human-interest stories that would become characteristic of De Santis's filmography.

In *Caccia tragica*, one can trace stylistic influences of French films; American Westerns and musical and gangster genres; as well as allusions to the films of Eisenstein and Dovzhenko. In his brilliant monograph on De Santis, Farassino[7] notes how the young director, after opening with a scene that is pure Visconti, moves on quickly to establish his own heterogeneous style, in which the various cinematic references and modes that were part of his artistic background are all well assimilated. The camera, carried by a crane, focuses briefly on two lovers embracing in the back of a truck and then rises to show the ambience. Aside from having artistic beauty, this camera sequence is also a narrative device used to shift from the personal to the social, integrating both levels into a specific physical setting. The significance of landscape as part of the *mise en scène* was referred to by De Santis in one of the articles he wrote in 1941:

The importance of a landscape and of its choice is a fundamental element inside which the characters should live, showing, almost, the signs of its reflections, just as our great painters understood ... How could it be possible to understand and to interpret man if he is isolated from the elements in which he lives every day, with which he communicates every day ...[8]

The film was well received by the critics. At the Eighth Venice Film Festival, it won an *ex aequo* Silver Ribbon for best director and for best starring actress (Vivi Gioi). At the same festival, it also received first prize as best Italian film. Notwithstanding this recognition in Italy, the film's release was preceded by long and harsh polemics between the two political factions competing in the upcoming national election: the National Popular Front, which supported the film, and the Christian Democrats, which, together with the clergy, ostracized it. In fact, for political and propaganda reasons, *Caccia tragica* was not released publicly until three days before the national election of 18 April 1948.[9]

After the defeat of the National Popular Front, the film would be shown only in provincial cities and in third-class theatres. The hostile climate which was responsible for its late release and the pessimistic mood of the defeated Left is a dramatic contrast with the film's optimistic storyline and political message. In the film, the solidarity and collaboration of the peasants are rewarded, and their success in recovering the stolen funds forestalls the landowner's attempt to crush their cooperative. After the election, the film was at first interpreted as statement of the Left's political thesis and national strategy, and was labelled as an unartistic hodgepodge of preconceived ideological dogmas.[10] However, *Caccia tragica* was not intended as a propagandist manifesto. It is a cinematic masterpiece in which De Santis shows his ability to infuse new cinematic and narrative elements into established modes, genres, and styles of filmmaking. With this, his first film, he broadened the Italian postwar film idiom and also renewed the Neorealist trend that, after only a few years of activity, was already in stagnation.

Caccia tragica is more than a glorification of class solidarity and achieved socialism; it is also an exciting and tragic story about how people recover from the devastation of war, how they heal their wounds and reconcile their differences. In the film, the Second World War has just ended and, in the Lower Po Valley, peasants working in cooperatives are removing the land-mines from the abandoned and ravaged fields in order to prepare the soil for planting. Giovanna (Carla Del Poggio) and Michele (Massimo Girotti), just married, are returning to the cooperative's farmstead aboard a truck that is also transporting funds to lease land and livestock. At the farm, excitement is running high in anticipation of this doubly festive occasion. The funds, however, are not destined to arrive. A band of gangsters driving an ambulance stops the truck and escapes with the money, taking the newlywed Giovanna as a hostage. In the course of the robbery, Michele recognizes one of the bandits as Alberto (Andrea Checchi), a former comrade and fellow detainee in a German concentration camp. The rest of the gag consists of Daniela / Lilì Marlene (Vivi Gioi), a former German soldier, and a driver. The bandits take refuge at a country villa, where they meet with their accomplices, the conservative faction of landlords. Upon returning to the cooperative, Michele discovers that these same land-owners have already repossessed the land and equipment and are evict-ing the peasants. He is nevertheless reticent about revealing details of the robbery and the name of his concentration-camp buddy. The other peasants are determined to mobilize and, before long, pursue the bandits. The villa hideaway is soon discovered and surrounded by armed peasants, but the bandits flee, using Giovanna as their shield.

Lilì Marlene transports Giovanna to the former German headquarters, which is protected by land-mine, connected electronically to a remote detonator inside the villa of the landowners. The gang decides to separate: Alberto and his male accomplices must catch a train, usually crowded with black-marketeers, in order to exchange banknotes for foreign currency, while Daniela / Lilì Marlene will stay hidden with Giovanna in the swamp. The bandits attempt to conceal themselves in a trainload of veterans crossing the Po Valley as part of a propaganda campaign for the National Popular Front. The train is stopped, and Michele spots Alberto and pursues him, eventually forcing him to reveal the location of Lilì Marlene's hide-out. The two men arrive at the former headquarters, where Alberto kills Lilì Marlene before she can detonate the mines. In the evening, at the farm, the peasants set up a Kangaroo court to try Alberto.[11] After lengthy discussions, they agree that he is not guilty, having been a dupe of the landowners, who have exploited his poverty, unemployment, despair, and alienation. The peasants tell Alberto where he can find work and, as he walks away, they pelt him with lumps of earth as a sign of good luck and forgiveness.[12]

In his first film, De Santis displays his ability to combine spectacle and social comment. For him, cinema is a medium capable of entertain-ing while it instructs. He does not record events as static reportage but shows the dynamics of conflicting forces engaged in the painstaking metamorphoses of progress. The opposing forces in *Caccia tragica* are the peasants and conservative element among the landowning class, who are in turn, aided by a few individuals who have been instrumental during the Fascist regime. The Italian war veteran Alberto, who has suc-cumbed to the charms of Lilì Marlene, is the key figure of the drama.[13] It is his change of heart and his act of self-liberation, represented by his murder of Lilì Marlene, which resolve a dangerous situation. Above all, his actions symbolize the triumph of reconstruction and national reconciliation over Fascism and Neofascism. The land-mines as well as the war wounds of the veterans are tangible symbols of the injuries that must be healed before life can resume its normal cycles. The reconstruction meant for De Santis a desire to forge a new national identity based on some of the ideals of the Resistance.[14]

Typical of the American Westerns that influenced De Santis was the simplistic reduction of conflict into a struggle between good and evil. From the Westerns also comes the image of the train, a symbol of progress, of territorial conquest, and of the linking of two coasts. The train full of veterans crossing the Po Valley also has another significance. In *Caccia tragica*, it becomes, as in the Russian cinematic tradition, a vehicle for spreading new political ideologies. Some features, such as a crane shot which takes in a crowd of peasants and then descends, isolating in individual frames the war veterans who are crossing the fields en masse, are similar to the techniques used to display group configurations in American musical productions. It was from the great American musicals that De Santis learned how to follow crowds and how to isolate the individual members among them in single shots.

By focusing on the veterans, both as individuals and as a background-filler which becomes part of the landscape, De Santis achieves an explicit, non-verbal condemnation of the Fascist war.

Another significant scene is the fight between Alberto and Michele, which De Santis has staged in a public square cluttered with bicycles left behind by peasants attending a nearby political rally. The fight, witnessed only by inanimate spectators – the bicycles – and accompanied by the off-screen voices and noises of the rally, unfolds in the fashion of a showdown in an American Western. Here again, De Santis is able to add a touch of his own. The use of abandoned bicycles instead of extras creates a symbiosis between men and their bikes. The visual effect has a stunning emotional impact: the rows of abandoned bikes bring to mind the devastation of the war in a suggestive manner perhaps unattainable with a pan shot over a screaming crowd. Indeed, as De Santis proposed in his 1941 article 'Per un paesaggio italiano,' the bikes are descriptive and essential elements that speak of the everyday lives of these men.

In 1946, while the other Neorealist directors were arguing for a cinema based on everyday life and on the objective representation of reality in the illusion that reality speaks by itself about a given and ongoing situation, De Santis was well aware that a film is, at best, an imitation of reality, the 'image' of reality. For him, news items and the documentary were only raw materials for creating plots which were then transformed into a new cinematic reality. De Santis comments on the dual real/illusory nature of film in a symbolic sequence in *Caccia tragica*: Michele and Giuseppe enter Alberto's house and are confronted by masked children playing and dancing in celebration of Carnevale.[15] Ignoring the surprise shown by the intruders, the children invite them to join in the celebration. When they refuse, the oldest child suddenly removes his mask, and a little girl pulls aside a curtain which conceals a gaping hole in one of the walls. Through the hole the adults can observe Il Camoscio, an accomplice of Alberto, who has just gotten out of his car and, unaware of the onlookers, is shining his shoes. Michele then interrogates the little girl on the subject of Lilì Marlene and Alberto, but, before she can reveal what she knows, the oldest child, Eugene, intervenes. In anger and frustration, Michele shoves Eugene to the ground. A brief struggle ensues, and Eugene, aided by the other children, gets back on his feet, replaces his mask, and resumes playing. Here, the interplay between reality and illusion is expressed by the removing and replacing of masks. De Santis's intention is to demonstrate that artistic reality is built on conventions, but that convention is likewise a reality. Giuseppe and Michele, by refusing to wear masks, are unable to take part in the children's make-believe. In order to enter for a moment into the adults' reality, Eugene removes his mask, which symbolically represents the world of games and fantasy. When the little girl pulls aside the curtain covering the hole, the protagonists glimpse another reality. In these scenes, De Santis is exposing some of the hidden assumptions of his medium. He is telling us that reality does not necessarily speak for itself in a way that is intelligible to all. It needs a setting, exposition, and a form. Like the masks, which represent the world of games and fantasy for the children, the camera becomes, for De Santis, a joyful instrument with which to explore and play.

Caccia tragica shows all the exuberance of a young director involved in his first film. It is, indeed, a story about the postwar period, about reconstruction, about the problems faced by returning veterans, and about land reform, but it is also a film about filmmaking. Here, De Santis puts into practice the techniques of great spectacle, the ideals of social commitment, and a self-conscious reflection on the nature of cinema. The film is optimistic. It is the only one of De Santis's films in which the reality examined is not at odds with the historical reality of the time. The film traces, in an upward trajectory, the visions of solidarity and social rebirth that the Resistance spawned for the Italian Left – expectations that faded away with the political defeat of the National Popular Front in 1948. The central message of De Santis's later films, beginning with *Riso amaro* (Bitter Rice), is no longer a reflection of the ideological and central debate of the period. In these films, the gulf between the cinematic message and the social-political historical moment widens and is never bridged.

5

And Then Came Silvana:
Riso amaro (1949)

La critica cinematografica di sinistra si mostrò veramente moralista. A proposito di 'Riso amaro' la stampa di sinistra si produsse in manifestazioni di moralismo zdanovista, veramente aberrante. Qualcuno scrisse addirittura che il mio film costituiva un attentato alla moralità delle mondine.

Leftist film critics proved to be truly moralistic. With regard to *Riso amaro* the leftist press showed a Zhdanovistic moralism, truly aberrant. Someone actually wrote that my film was an immoral offence against the rice workers.

Giuseppe De Santis

In late October 1949, in the pages of the Communist paper *L'Unità*, Davide Lojola started the first national debate on a film. The majority of the Italian critics involved showed their unpreparedness to deal with a film as exuberant as *Riso amaro* (Bitter Rice), which was soon to become a worldwide commercial success. The criticism was levelled at the credibility of the story and at the improbable fusion of a melodramatic love story and a socially committed theme.

The main cause of the critics' bewilderment was the protagonists' overt sexuality, which motivated their actions, and the explicit eroticism displayed by the then unknown eighteen-year-old Silvana Mangano (Silvana Melega in the film).[1] Such distractions, socially engaged critics complained, diverted the audience's attention away from and overshadowed the political message of class unity and solidarity. The harsh words of the prudish critic Guido Aristarco probably still resound in the director's ears: 'The workers cannot be educated with the bare legs of Silvana.'[2]

Some leftist labour-union leaders defended[3] the *mondine's* (rice workers') innocence and morality by reaffirming that it was their custom and desire to dance to the comforting tune of traditional folk music rather than to the corrupting American boogie-woogie, as shown in the film. De Santis was so deeply affected by the attacks that he waited almost two years before replying.

The moralistic attacks from the Left[4] were shortly followed by the uncompromising judgment of the Vatican censors, who, in order to preserve audiences from the temptation of Silvana's sensuality, placed the film on the list of forbidden works. Among the other negative reviews from the Right, Ennio Flaiano's slanted remarks[5] remain the most representative evidence of the distance between De Santis's film and the sensibility of some of his colleagues.

Nowadays, in the canon of American film criticism *Bitter Rice* is remembered as the film that marked the beginning of the return of Italian postwar cinema to the star system, to colossal production, to the use of professional actors, and, most important, as the film that, with a hybrid style recognizably indebted to Hollywood, betrayed the newly formed Italian Neorealism.

These charges become even more serious if one considers the fact that the film was made by Giuseppe De Santis (in collaboration with former members of the journal *Cinema*), the most politically and ideologically committed Communist of all the Italian filmmakers of the time.

This is how one American critic describes the paradox: '"Bitter Rice" rejects the more optimistic vision of Italian–American relationships found in Rossellini's 'Paisan' and goes far beyond the criticism of the American way of life in Lattuada's "Without Pity," but it is, paradoxically, the neorealist film most obviously indebted to the American cinema and its rich generic traditions.'[6]

The fact that De Santis and his two main collaborators, Gianni Puccini and Carlo Lizzani, were Marxists, and that one of the film's intentions in using Hollywood's cinematic conventions was to undermine and denounce the corrupting effects of embracing popular American trends in lifestyle must not be considered paradoxical.

Puccini, De Santis and Lizzani, schooled as cineastes, had watched and appreciated the great American films of the 1930s. As was the case for many other intellectuals of the period who opposed Fascism, American culture and literature meant freedom and cosmopolitanism. The cultivation of a taste for things American was a sort of intellectual rebellion against the provincialism of the regime.

To get a sampling of their personal views on this issue, one needs to turn to some of their film reviews and major articles written for *Cinema*. These sources reveal that American films were often a reference point as they sought ideas for how to make national cinema more authentic. For example, in De Santis's largely neglected, 1945 article 'Cinema e narrativa' (Cinema and Narrative), the American practice of making use of popular fiction and folk heroes in the Western genre is cited as a stimulating model for the promotion of a new type of national cinema – a cinema that 'by drawing on the popular narrative mode and on indigenous tales could ... speak the language of the masses and stir their sentiments.'[7]

After the war, Puccini, De Santis, and Lizzani reaffirmed on various occasions their positions regarding American culture. For example, during a lecture in Pisa, on 18 February 1989, De Santis stated:

My position vis-à-vis American culture reflected the views of other intellectuals, such as Cesare Pavese and Elio Vittorini [Neorealist writers], who aimed at reconstructing the image of Italy through that culture. America was for us the great democratic system of the New Deal – an absolute reference point which we wanted to absorb first and later re-elaborate in order to adapt it to the local culture of Italy. For example, the 'mondine' [rice workers] in *Riso amaro* sing, instead of talking, to communicate. This is a reference to both American musicals and the Black American culture that I learned to love in American films. America was the great myth for us. It was the introduction to mass culture with the arrival of the American troops in Italy. Before *Riso amaro*, I worked with Visconti, as scriptwriter and assistant director, for *Ossessione* [1942; Obsession]. The topography of the Po Valley [in the film] referred to the great American plains. Another important cultural reference for me were King Vidor's films. However, the character of Silvana in *Riso amaro* was not modelled on any protagonist in American literature, but on the character of Padron 'Ntoni of Giovanni Verga's *I Malavoglia*. When *Riso amaro* was nominated for an Oscar award in 1949, the United States denied me a visa to enter the country because of my political allegiance to the PCI [Partito Comunista Italiano]. At that time [1949], many things had changed.[8]

As De Santis says, in the late 1940s the political situation had changed. The world was divided into political blocks controlled by the Soviets (the Warsaw Pact countries), and the NATO alliance. This polarization set the climate for the bitter confrontation of the Cold War. On a personal level, the love and admiration that De Santis felt for the films of John Ford, King Vidor, Howard Hawks, Charlie Chaplin, and Frank Capra was an indelible part of his own cinematic vision and had shaped his conception of filmmaking to such a degree that it could not be changed by the new political atmosphere.

De Santis's own notion of filmmaking is tied to his intellectual and political commitment to making films that could communicate to everyone. His main concerns were to entertain and to denounce; his films are never passive witnesses to social injustice.

De Santis never employs heavy-handed allegories; rather, he uses simple metaphors, such as the necklace in *Riso amaro*. Equally, in his quest to underscore social problems and point out their causes, he did not care to resort to the rigidity of surface accuracy and authenticity.

Obviously, if one of De Santis's primary concerns was to promote a national cinema that could appeal and communicate to any audience, he had to use the generic American cinematic forms that movie-goers knew, understood, and enjoyed most. De Santis was never interested in making esoteric films that appealed only to the critics. His works were all spectacular and metaphorical pieces directed towards extra-aesthetic ends. These notions are fundamental in understanding the director's view of filmmaking and his role within the Neorealist movement.

These notions also explain De Santis's adaptation of cinematic melodramatic patterns in *Riso amaro* and his depiction of Silvana Mangano as the Italian counterpart of the 'American atomic bomb,' Rita Hayworth.[9] I will return to that idea later in this chapter in the analysis of Silvana Mangano's rise to stardom. First, though, an examination of the turbulent period that accompanied the making of De Santis's best-known and most successful film will help elucidate the director's love–contempt relationship with American culture.

The storyline for *Riso amaro* was written in October 1947, and the film treatment during winter 1947–8. The final script was completed in April 1948. The film was shot during a crucial historical moment for the Italian Left. The PCI, led by its general secretary, Palmiro Togliatti, had broken with the De Gasperi government and gone over to the opposition. The political situation was so dramatic that the film's production was held up for two months after the great electoral defeat of the National Popular Front on 18 April 1948.[10] The defeat marked, from a leftist prospective (and for De Santis), the onset of the twilight of the Resistance's dreams for a progressive / leftist reconstruction. After 1948, the conservative forces, supported by the American government through the Marshall Plan, started a period of reconstruction / restoration marked by the semi-democratization of the Fascist legislature. For the director, the forces of reaction had defeated the forces for change.

During these turbulent years, Italy was also undergoing a cultural transformation. In the late 1940s, customs were changing. The populace had a great desire to forget the war, to enjoy life, and to adopt new foreign modes of life and fashion after the autarchical economic restrictions imposed by the regime.

The national circulation of the first photo-romances, *Bolero Film*, *Grand Hôtel*, and *Confidenze di Liala* (*Grand Hôtel* first came out as a comic strip in 1946), among the poorly educated stratum of the populace can be regarded as one of the many signs that the nation was in the midst of a cultural transition.

These new forms of mass communications had a direct impact on the film industry as well, creating a period of transition in the history of Italian cinema. Commenting on this new phenomenon, one Italian critic remarked: 'The turning-point of our cinema can be found, not so much in the ten or fifteen films of Visconti, De Sica, and Rossellini that by now we know by heart, but in the popular films in Neapolitan and Venetian dialects, or Matarazzo's, Brignone's, and Mario Costa's films.'[11]

As a case in point, in 1949, Raffaello Matarazzo's *Catene* (Chains) was the most viewed film, grossing 735 million lire; *La terra trema* (The Earth Trembles), made two years earlier, grossed 38 million lire.[12] Matarazzo's films, such as *Catene*, *Tormento* (Torment), and *I figli di nessuno* (Nobody's Sons) reidentified social taboos and appealed to the public's taste and imagination by chronicling some social changes.

By concentrating on themes such as love, death, violence, and fears linked to the ancestral sins of abortion, rape, adultery and incest, this new cinematic form became, by the early 1950s, a codified genre.

At the centre of these dramas was the family, consistently presented with overtones of sex-phobia and a rigid Catholic moralism in combination with a strong sense of honour, which effectively made of the family an institution that repressed any form of individualism, independence, and personal fulfilment.

Generally, in these films women are victims of males' prejudices and false sense of honour. Often, women are also victims of some misunderstanding which serves to drive the plot. But, by the end of these films, the confusion is resolved, and everyone's honour is preserved and saved.

Rather than using the melodramatic mode, as Raffaello Matarazzo does in his social-conformist films, De Santis demeans the photo-romance's messages and challenges social conventions in *Riso amaro*.

When *Riso amaro* was filmed, the photo-romance was the most important means of communication and the most powerful medium for reaching the female public, even though the genre was snubbed by the intellectuals, who relegated it to the realm of subculture.[13] Commenting on the medium, Damiano Damiani, one of its creators, stated: 'We concentrated on increasing the number of readers and their acculturation by using stories recognizable and understandable because they corresponded to values and feelings then well diffused. We did not believe that what had success among the masses necessarily had to be a subcultural product, as defined by an élitist vision of culture rooted in Italy.'[14]

As the quote suggests, the readers of photo-romances belonged to a particular social class. Lower- and working-class women between the ages of fifteen and twenty-five were the most avid readers of these new publications. The typical female reader had no job skills, and most probably had not even finished elementary school.

In these 'recognizable and understandable' stories, the action centres around the male who renews the myth of Prince Charming. The female protagonist often serves as a cultural reference model of accepted values. Her main aspirations are to marry and to have a family. In order to intensify the identification process between the reader and the protagonists, no specific location is ever revealed.

Love is the predominant theme. It will overcome all obstacles but class barriers. Conformity can solve all existential and psychological problems. When sociopolitical realities such as labour and class conflicts are touched upon, they are always minimized.

De Santis saw this new medium as promoting the Americanization of the Italian lower class. He did not trust the messages or the values presented, which, to him, exemplified a threat to the simple, natural life of rural Italy, the culture of De Santis's cinematic characters, who politically were the majority of his party's supporters.

In making *Riso amaro*, De Santis's intentions were to undermine the addiction to certain American individualistic ideas, considered antisocial and disruptive of class solidarity. The film demonstrates how the addiction to induced desires, exemplified in Silvana's drive to possess the necklace and to stay in beautiful hotels, will lead to betrayal and theft.

The film's success is not attributable to its moralistic and propagandistic schematization of hard work and class solidarity against selfishness and theft, but rests in its capturing of the cultural atmosphere of the time. Its modernity consists in its having attempted to deal with what could be called 'the onset of cultural imperialism,' or in a Marxist sense, the overwhelming power of the overstructure.

The film's discourse concerns the social changes taking place in a culture struggling for a new identity. The new sexual freedom of young people, the influence of the new cinematic medium, and the impact of more liberal ideas imported from the other side of the ocean are manifestations of the new modes of life.

More than any other postwar Italian film, *Riso amaro* shows a society in transition. In this work, De Santis continued and broadened his reflection on the influence of mass media on culture and on its power to shape the audience's desires and aspirations. The film is a groundbreaking attempt to deal with the first effects of induced desires on the working class.

The insightfulness of *Riso amaro* returned Italian cinema to international prominence. In the United States, the film was nominated for an Academy Award for best original story, and internationally it surpassed even the fame of Rossellini's *Paisan*.

The film's release was preceded by a great deal of publicity and curiosity. It was announced as a colossal production by Lux Film, and Robert Capa went to Veneria di Lignana, where De Santis's cast was filming, to research a special report for *Life* magazine.[15]

The clamour continued during the seventy-two days of filming, and reached its peak with the beautiful drawings specially made by Renato Guttuso, one of the most famous realist painters of the time, for the film's release.

The film also marked the birth of a new star. Even today, many film critics wonder how a rigid and structured script intended to denounce induced desires could have achieved such popularity. Since other studies have concentrated on the dualistic melodramatic and documentary modes of *Riso amaro*, I focus here on how the form interconnects cinematically with the message by condemning Silvana's fancies and redeeming Francesca. This examination of the condemnation of Silvana's induced desires also shows that the images and the presence of this newcomer to the screen not only superseded the director's ideology but led to the clamorous rise to stardom of the actress. Silvana was supremely suited to achieve stardom through this film because she embodied all the contradictions inherent in the cultural transition then under way in Italy. Her confused actions stand for the existential struggle for a better life with no assurance as to what lies ahead. Sylvana's existential struggle is that of an adolescent coming of age.

By De Santis's own account,[16] the idea of a film about the rice workers was suggested to him by Libero Solaroli, who, knowing the director's predilection for rural and choral themes, mentioned a film on the annual migration of thousands of girls to the rice fields to plant the rice. That suggestion became a reality only much later. In Milan, in the early hours of a September morning, as he returned from France, where he had attended a première of *Caccia tragica*, De Santis was astounded to discover at the train station a crowd of rice workers comprising women of all ages and from various parts of northern Italy on their way home after having spent more than a month in the rice paddies.

The experience had a lasting impact on De Santis, who immediately set to work on a story with his best friend, Gianni Puccini, and Carlo Lizzani. Once the storyline was completed, they departed for Turin to search for a good location. In need of advice, they called on the writer Cesare Pavese, and Davide Lojola, the editor of the Turin edition of *L'Unità*, who referred them to one of his subordinates, Raf Vallone. This young and relatively unknown journalist, editor of the third page of *L'Unità*, helped them in contacting the local rice growers.[17] After a long and difficult search, the Agnelli family agreed to let them film on its estate.[18]

Two years had passed since De Santis's fateful encounter with the *mondine* before the three young cineastes completed the screenplay. At the request of Lux Studio, Carlo Musso and Ivo Perilli were brought on board as co-writers. Later, Corrado Alvaro, a well-known realist writer, was brought in to rewrite the dialogue and the songs.[19]

The ideas of the three friends, who had also worked on De Santis's first film, were varied. They wanted to create a film that would include all of their much-debated concepts – a spectacular, popular, realistic, social, and political film that could reach everyone and not only viewers of art films.

The dilemma that they faced was how to reconcile the realistic, political, documentary, and social program with the delivery mode of spectacular, melodramatic entertainment. These rival impulses are evident in the opening film titles, which announce: 'This film tells two stories: one, of the hard work, and the other, of the flow of emotions generated by thousands of women who pick and plant, pick and plant for forty days. It also tells about their long, long nights.'

The two rival impulses that the film proposes to follow are the capitalistic exploitation of the *mondine* by day and the sexual drives that take them over at night – the collective and the private.

How does the finished film show what its authors had successfully reconciled in a rigid and well-structured script? Could the images follow and reflect these two opposing drives in order to demonstrate the ideological theorems that support the intentionality of the story?

As Carlo Lizzani has described in his meticulous study of the making of *Riso amaro*, the scriptwriters had to make the story fit De Santis's already well-established and -tested model for reconciling the personal with the social. In De Santis's pattern, a syntactic crescendo builds, linking individuals, voices, or sonorous signals, to trigger off, at a specific moment, a type of image that is no longer the sum of the preceding ones but a new event in choral dimension.[20]

This structural and visual device enables the director to reconcile the various tensions in the film. But most of all, it enables him to link the melodramatic mode with Silvana's behaviour, which leads to her expulsion from the group, and with Francesca's redemption through assimilation with the hard work of the rice workers.

In the film, form brilliantly represents and operates as a function of content. The unhealthy lure of the photo-romance's ideals and attractions (Americanization) is opposed to the hard work and good values of the working class, and these two elements are also contrasted through their association with the protagonists – Francesca (Doris Dowling) and Walter (Vittorio Gassman) on one side, and Silvana and Sergeant Marco Galli (Raf Vallone) on the other. Thus, corruption contrasts with traditional values, and theft with labour. As the story progresses, the roles of the female characters are reversed. The passage from one role to the other is a pendulous movement in a pattern comprising several individual crossed courses. As Francesca is slowly incorporated into the group, Silvana is expelled, and the rise and fall of the two female protagonists is charted. The transition drives the narrative and demonstrates the director's ideology. His ultimate goal is to go beyond the discrediting of Silvana's dream and to attack its source, America, the land where everything is electric, including the electric chair, as Marco, the positive hero, says to Silvana.

In the introductory preamble, Francesca is presented as Walter's partner in crime. They have just robbed a jewellery store and are fleeing from the police. At the boarding for the rice fields, Walter spots the beautiful Silvana Melega dancing the boogie-woogie and chewing gum.

Walter joins her to avoid being recognized. Later, in order to escape, he uses Francesca as a shield from the policemen's bullets.

The stage is set. The photo-romance (the melodramatic mode associated with Silvana's dream) and its distinguishing components – adventure, romance, action, suspense, escapism, conflict, and beautiful protagonists – are all present. The characters will be defined by their actions, looks, and clothing.

Silvana is not only an avid reader of *Grand Hôtel* but also a poor peasant girl in search of a life more enjoyable and interesting than weeding and planting in the paddies. In her fantasy, Walter appears to be the Prince Charming of the *Grand Hôtel* she reads. However, the love triangle typical of many photo-romances turns into a square when Sergeant Marco Galli appears at the arrival at the rice field. He will be the positive antagonist of Walter, the petty thief.

In the course of the action, the two women aspire to be what they're not. Each wants to be in the other's shoes. Their desires are enhanced and paralleled by the filming techniques used: a rhythmic structure created by the pendulous movement of the role transition accompanied by a meticulous Griffith-like montage and contrasting of backgrounds.

Realistic scenes depicting the workers are used frequently as a contrast to the melodramatic ones. These different types of shots are interspersed throughout the film, giving it a background–foreground visual base. Their purpose is not only to tell the story of women slaving in the rice fields but also to highlight Francesa's transition into the work force and Silvana's self-exclusion from it. In this meticulous structure, the screen newcomer also shows the character's multidimensional and complex personality. The contradictory and multifaceted character that sets her apart from the one-dimensional *mondine* is obvious from the start.

Silvana's distance is not only visual but behavioural. When she first sees Walter, she is intrigued by his photo-romantic / cinematic good looks, to which he draws further attention by donning a straw hat, and his ability to dance the boogie-woogie. The police chase and the shots fired at Walter only increase her attraction to him. Her curiosity is further sharped when she sees Francesca making a conspicuous effort to reach Walter. Then, just in case we miss the message, the film adds to this reading with an intercut of a man selling copies of *Grand Hôtel*. As if that were not enough, immediately after the shot of the stolen necklace, a knock is heard at the door and a young woman holding up a copy of *Grand Hôtel* is seen standing there. It is Silvana. Her vision of Francesca and Walter as characters in her fictional world is completed.

A short conversation between the two women is followed by completely different background shots. As Francesca moves down the train aisle, the camera pans across some of the 'real rice workers.' These women are plain. Some are sleeping; one woman is distraught and anxiously eats a piece of bread; another is drinking. Yet another woman serves as a striking contrast: seated at the back of the car, she is trying to apply lipstick to cover her ugliness. The contrast with the world of photo-romantic fantasy reaches its peak when Amelia tells Francesca that someone has thrown up nearby.

Francesca is presented analogically with the world that she will enter. This pattern of switching style and content in association with two main female protagonists continues throughout the film and peaks once they arrive at the rice field, where the metamorphosis of Silvana and Francesca occurs.

The next day, many women are told they cannot work in the fields without a contract. Led by Francesca, they try to win one by working twice as hard as the women who have been legally hired. Francesca displays her personal strength and slowly affirms her leadership. This transformation is visually demonstrated by the beautifully choreographed sequence of the hat distribution.

The scabs are standing in a clump together. Francesca is front and centre, and she stares intensely at the edgy Silvana. Then Francesca moves closer to the camera, becoming more dominant. In contrast, Silvana is seen putting her hat on, not in the midst of a group of other rice workers, but almost in isolation. Whereas Francesca stands with the workers, Silvana stands apart from the group, as if to underline her individualistic drives. Her stance is a visual reminder of Silvana's ambiguous role and personality. Her body actions, facial expressions, and behaviour exemplify her uncertain and complex nature, which makes her an attractive character.

Later, as the scabs are trying to outwork the other women, Silvana is seen in a boat, distributing the rice plants. She leads the rice workers in song to voice their disapproval of the scabs. Francesca and the other illegal workers respond, asking the other group to be more understanding of their desperate state. Their appeal for class solidarity is answered with attack by the hired workers. Silvana tries to direct the hired workers' anger against Francesca, who is saved from a lynching by the providential arrival of the positive hero, Sergeant Marco Galli, who exhorts the women to work together instead of fighting against one another.[21]

As a visual reference to Silvana's estrangement from the 'real *mondine*,' she, the fomenter of the attack, does not take part in the wrestling in the mud. Rather, she is shown standing apart, screaming but unscathed.

The role change between the two female protagonists continues. The scene inside the former barracks brings the transformation a step closer to completion. The brilliant interplay of the contrasting black and white of Silvana's and Francesca's petticoats renders visually the pattern of their individual crossed courses.

The scene begins with a shot of Francesca telling Silvana the story of her relationship with Walter. For Silvana, it is like the realization of her fantasy world. She overlooks completely the tragic element. For Francesca, it is the confession of a shame that she wants to rid herself of. Visually, they seem to be in a Catholic confessional, and Silvana listens eagerly without giving any comfort. Their conversation is interrupted by the moaning of one of the *mondine* who has taken ill. Promptly, Francesca runs to help, leaving behind, with Silvana, her past, now transformed in Silvana's fantasy to a glamorous life. Francesca is shown among her fellow workers, trying to help the ill woman; Silvana is alone, stretched out on her bed, showing an expression of disgust and annoyance at the interruption. Her individualistic attitude is further emphasized as she plays a dance record, snapping her fingers as she waits for Francesca to resume her story.

The interplay between them goes a step farther. One crucial scene marking Silvana's indulgence in her fantasies is the dance with Walter. Mirroring a dance pattern from one of De Santis's favourite filmmakers, King Vidor,[22] Marco steps in to save Silvana when he sees her, radiant with the excitement of the music and her own daring, dancing with the stolen necklace on. Walter intercedes, and the famous fight between him and Marco takes place.[23]

In Marco's actions, there is an attempt to stem the allure of materialism, as his ripping the necklace from Silvana's neck attests. Marco beats Walter in the fight, to the pleasure of the 'real rice workers' and Francesca, but not of Silvana. She does not give up her pursuit of easy life and happiness alongside her 'Prince Charming,' Walter.

The changing of roles reaches its climax and completion during the paralleled scenes of Silvana's rape and the miscarriage of Gabriella (Maria Grazia Francia). In these much-discussed scenes, De Santis is able to show, in dramatic and brilliant images, the complete expulsion of Silvana from the working class.

It has been raining for days. The older rice workers decide to work, despite the weather; Francesca, after a little hesitation, joins them. In a beautiful setting worthy of De Santis's enthusiasm for spectacular, plastic effects, the *mondine* emerge from the farmhouse with sacks on their heads. They look like vestal virgins ready for a rite that will be soon performed around the desolate body of Gabriella. Meanwhile, Silvana, in her best form, followed by Walter, has entered a woody area adjacent to the rice paddies. She has a switch in her hand to tease and keep Walter at a distance. In the pouring rain, Walter forces her into submission, and Silvana is now on Walter's side. The identification with the female characters of her stories is completed. She is seen again, alone in desperation, unable to succour her friend Gabriella, who is in pain.

In the nearby fields, the *mondine* are working in order not to lose another day of pay when the pregnant Gabriella, in agony, starts to lose her baby. The rest of the *mondine* try to cover her screams by singing.

The sequence is a powerful representation of mourning, portrayed in a highly symbolic and spiritual manner. The *mondine* with the sacks over their heads, make a circle around Gabriella's tortured body to show support and to protect her from losing her job. The content is a display of working-class solidarity and peasant choral participation in the sorrow. When the circle opens, it becomes clear that nothing else can be done for Gabriella, and a funeral lamentation starts.

The composition of the scene is similar to a painting of the Lamentation.[24] An older *mondine* in the centre of the frame assumes a posture similar to that of the Virgin Mary. She looks down on Gabriella and later turn her eyes to the sky, joining her hands together as if to invoke help and protection from heaven. Her rhythmic motion is taken up by the rest of the *mondine*. De Santis is putting into practice his ideas on how filmmakers can profit from the rich patrimony of Italian paintings.

The *mondine* head back to the farmhouse, Francesca carrying the body of Gabriella as Silvana walks away from them in desperation. Her exclusion is visually reinforced by the rice-paddy channel that separates her from the group.

The reversal of roles is now final. Francesca is one of the leaders in the rice fields, and Silvana has taken her place next to Walter, having abandoned her social class. By intercutting shots of a solitary Silvana with those of the *mondine* surrounding Gabriella, De Santis has visually staged in cinematic form the peasant system of ostracizing community members who have strayed. Carlo Lizzani, in his study on the making of *Riso amaro*, compares De Santis's visual enactment of Silvana's expulsion to the studies that the anthropologist De Martino was conducting on peasant ways of dealing with malefic behaviours.[25]

Silvana's rape is her initiation into a world that she had imagined was easy and glamorous. She has been betrayed but is not yet conscious of it. In fact, Silvana is simultaneously the betrayed and the betrayer, but before the catastrophic end she is given one last chance to open her eyes and see the motive for her betrayal.

Back in the storage rooms, Walter discusses his plan to steal the rice. Bent on convincing Silvana to flood the fields during the celebration that marks the end of the harvest, he gives her the stolen necklace as an engagement gift. Then, Francesca arrives and confronts Walter. As they argue, Silvana stands between them, her gaze moving nervously between the two. In this scene, De Santis reverses the role that destiny plays in the photo-romance and in the cinematic melodrama.

Walter tells Francesca that her place has been taken by Silvana but, at the same time, warns her that her fate is still tied to his. He says: 'Remember. Whether *mondina* or maid, you will always be tied to me, all the way to jail.' Francesca makes a choice: she rebels against Walter and the world of the photo-romance by choosing to remain in her new role on the side of the working class.

Silvana also makes a choice, by staying with Walter even though she is well aware that he is a thief. Her materialistic greed and desire for an easy life are stronger than her solidarity with the rest of the *mondine*, who will be soon deprived of the fruit of their hard work.

The betrayal motif comes to its conclusion in the last sequence as Silvana's fantasy world collapses around her. The final catastrophe begins with Silvana carrying out Walter's plan: she opens the irrigation gates and floods the rice fields, distracting the workers as Walter's male accomplices drive away with the rice. The workers discover the flooding just as Silvana is crowned Miss Mondina (Rice Queen) 1948. As everyone rushes to save the rice plants, Silvana, in an emblematic shot, is seen alone with her crown. The message is clear that there is no happiness for anyone outside of his or her own social class, especially for traitors. Silvana in isolation is contrasted with Francesca, who is seen in the midst of the struggle against the gushing water, working alongside Marco, the positive hero.

The final showdown between the two couples takes place in a slaughterhouse. In this much-criticized scene, said to be the 'epitome of bad taste' and in the style of the serial, Walter meets his demise.

Walter stabs Marco and, in return, is shot by him. In this dramatic duel, Francesca stands above everyone. She retains her strength and coolness. She walks over to Walter and Silvana and kicks the necklace into a drain, telling Silvana that it was only fake. Disillusioned and enraged, Silvana kills Walter and, in a daze, runs out. In a dramatic close-up, her tear-stained face and her disillusioned expression are one more reminder of her betrayer / betrayed role.

Silvana kills herself by jumping from the platform on which she had been crowned Rice Queen. Even her last act is consistent with the role she had assumed on entering the photo-romance world of her dreams. But she is more than a character from a photo-romance. She kills Walter and herself, not only because she has discovered the emptiness and falsity of her fancies, but because she realizes that she can never return to the solidarity of the *mondine* and that she had taken the wrong path in seeking to escape a life of toil in the knee-deep water of the paddies.

The film ends with a symbolic reinstating of Silvana into the class of the *mondine*, represented by the handfuls of rice they toss over her dead body. Each grain of rice is a symbol of life never wasted.

De Santis again employs his favourite stylistic module in using a rising crane shot of the entire group. The effect is obtained through a syntactic concatenation of a series of single frames containing an ever-increasing number of people. At a specific point, a new type of image that is not the sum of the preceding ones but a new event, of a choral dimension, ends the camera movement.

The camera focuses, first, on Silvana and, in crescendo, moves to enclose the rest of the group, then later returns to her dead body surrounded by even more *mondine*. The meaning of the new frame is totally different: it seals the victory of the social over the personal drive that had led to Silvana's betrayal and death.

The film ends with a shot of Marco and Francesca as they walk away together. The happy ending is not the traditional, generic, open-ended finale offered by the other films of the time but is the culmination of the dialectical forces at work in the story, reflecting De Santis's interpretation of cultural conflicts.

Riso amaro is a very tightly plotted film in which the form explains the content. As this discussion has shown, this interplay between content and structure carries De Santis's message right to the end. Silvana's desire to abandon her working-class life and pursue the false ideals of fantasy is counterpoised with Francesca's desire to redeem herself from a tragic life. These contrasting desires are accompanied by different backgrounds. Francesca, as she moves closer to the working class, is associated with hard work and the simple life. Silvana, as she struggles to move beyond her class, is isolated or shown to be consumed by false values and frivolous mode of life.

This rigid scheme conforms with the director's intention to condemn the new values connected with the photo-romance and Americanization; thus, Silvana's individualism loses out to the collective. However, to audiences the world over, she is the real winner, for two reasons.

As a film critic, De Santis had theorized the rebirth of Italian cinema through two main components: an authentic landscape that shows and bears the signs of its inhabitants, and characters who reveal their cultural background in their physique.[26] This conception explains his preference for types in his films. Actors and actresses merge perfectly with their characters, not by means of the capacity for naturalistic recitation, but in so far as they mirror the physical type required by the story. De Santis sees in the actor the possibilities that a certain facial or body type offers in invoking its past and its social class.

In this general idea there is already the base of what will be De Santis's future approach to choosing actors for his films and using them to advantage. He never believed in or followed Zavattini's idea of casting unprofessional actors to seem more realistic.

De Santis chose Silvana Mangano for her beauty and personality. In the director's mind, she had to be the Italian physical counterpart of Rita Hayworth. She had to represent a girl with a head full of fancies but also a very complicated character on a quest for something new. She is one of the most complex female figures of postwar Italian cinema. As one critic says, she is 'generous, supportive, thief, betrayer, betrayed, friend, confidante, rival, accomplice, seductress, seduced, guilty, innocent, object of desire, sacrificial victim, et cetera, et cetera.'[27]

Silvana Melega had to be, at once, the leader of the *mondine*, an admirer of the 'electric' ways of American life, and the potential dedicated wife of Marco and the mother of his children, but she was, most of all, a restless individual. Not knowing what lay ahead, she tried to move away from the old to embrace a foreign culture which promised a better life lived to the rhythm of boogie-woogie. In her confusion of aspirations, Silvana becomes a testament to the persuasive power of induced desires. De Santis demanded of his actors that the body be an instrument and form of communication. Silvana, with her perfect and opulent form and personality of contrasts, is the visual embodiment of a modernity that the schematic patterns of the film's structure could not suppress.

6

Myth and Reality among
the Shepherds of Ciociaria:
Non c'è pace tra gli ulivi (1950)

In realtà accadde questo: volevo esaltare con intenzione questo contesto tanto semplice, popolaresco, elementare, nobilitando con una forma raffinata che potesse dare una connotazione di livello culturale rispetto a una storia un pò da fumetto.

In *Non c'è pace tra gli ulivi* ... I wanted to exalt the content; so simple, folksy, and primordial, by ennobling it with a refined form that might give the film a sense of higher culture – a culture higher than the one implied by the simplicity of a plot a bit like that of a comic-strip story.

Giuseppe De Santis

In 1949, De Santis finished his third film *Non c'è pace tra gli ulivi* (No Peace under the Olives), produced by Domenico Davanzati, and distributed by Lux. The story was based on a news item written for the local Roman newspaper *Il tempo* by the journalist Galluppi. As in his previous films, De Santis wrote the treatment in collaboration with his friend Gianni Puccini, and they wrote the script with Carlo Lizzani. The nationally known poet Libero de Libero wrote the words for the folksongs and the dialogue. *Non c'è pace tra gli ulivi*, a visually beautiful film, is based on primordial conflicts, which are depicted through experiments with form and narrative. The story concerns a Ciociaro shepherd, Francesco Dominici, who, after three years of war and three more spent as a prisoner, returns to his mountain village and finds that his flock has been stolen by the local despot, Agostino Bonfiglio, who is now also planning to marry Francesco's fiancée, Lucia. Left without his flock and unable to find work, Francesco decides to reappropriate his flock with the help of his elderly parents and his seventeen-year-old sister, Maria Grazia. On the night of the theft, as the Domenici family attempts to slip away with the sheep, the pursuing Bonfiglio overtakes and rapes Maria Grazia. The following day he has Francesco arrested. At the trial the local shepherds, bribed by Bonfiglio, testify against Francesco, who is sentenced to four years in prison. When his mother informs him of the rape, Francesco escapes to carry out his revenge. In the meantime, Bonfiglio has pushed his exploitation of the shepherds to the limit, and now these men, moved by anger and a common urge for vendetta, rally to Francesco's side. Bonfiglio flees with Maria Grazia, but when she tries to abandon him, he strangles her. Bonfiglio is nevertheless tracked down by Francesco and meets his death by falling off a cliff. Francesco is arrested again and faces a retrial, but this time he can count on the testimony and the support of the entire village. Unity and solidarity have prevailed over bribery, usury, and fatalism.

The criticisms that followed the film's release[1] in Italy concentrated on its political message and on its formalism, and called into question the verisimilitude of the story. To confirm the authenticity of the film, Massimo Mida Puccini, Gianni's brother, wrote an article titled 'Le quercie'[2] (The Oaks) about his experience among the shepherds during the shooting of the final scenes. Anna Gobbi,[3] the film costumist, protested the manoeuvrings of the film's distributor to have the film's title changed. According to Gobbi, the title, *Non c'è pace tra gli ulivi*, had been chosen, in a democratic referendum, by the local shepherds themselves; therefore, it was more authentic than the sensationalist and commercial title 'Pasqua di sangue' (Bloody Easter) that Lux wanted to impose. Among the numerous film reviews and articles, several stand out for the manner in which they address the film. Ennio Flaiani, writing for *Il mondo*,[4] placed the film within the rhetorical tradition of the twentieth-century narrative, when, according to him, the first socialist artists discovered peasantry and rural life and went about transforming the spontaneous and sincere gestures of the people into empty and unpoetic intellectual mechanisms. Another article, by Alberto Moravia,[5] praised the camera work and the richness of the compositions, which he found, none the less, to be inconsistent with the simplicity of the story.

De Santis intervened personally to defend the authenticity of his characters against the attacks of the critic Adriano Baracco.[6] This critic accused the film of *dannunzianesimo*, comparing it to the *Novelle della Pescara* of Gabriele D'Annunzio. In defence of his film De Santis wrote:

It was worth it to just show my Ciociaria, which is so remote that many critics confuse it with bordering regions, especially with Abruzzo. I wanted to show, not only the region, but also the mannerism of its people and the shepherds, who are seen by some critics as remnants of 'dannunzianesimo' and aestheticism. By using this type of criticism, the critics make out of 'dannunzianesimo' a formalistic problem rather than a way of living, a way of looking at the world and a way of placing man in a hopeless fatalism, which is the complete opposite of the natural content of my film.[7]

After treating the seduction of the American way of life in *Riso amaro* (Bitter Rice) De Santis comes back, in *Non c'è pace tra gli ulivi* to the problems of the returning veterans and banditism, themes which he had already taken up in *Caccia tragica* (Tragic Pursuit) but in a sociopolitical situation that was completely different. Unlike Alberto and Michele of *Caccia tragica*, Francesco Dominici lives in a remote society shut off from the social unrest and political contradictions of postwar Italy. The shepherds of Ciociaria are faced with the persistent struggle against exploitation, poverty, and usury. They act out of fear and self-interest. Poverty and unemployment often force some of their numbers into banditry. Unlike the gangsters of *Caccia tragica*, or Walter in *Riso amaro*, Francesco, in committing his 'crime,' feels morally innocent. *Non c'è pace tra gli ulivi* marks the beginning of what could be called De Santis's 'southern films' (*cinema meridionale*), since, from this point on, all his films, with the exception of the ones filmed abroad, concern southern themes. De Santis[8] had always aspired to make films about his part of the world; therefore, this story about the Ciociaro shepherds cannot be considered a mere reaction or a response to certain critics who saw in the peasants of *Caccia tragica* and the *mondine* of *Riso amaro* a dubious authenticity unworthy of Neorealism. The decision to return to a well-known location and a familiar situation must also be seen within the context of the ongoing sociopolitical and cultural debate on populist culture, and the influence of socialist realist paintings, cinema, and narrative.

In the late 1940s, the newly founded Fronte Nuovo delle Arti was promoting socio-realist representation, and Marxist typification, characterization, and prudishness, in the arts. As his films testify, De Santis was never interested in accommodating maxims and never hesitated to transgress rules. He was, nevertheless, idealistically and ideologically tied to the discussion of those problematics. He was a filmmaker driven by a great love for freedom of expression, who saw in cinematography an instrument to entertain the masses and at the same time to promote social and political reforms. De Santis has said on this matter:

We were all involved with socialist realism. All the Communist intellectuals of the time were, and not only Communists ... Few of us were capable of discerning that what was expected of us was part of a dictatorial, tyrannical, and oppressive undertaking ... . I kept to a simple cinema, clear and understandable to all ... anyway, we were all conditioned by socialist realism.[9]

In order to reconcile the social-realist discourses with his own cinematic project, De Santis abandoned his previous narrative modes and took up experimentation with narrative based on peasant folk-tales. He mixed components of the *sacra rappresentazione* (the miracle play), used by the great Italian painters of the past, with those of *la rivista* (the revue theatre), turning to the former for the visual rendering of the film, and to the latter to alleviate the tension of the plot. The critics have pointed out the extreme stylization of *Non c'è pace tra gli ulivi*. Its positive characters are framed in monumental stances, reinforced by low-angle shots to emphasize their moral superiority and their physical strength. The negative characters, according to the canons of Russian socialist realism, are often shot high-angle to stress their moral inferiority. Without refuting these valid stylistic techniques, one can still read *Non c'è pace tra gli ulivi* as a peasant folk-tale about banditry enriched by cinematic visual stylization, and narrated by a committed storyteller.

The movie starts and ends with the off-screen voice of the director relating the misadventures of Francesco Dominici. His intent is also to tell a moralistic tale about the privileged and the underprivileged, in which the shepherds finally break out of their cycle of fatalism and resignation. His comments are directed at the viewers to remind them that the film shows the general sociopolitical conditions of his remote region, and that he has portrayed the reasons for its ancient state of poverty and human exploitation in an attempt to create a victory for the shepherds. In spite of the director's comments, the film's content remains a typical southern Italian story about primordial conflicts. Unlike *Riso amaro*, which proposes to tell two stories, one about a harvest and one about love, using two distinctive narrative modes, documentary reportage and the melodrama, *Non c'è pace tra gli ulivi* has only one narrative mode: the folk-tale. As in the oral folk-tale tradition, the characters are schematically divided into good and bad and are stylized to make them more recognizable as types. Bonfiglio stands for evil, cowardice, lust, and perversion; Francesco stands for goodness, courage, purity, and simplicity. Francesco is simple, impulsive, honest, and courageous. As is typical of the simple, good man, he does not trust the authorities. He acts out of revenge, and in recapturing his flock he is following an ancient belief that repossessing what has been stolen is not theft. Bonfiglio is also a product of this land. Once poor, he has prospered during the war by being unscrupulous, ambitious, and malicious. He now represents the antisocial elements of the community. Lucia is passionate and honest but is a victim of her parents' poverty and the repressive conditions in which women are forced to live in primitive societies that treat them as commodities. Maria Grazia is naïve, young, and spontaneous. As a typical young female in a repressive society, she thinks of herself as Bonfiglio's property after he rapes her. She feels bound by his violence, and obeys without question, simply accepting life at his house as his maid. She follows Bonfiglio passively, as his flock does, and at the end, when she is slain, she symbolically becomes the sacrificial lamb of Easter.

Salvatore is a character from *la rivista*, and his role is to bring comic relief to the tense scene of the manhunt in the mountains. In these sequences, the shepherds and their flock are the centre of the drama. At times they assume the role of a chorus. The flock is the object of contention and, as we will see, it becomes a symbol of destiny. All the characters lead their lives without introspection or psychological development. They move and act as if controlled by an ineluctable outside force, which is comparable to peasant fatalism. Even during the witnesses' false testimonies, Francesco appears subdued. As in a folk-tale, the intentions of the characters are revealed by simple dialogue or monologues, followed immediately by action. Francesco's trial is an example of this fatalism. A high-angle shot conveys his state of resignation. His face registers little emotion until the moment at which he is betrayed by the testimony of his girlfriend, Lucia. Even as his facial expression shows the pain he feels in hearing her false deposition, he behaves as if restrained and silenced by an outside force. This dramatic confrontation between the two lovers takes place before a courtroom full of onlookers, many of whom are also shepherds. They, too, submit passively to Bonfiglio's exploitation and schemes in a similar fatalistic manner.

The landscape becomes the stage on which the brewing conflicts are acted out. The film's tension is maintained by a series of confrontations. First, there is the dispute between Francesco and Bonfiglio over the sheep. Their conflict is aggravated by Bonfiglio's plans to marry Lucia,

Francesco's girlfriend, and, when Bonfiglio rapes Maria Grazia, a new conflict is generated between the two men. The continuous build-up of tension is punctuated with moments of comic relief, such as the folksong sung during Bonfiglio's engagement ceremony with Lucia. With Francesco's arrest, the confrontation seems to have been resolved in Bonfiglio's favour. During the phase of transition that follows, new conflicts evolve, this time between Bonfiglio and the other shepherds, setting up the cause of their rebellion, which is symbolically tied with the coming of spring. When Francesco escapes from prison, the conflicts between him and Bonfiglio explode. Now, Francesco has the shepherds and Lucia on his side, whereas Bonfiglio is isolated. The tension of the film is kept alive by a series of actions and events tied to this conflict and builds until Bonfiglio's death at the end of the film. The resolution of the conflict is preceded by a transitional sequence depicting the Good Friday procession.

Throughout these events, the landscape, raw, beautiful, and overwhelming, seems to be populated with elemental beings; both hero and villain are immersed in a mythical atmosphere, and the improbable and the forces of nature come to the aid of the hero. For example, when the *carabinieri* endeavour to hunt down Francesco, the shepherds succeed in confusing them by letting their sheep run loose over the hills. At this point, the rocky mountains of Ciociaria become a fantastic stage in which primal conflicts are acted out. As in a folk-tale, Francesco, the force of good, takes justice into his own hands and avenges himself on his own terms. Bonfiglio, the force of evil, is defeated by the common effort of his former victims, who mobilize in order to aid Francesco. The slow and often weighty rhythm of the sequences reinforces the timeless atmosphere of the tale. Even the religious procession, inching along a serpentine mountain road, contributes to this mythical ambience. The procession exudes an atmosphere of intense devotion that mixes pagan and Catholic elements. The scene in which the statue of the Virgin, papered with banknotes and followed by a gaggle of the crippled and the lame, reveals a quiet desperation and a religiosity tinged with superstition. The contrast between the whiteness of the sandy road and the black dresses of the women is visually striking.

This stark contrast is repeated with more dramatic effectiveness in other sequences. Lucia, elegant in her white wedding veil, passes along the narrow streets of the town thronged with black-clad townspeople pressed against the walls of their white-washed homes. Before she can reach the church, she is confronted by the pregnant Maria Grazia, who emerges unexpectedly from the crowd to denounce Bonfiglio. In the scene of Bonfiglio's flight from the pursuing Francesco, the counterposing of black and white has an emblematic significance. Dressed in predominantly black clothing, Bonfiglio is encumbered by the swirling motion of the white flock surging around him. The dust that rises from the multitude of trampling hooves betrays his movements to Francesco and is suggestive of a curse hanging over his head. As in the folk-tale tradition, his fate is sealed by the things that he has stolen and most coveted. Symbolically the sequence offers another interpretation: it was Bonfiglio's theft of Francesco's flock that created an injustice; now, the flock becomes part of a hidden act of justice to punish him.

In all moments of immobility, the characters' blocking is theatrical and elaborate. Single frames frequently consist of two or three smaller, well-balanced internal compositions, arranged within the larger whole with spectacular symmetry. This particular experimentation with formal composition some critics have referred to as statuesque and monumental.[10] It is not my intention here to pass judgment on the director's experiment, or on the critical doubts expressed by others, but to point out that the positions assumed by the actors in the shots in question make them appear to be the symbolic living embodiment of the *presepio* (Nativity scene) of the southern Italian tradition. One example of this type of composition is the shepherds' arrival at the cave which is Francesco's hide-out. He emerges and is confronted by the group, its members artfully posted along the slope of the hill in a staggered configuration, similar to the pastoral scene in which shepherds surround the newborn Jesus. Another scene that recalls the popular religious tableau presents itself when the news of Francesco's escape from jail reaches Lucia's parents. Fearful of his vendetta, they decide to flee from their village, and their hasty departure with few belongings and a donkey is staged in a way that recalls Joseph and Mary's flight from Herod in Italian paintings.

The film's stylistic and formal experimentations are an integral part of the story and do not conflict with the simplicity of its content. The complicated camera movements, such as rapid shifts from a close shot to a medium shot, followed by a long shot which then returns to a close-up, are used skilfully by the director to show how an individual's destiny is tied to the community's values. Technically the various shots are also useful for filling the screen with elements linked to the action. The film starts with a deep shot, used to establish a general description of the environment, followed by a pause to introduce the Domenici family. De Santis also uses panoramic shots and travelling shots in combination to follow the movements of the protagonists. It is not uncommon for the camera to follow a new character encountered by a character on whom it was previously focused. For example, during Francesco's trial, the camera begins by tracking Lucia's entrance into the courtroom; when she passes in front of Francesco, the camera lingers on his face to show us his reactions. Similarly, during moments of conflict or intense action, the camera's movements mirror the dramatic movements of the scene to increase the effect on the viewers. Suspense is created by paralleling actions and montage. For example, at the end of the film, before the final showdown between Francesco and Bonfiglio,[11] suspense is built up by interspersing scenes of Francesco's pursuit with shots of the facial expressions of Bonfiglio's mother and Maria Grazia's. As in most of De Santis's films, the scenes contain a profusion of details based on background–foreground composition. *Non c'è pace tra gli ulivi* features two techniques new to Italian cinema: infrared film stock is used for the dark scenes, and pan focus is used systematically, to allow the director to exploit the background to full effect. The pan focus combined with low-angle shots allows him to link Francesco and all the other characters with the landscape and the locale in a way that suggests they share a natural common destiny. Thanks to the expertise of Piero Portalupi, the director of photography, this film displays a distinctive quality of light and a dislocation of visual planes unusual for its time in Italy.

In *Non c'è pace tra gli ulivi*, De Santis seems more aware of the difficulties presented in preserving the authenticity of his characters' language than in his previous films. In fact, in this film, an effort is made to give to spoken language local colour and to reproduce the dialect of Ciociaro actually spoken by the local shepherds. The dialogue of the minor characters is often in dialect, as are the songs and the refrain verses that accompany the action. For example, when Francesco, who is looking for work, asks another shepherd if he can go down to the valley with his flock as a helper, the other replies: 'Non può essè. N'te dispiacè. E poi tu ssì n'àta vocca da sfamà, qualche soldo pure te lo dovrei dare. Tu mica ci puoi venì per niente'[12] (It is not possible. Do not take offence. After all, you are another mouth to feed, I should even give you some money. You cannot come for nothing). Here, 'essé,' is dialect for 'essere' (to be); 'N'te dispiacè' for 'non lo prendere male' (do not take it hard); 'tu ssì' for 'tu sei' (you are); and 'n'àta vocca' for 'un'altra bocca' (another mouth). The dialogue between the main characters is either in a syntax closer to dialect or in a mixture of Italian and dialect words, and is often introduced by interjections such as 'Eh!' or 'Oh!,' which are typically used in dialect to address someone. For example, during the first encounter between Francesco and Lucia, Francesco says: 'Domattina me ne parto' (Tomorrow I'm leaving). 'Me ne parto' is the Italian transcription of the dialectal form 'm'n'part.' When Francesco's sister, Maria Grazia, interrupts their conversation, Francesco says: 'Mo vengo' (I will be right there). 'Mo' is the dialect and ancient form of 'adesso' or 'ora' (now).

The songs are all drawn from the regional folklore and are sung in dialect. They are often used as a counterpart or counterpoint to the action or dialogue. Among the many examples in the film is the sequence inside Bonfiglio's house on the night of his official engagement to Lucia, which is also the night when the Domenici family will reappropriate the stolen flock. Lucia is standing near the window, trying to avoid Bonfiglio's caresses. At the same time, she is gazing desperately out, trying to spot Francesco in the dark. Two folk musicians are singing about a rich man who is the only one with enough money to buy the best mare around. The refrain asks in a rhetorical manner who this mare might be: 'E chi la pò comprà questa cavalla / di tutta la montagna è la più bella' (And who can buy this mare / She is the best-looking one of the entire mountain). The allusion to Lucia is even more evident since, in dialect, a young unmarried woman is often referred to as a mare.

Non c'è pace tra gli ulivi is a portrait of the sociopolitical and cultural conditions of a remote part of Italy, which also exposes some of the forces responsible for the region's perennial poverty. A large part of the shepherd's life is poverty, exploitation, and usury. The chief motivating forces of these people are fear and self-interest. In order to be more faithful to the content of the situation in this film, De Santis has left out the meditation on mass media and on the effects of modernism on Italian peasant culture. Instead, the director has chosen to take into account the anthropological factors that shape that part of Italy. In fact, the film shows the superstition, the fatalism, the mannerisms, and the customs of the Ciociaro shepherds. The scene in which Francesco and Lucia meet and converse without looking each other in the eye has been labelled by the critics as an example of aestheticism. However, De Santis's intention was to show a reality and a custom of the time which prescribed such behaviour for young, unmarried people. This film is a peasants' story, narrated in cinematic form, and concluding with a political and a moral lesson. Like the straight-on stares into the camera of the film's protagonists, which broke the cinematic code of the time,[13] the shepherds' victory over their situation breaks with tradition, altering the fatalistic cycle of peasants' resignation. The film is unique in its time for the stylized composition and the advanced technical and visual means used. It is also the first Neorealist cinematic work that has shepherds as protagonists. Twenty years would pass before this subject was featured again on the Italian screen with Bertolucci's *Novecento*, the Tavianises' *My Father, My Master*, Zavattini's *Ligabue*, and Olmi's *The Tree of Wooden Clogs*, all made in the 1970s.[14]

7

The Stairway of Dreams
and Illusions: *Roma, Ore 11* (1952)

Un significato particolare assume la larga partecipazione di attori di cui '*Roma, Ore 11*' si vale. Ciò dimostra che gli attori hanno compreso quale sia il loro vero posto in un cinema realistico. E posso testimoniare che ognuno di questi attori ha sostenuto, per partecipare al mio film, più d'un sacrificio. Di questo li ringrazio vivamente.

The fact that *Roma, Ore 11* features a large number of professional actors indicates a distinct meaning. It shows that actors have understood their true role in realistic cinema. I can attest to the numerous sacrifices that these actors endured in order to make my film, and I thank them for it.

Giuseppe De Santis

In 1952, unable to find a producer[1] for 'Noi che facciamo crescere il pane,' a saga about the exploitation of the southern peasant, De Santis shot *Roma, Ore 11* (Rome, 11 O'clock), soon acclaimed[2] as his best film to date in terms of content and balance. The story is based on a tragic event that occurred at Via Savoia 31, in Rome, 15 January 1951, which shocked the public. On that cold, winter day, a building staircase collapsed under the weight of about two hundred women who had travelled there from almost every section of the city to be interviewed for one low-paying job as a typist. The accident resulted in one death and more than sixty injuries. The event immediately caught the attention of the Italian cinematographers of the 1950s, always on the lookout for sensational news items. Rumours followed about two upcoming films based on the tragic story of the young women crushed under debris. Two 1951

ANSA bulletins[3] reported contrasting items, statements released by Giuseppe De Santis and Augusto Genina about their respective projects. Unlike Genina's film (*Tre storie proibite*; Three Forbidden Stories); De Santis's *Roma, Ore 11* is not centred on the private love stories of three women who happened to be at Via Savoia 31 on 15 January but is a thorough investigation of the reasons and motivations that forced so many women to seek the job. Although it takes its inspiration from the event, De Santis's film goes beyond simple exposition of the incident. By exploring the personal motivations of each woman, his film places blame for the incident on the government and the party in power and accuses them of inefficiency in resolving the serious problem of unemployment.[4]

De Santis states[5] that, after he learned about the accident, he appointed the then young reporter Elio Petri,[6] who was working for the Rome edition of the communist newspaper *L'Unità*, to investigate. After conducting research for six months, Petri submitted a long and detailed account, including background information on the women involved in the incident supplemented with personal interviews with bystanders, policemen, and firemen who had rushed to the scene. With this useful information in hand, De Santis, Gianni Puccini, Cesare Zavattini, Basilio Franchina, and Rodolfo Sonego secluded themselves for three months in a villa at Fregene to work on the film treatment and its final script.

The film was produced by Paul Graetz for Transcontinental Film and Titanus and is remembered as one of the most expensive Italian films made in the 1950s. De Santis assembled some of the best-known actors of the time, such as Massimo Girotti, Raf Vallone, Paolo Stoppa, Armando Francioli, Checco Durante, and Alberto Farnese, together with some of the most popular female counterparts: Lucia Bosè, Carla Del Poggio, Maria Grazia Francia, Lea Padovani, Delia Scala, Elena Varzi, and Paola Borboni. The well-known French artistic director, Léon Barsacq, was engaged to reconstruct, in Titanus's studios, the entire district and the street on which the accident had taken place. The outcome is a film which combines Zavattinian faith in reality with De Santis's belief in reconstructing news items with imagination and a basis of perfect understanding of the event and the situation.

Roma, Ore 11 is an investigation of the inhuman social and economic conditions that forced all those women to gather on the stairway. The message of the film is captured in the brief final dialogue between a disappointed newspaper reporter looking for a sensational headline for the morning paper, and the police commissioner investigating the crash.

In response to the journalist's question – 'Whose fault is it?' – the policemen replies, 'Here, look ... Think about it,' as he points to one of the girls who is still standing at the building's entrance, in hope of getting the job.

Roma, Ore 11 has a firm unity of time and action and a circular development. In fact, it starts and ends in front of the gate that leads to the stairway, and covers the time span of a day – from 8:00 a.m. to 8:00 p.m. The film is divided into two parts, each set in a separate place, but the story is unified by the investigation. The first part takes place on the staircase and ends with its collapse. The second part starts in the hospital and ends with the women's return to their homes. During the long wait on the staircase, the characters are introduced. These introductions are preceded by a sort of interlude outside the building where the women gather, accompanied by their friends, lovers, or relatives, who will be seen again in the hospital after the accident. The wait on the stairway is followed by the typing test, which highlights the perverted practice that forces women looking for work to be not only qualified but attractive and charming. For example, in the scene where a nameless older and unattractive woman is test-typing, the camera angle tilts to contrast her with a large publicity poster of Riccadonna sparkling wine on the wall behind her, which shows a young and seductive woman; the contrast highlighted stands as a silent commentary on the exploitation of women in the workplace. In spite of her typing skills, the older woman would not get the job because she is unattractive. The fact that her name is never revealed stands as a further indictment of the conditions faced by older women in the 1950s Italian job market, where beauty and youth are prerequisites for employment. The newspaper ad for the job made no mention of typing speed but cited 'Bellissima presenza' (very beautiful appearance) as a requirement, stressing the superlative 'bellissima.'

The typing test is interposed with vivacious and colourful remarks and small talk among the women waiting to be called. The various conversations allow the audience to learn more about the social background of the group. The camera moves vertically, following the various landings on the stairway. Metaphorically, the stairway stands for the dreams and aspirations of the women – an image reinforced by the women's upwards stares towards the office door. As soon as one enters, the rest try to catch sight of the office inside, but the door is quickly shut on their dreams and curiosity. A camera set up at the office door focuses on the facial expressions of the group left outside, whose members anxiously listen to the click-clack of the typewriter keyboard to assess the competitor's skill. The few seconds of motionless silence are followed by eloquent facial expressions, showing confidence or discouragement. The sudden collapse of the stairway brings an end to the film's first part. The rashness of one of the women, who pushes ahead of the others, provoked a major uproar, and the resulting squabble caused the stairway to collapse. At first, Luciana (Carla Del Poggio) seems to have caused the crash, but by the end of the film it becomes clear that her behaviour is only the apparent cause and that she is, if not a scapegoat, the emblem of a broader and deeper problem – unemployment and the lack of social measures to assist the needy, as is reaffirmed by her unemployed husband, Nando (Massimo Girotti), who tries to comfort her.

The accident brings to an end the women applicants' dreams and illusions. The catastrophic event is a further testament to De Santis's commanding camera skills. The director does not make a spectacle out of it, but keeps the coverage of the crash at the level of a news event, showing its import without resorting to the sensational. The arrival of the ambulances, the firemen, and the rescuers is presented with camera work similar to that used in documentary reportage. A descending camera shows the women covered with debris and slabs of concrete that were part of the stairway that led to their dreams of employment and happiness. The stairway has become a tombstone; the promised land an inferno. This imagery is foreshadowed in the titles and opening credits, where the sounds of an organ playing a grave tune ominously blend with the sound of a typewriter's keys. The image of hell is bolstered by the descending camera, which pauses on the victims to augment the infernal atmosphere. The final scene of the sequence is shot from the opposite side of the entrance gate. Yells and screams are heard, until a woman with torn clothes staggers out of the building shrouded in dust and collapses on the pavement.

There are many examples in this film of De Santis's distinctive and forceful style. The opening frame is a close-up of a young sleeping woman who is abruptly awakened by the rumblings of a machine. The camera pulls back to show a full shot of the girl standing up, then tracks her to a vendor's stand, and then to a news-stand. The camera movements serve as establishing shots. As the camera follows the young woman's movements, we see another girl approaching the gate; when she crosses the middle of the screen, the camera focuses on the newcomer. The same technique is used to present the rest of the women who assemble in front of the entrance. Another well-shot sequence is the scene following the arrival of the *ragioniere* (accountant) who will conduct the interviews. When one of his subordinates enters the elevator, carrying coffee for him, the camera adopts his point of view; as the elevator goes up to the fifth floor, the audience sees the long line of aspiring women lined up along the staircase. In spite of Guido Aristarco's criticism[7] of the scene (he found it too aesthetic and cerebral), the moment is complex, at once suggestive and beautiful. It is a scene full of dramatic force – reinforced by the silent stares of the women, the rising elevator carrying the subordinate appears as to be unreachable goal from the standpoint of the unemployed women.

The second part tells the story of nine of the women on the stairway. We see them at the hospital, and later, as they leave the hospital, we are shown scenes that illuminate their private lives. For instance, the viewer discovers that Caterina (Lea Padovani), the prostitute, is tired of her degrading job and is looking to redeem herself. At the start of the film, she is dropped off by a customer, who in a sardonic prophesy replies to her comment about finding a new life by saying, 'I doubt it very much.' On the stairway, she tries to hide her real identity, but her attempt to change fails. After being released from the hospital, she goes back to the scene of the crash to recover her missing umbrella and purse – objects that were part of the profession she now has to resume. She is picked up by a man, and together they go to her house in Tormarancia, one of the most destitute *borgate* (slums) of Rome. Once there, the well-off client, frightened by the poverty of the place, runs away, leaving behind some money. The sequence caused De Santis problems with the producer and the state censors, who wanted the prostitute's return home edited out. A long dispute followed, which ended up in court. Titanus used Zavattini's testimony to prove that De Santis had wasted time and money to shoot the episode. However, despite the scriptwriter's testimony, the court decided in favour of De Santis's artistic right to self-expression, and the sequence remained in the final version of the film.

A similar discovery is made in the episode featuring Adriana (Elena Varzi), the woman seduced and abandoned by her employer. During the typing test, she tells the *ragioniere* why she quit her former job, then she flees in tears. At the hospital, with her father (Checco Durante) at her bedside, the audience learns from the doctor that she is pregnant, and that the fall has not caused any damage to the expected child. During their ride home, their family drama explodes. Her father tells her to leave the family house forever, but when they are greeted by all the neighbours, who are delighted to see Adriana alive and well, her father has a change of heart and comes to understand the meaning of life and humanity, without a word leading his daughter inside.

The episode of Cornelia (Maria Grazia Francia), one of the youngest women in front of the gate, is tragic and completely different from the others. She seems like a character from the comic-strip magazines. During the wait, she meets a sailor who is about to leave for Mogadiscio, a far-away and mysterious place for young Cornelia. They hardly say anything to each other, but their glances and smiles reveal Cornelia's innocence. From one of the floors inside the building, the camera assumes her perspective as she looks out of the window to see if her sailor is still outside. This scene is followed by a camera shot from the street, which shows her from the sailor's point of view. From his perspective, she appears as an ethereal angel surrounded by the stone wings on both sides of the round window from which she is looking out. Cornelia's dream of love will never be fulfilled. The destiny that gave her love at first sight would later give her death, as was suggested by the image of her with stone wings, an allusion to cemetery monuments.

A desperate story is revealed in the episode of Luciana (Carla Del Poggio), the wife of an unemployed worker (Massimo Girotti). In desperation, she forces her way inside the office in an attempt to find a job to support her family, and thus becomes the apparent cause of the accident. After learning about Cornelia's death, she tries to commit suicide but is saved by her husband and some of the women who accept her innocence. Luciana is the most dramatic character of the film; her role is designed to lead the audience to an understanding of the real cause of the accident.

There is also the happy-ending story of the young daughter of a proud and strict state employee, Clara (Irene Gelber), who conceals her secret dream of becoming a professional singer. At the start of the film, after she leaves her father (Paolo Stoppa), she runs to the news-stand to buy *Il canzoniere* (a song-book). At the hospital, she falls in love with her rescuer. During the National Radio report on the crash, conducted live inside the hospital, Clara sings 'Amado mio,' imitating Rita Hayworth's performance in *Gilda* (1947). Her father takes advantage of the report to complain about low government wages but, much to his disappointment, the comment is left out of the evening news broadcast.

Amidst the major stories, there is also the stirring episode of Loretta (Loretta Paoli), the provincial girl from Viterbo who has become the laughing-stock of her town for her daily trips to Rome in search of employment, which have earned her the nick-name 'Round-trip.' Loretta cannot type but, in order to get a job, is willing to render favours to her employer. After the accident, she resists medication as she is ashamed of the cyclist shirt she wears under her Sunday clothes. However, nothing can be concealed from the cynical media: a merciless reporter takes pictures of her shirt as another notes: 'Great story. Young girl in search of work in order to buy a new shirt!' Luckily, Loretta finds a job as a maid, replacing Angelina (Delia Scala), who, after the accident, finds enough courage to quit her job and return home to her family. She is tired of enduring sexual harassment from her employer and his son. The verbal exchange, in two different dialects, that takes place between Loretta and Angelina concerning the job and the meals adds another tragic element to their human drama.

The episode featuring Simona (Lucia Bosè) focuses on the only woman of the group who comes from a rich family, a distinction that is immediately apparent from her looks and clothing. She is looking for work to gain independence from her rich family. Her family comes to the hospital to take her home, but, during the ride back in an expensive and luxurious car, she tells her father to stop, and walks away to return to her lover, an unemployed artist (Raf Vallone). The sequence in which Simona enters the apartment and wordlessly sets about doing little chores before sitting in a rocking chair that gently keeps time with an American jazz tune playing on the radio is one of the most sentimental, tender, and loving moments of the film. The sequence is a montage of close-ups of the two protagonists, Simona and her lover, which serves to eliminate the distance created between them at the hospital, when Simona's parents told her lover to leave her.

Interspersed among these major stories are others of nameless women from the group seen on the stairway. Besides that of the nameless typist who is not hired because of her age and appearance, there is also the story of the girl who starts and ends the film. She is timid and must be pushed by her mother. When her mother is hospitalized after the accident, the young girl finds the courage to run back to the gate, hoping to be hired. After she buys a few roasted chestnuts, sadly she sits, and the camera pulls back, using a technique which is the opposite of the one used in the opening frame of the film. The frame of the lonesome girl will remain with the audience, as will the film's point. The audience is left to think about unemployment and poverty.

Roma, Ore 11 brings Italian postwar cinema to a new height. By using the narrative mode of the investigation, De Santis and his collaborators created a protest against poor social conditions in Italy, but, most of all, they created a persuasive choral film. The various characters are equals, and there are no primary protagonists. The choral aspect of the film is always kept in balance and never disintegrates into a mere series of sketches. The central tragedy serves to converge and hold together the various backgrounds of the women / applicants for the typist's job. In this film, De Santis proved that Neorealism could continue without reliance on the use of real people from the street. It also proved that excellent professional actors and studio sets can be used to make news items memorable and moving.[8]

8

Could an Italian Male
Marry an Everyman's Woman?
Un marito per Anna Zaccheo (1953)

Provate a essere donna, per un giorno solo, provate la leggerezza, l'oltraggio, la denigrazione che si sono fatte carne della carne e nessuno ci bada più per niente affatto. Provate a cercare un posto, un lavoro che non sia di asina da soma, che non sia l'esposizione e la vendita di una pelle levigata che aggrinzisce al primo autunno. Provate a servire, quando la servitù vi è comandata come una necessità, un'antica innata tendenza del corpo femminile.

Experience being a woman, for just one day, feel the lightness, the outrage, the denigration that have made themselves flesh and blood and nobody takes notice at all, any more. Try looking for a position, a job that isn't for a beast of burden, that isn't the displaying and selling of a smooth skin that shrivels up in the first days of autumn. Try to serve, when servitude is demanded of you as a necessity, as an ancient innate tendency of the female body.

Dacia Maraini

After the critical recognition given *Roma, Ore 11*, De Santis once again tried to film 'Noi che facciamo crescere il pane,' his saga about the peasants' rebellion for land and reforms in Calabria, but he was unable to find a producer, even in 1953, when he was at the peak of his career (Goffredo Lombardo, director of Titanus Studio, gave him credit for the supervision of two minor films with the sole aim of promoting them, although De Santis never worked on the productions).[1] Elio Petri recounts that, as he was working with Gianni Puccini and De Santis on finding locations for a future film (a love story to be set near Gaeta), the producer Domenico Forges-Davanzati gave the director a short story written by Alfredo Giannetti and Salvatore Laurani titled 'Una corona per Anna Zaccheo' (A Crown for Anna Zaccheo). De Santis found the story interesting and, with the collaboration of Puccini, Petri, Zavattini, and the story's authors, rewrote parts of the plot for a film script.[2] Prior to the film's release, during one of his visits to the Soviet Union, De Santis held a press conference in which he announced that he was working on a film about the exploitation and objectification of female beauty in a capitalistic society; however, Anna's complex story transcends this propagandistic explanation arising from traditional male prejudices.[3]

The story takes place in Pignasecca, one of the working-class neighbourhoods of Naples. Anna Zaccheo (Silvana Pampanini) is a beautiful twenty-three-year-old woman, daughter of a cable-railway worker. Like many other girls of her age and social status, Anna dreams of finding love and happiness. Her low-income family hopes that she will use her beauty and virginity wisely since she does not have a dowry or a job. On the same street lives Don Antonio Percuoco (Umberto Spadaro), a rather ugly older man who has made a fortune for himself in the fish business. The Zaccheo family considers Don Antonio a good prospect and encourages his persistent courtship by accepting his daily bouquet of flowers. Anna's dreams come true one day when she meets Andrea (Massimo Girotti), a handsome sailor from the city of Ancona, whose ship has anchored in Naples for one day. Like a knight from a fairy-tale, Andrea rescues Anna, who has been caught swimming nude in the sea by a group of fellow sailors. Andrea fights them off, salvages her clothes, and kindly and bashfully helps Anna get dressed. Afterwards they spend the rest of the day together. They have lunch on a terrace overlooking the sea, while musicians play Neapolitan songs. After a long walk together, they attend a play at the local theatre and part after a long farewell embrace, including all the inevitable promises of eternal love and marriage. Since Anna's family does not have enough money for the wedding, she has to find a job to buy new clothes and, if possible, a few pieces of furniture. Her beauty helps her find a job modelling for Dr Illuminato (Dr Enlightened; Amedeo Nazzari), a Milanese businessman who has moved south to organize and promote underdeveloped southern craftsmanship. After the sexual harassment endured at her previous jobs, Anna is delighted to work for such a kind and decorous man. One day a heavy cloudburst interrupts the outdoor photo shoots, forcing a drenched Anna to take refuge in the car of Dr Illuminato. He encourages her to share his liquor for warmth and takes advantage of the circumstances, and her inebriated state, to seduce her. On their way home, he tells her that he is married and has children and cannot do much to help her. When she arrives home and sees her nuptial furniture, just delivered, Anna attempts suicide. At the hospital, she is visited by Andrea, who, when he is told of her lost virginity, abandons her forever. Anna moves out of her family's house and, unable to sustain herself, becomes Don Antonio's fiancée. Soon she discovers that he considers her a beautiful toy, exclusively at his disposal, and a bolster to his ego. Anna finds enough strength to break their engagement, but, left without any financial help, she is forced to work as an archer for an amusement park for men. One day, Andrea happens to be among the spectators and, seeing Anna, invites her to spend the day with him. Again they go to the theatre to see a Neapolitan play (sceneggiata),[4] but this time Anna invites him to spend the night at her little rented room. Andrea promises her love, marriage, and happiness, but in the morning he is overcome by male prejudice. He is jealous that she has been Don Antonio's fiancée and reproaches her for having taken the initiative in asking him to spend the night. His temper boils over at the sight of a publicity poster for hosiery which shows Anna with her skirt raised, displaying her legs. He cannot marry her because he cannot endure the thought that she is everyman's woman. They part and, when a male passer-by tries to comfort the sobbing Anna, she slaps him. The film ends with Anna, who has returned to her family's home, looking out over the city from her bedroom, where we first saw her at the beginning of the film. In a voice-over, Anna tells us that there are many other women all over the city who have endured the same experience, but one must not give up, because life is worth living.

The film's title refers to the sad reality that marriage was often the only option women had in an underdeveloped society. Anna Zaccheo's predicament typifies the position of many young Italian women, as the initials of her first name and surname are intended to signify. De Santis was well aware of the objections and criticisms that a female-centred story about a beautiful woman might raise,[5] especially in the Italy of 1953, where film criticism was heavily political, and national cinema was engaged in continuing the battle for Neorealism. As expected, the critics from the Left accused De Santis of having gone back to the decadent eroticism and sex appeal of *Riso amaro* (Bitter Rice). These puritanical attacks were mainly aimed at the opening scene, in which Anna Zaccheo (Silvana Pampanini wakes up and gets out of bed wearing a petticoat, and proceeds to dress herself in a provocative manner before the mirror. The other scene which caused a wave of letters of protest expressing indignation to *L'Unità*, the official communist newspaper, is that in which Anna swims nude. One of these letters stands out; it was submitted by the feminist writer Fausta Terni Cialente, who sarcastically referred to De Santis's film as 'Anna Zaccheo, or the triumph of the legs (*Il trionfo delle gambe*), a film made with the only purpose of undressing the actress, Pampanini.'[6] She concluded by calling for films which would shine light on the more positive aspects of the rich life of contemporary Italian women. De Santis responded[7] with a long polemical letter in which he defended his intentions and those of his collaborators in making the film. He went on to say that they wanted to show that *today's* male should start by asking the woman not to be so much a female (*femmina*), and only a female (*femmina*), but rather by learning how to consider her and value her for other reasons.

The critics from the political Right added their own objections and reservations, citing the political and moral intentions of the film. Writing for the *Fiera letteraria*, the journalist Feraldo Feraldi[8] asked, in rhetorical fashion, what else a bourgeois society could have in store for a woman, besides problems? He stated that, to a Marxist such as De Santis, art means little compared with the need to give political meaning to everything. The ostracism of the film started even before its release. In fact it forced the producer, Forges-Davanzati,[9] to reply to the accusation that he was a leftist. In his defence, he stated that he had not been moved by political affiliations in his choice of directors or subjects for his films, but by the aspiration to make high-quality films. He also affirmed that, in choosing De Santis for *Anna Zaccheo*, he had based his decision on the fact that the director was an internationally known figure. He added that he did not believe that the activity of a film director acquired a specific political colour just because his films, instead of being mere Sunday pastimes, focused on social problems or on certain social customs.

Un marito per Anna Zaccheo (A Husband for Anna Zaccheo) attempts to show the complexities of being female – an issue not given adequate attention in the political programs of the democratic movement or in the primary preoccupations of intellectuals. The film's ultimate goal is to condemn the characteristic social custom whereby women are reduced to mere objects of male desire by having their sexual drives and desires negated. The Italian general public in the 1950s was not sensitive to the problem, as the critics' polemics surrounding the film attest. For instance, Vittorio Spinazzola has stated: 'la questione femminile non riusciva a occupare un posto adeguato nei programmi politici del movimento democratico, né gli uomini di cultura se ne facevano un assillo particolare."[10] Women were present in Italian Neorealist films, and even in the comedies, in specific roles: as wives and mothers; as the remorseful victims of sexual temptation; or as persecuted temptresses and martyrs sacrificed in the name of family honour. Anna Zaccheo's character confirms De Santis's concern with the female social role, a theme he had already addressed in *Riso amaro, Non c'è pace tra gli ulivi*, and *Roma, Ore 11*. As he did in those films, in *Anna Zaccheo* the director also reaffirms his belief in the power of cinema to shape a progressive social consciousness. In fact, the story of Anna Zaccheo is a commentary on Italian culture and customs. In order to carry on the social commentary and to communicate with the masses in this film, De Santis takes advantage of popular forms of entertainment. In *Anna Zaccheo*, De Santis adopts the narrative clichés of the Neapolitan popular theatre (*sceneggiata*) and the melodramatic *romanzo d'appendice* (serial) but reverses their conservative and conformist social messages.

The film takes place in Naples, the city where the *sceneggiata* and the *romanzo d'appendice* are part of the people's collective imagination. In order to stage the objectification of female beauty, the director needed a city such as Naples, where life is lived outdoors. In the first part of the film, when Anna leaves the house, walks down the street, and passes through the outdoor market, every head turns, and every vendor makes a comment on her beauty. Thus the audience sees how female beauty is appreciated and displayed, and how a woman becomes an object of desire. Anna's character combines the purity and the innocence associated with the good girl of the Neapolitan *sceneggiata*, but at the same time her beauty is a characteristic associated with the antagonist, the femme fatale or temptress. Thus, beauty is detrimental to her happiness in a male-dominated society that adores female beauty and at the same time is frightened by it. Andrea, the handsome sailor and outsider, has also all the qualities associated with the seducer in these popular forms of entertainment. They meet when Anna is bathing nude, floating in the rising foam as the goddess Venus. In this symbiosis of water and body, Anna shows her innate innocence and purity; only the sailors' gazes give her a sense of shame and guilt. Andrea helps her, and Anna finds his gentle actions reassuring. During their walk on the seashore and their lunch on the terrace, De Santis covers all the narrative clichés of the *sceneggiata*, culminating when, at Anna's request, they go to see a real *sceneggiata* at the local theatre. As she watches the play, Anna relives her own feelings and emotions, identifying with the staged play. She believes in the sentimentality of the theatrical conventions. In fact, she says to the sceptical Andrea, who, being a man and from another cultural background, laughs at the play, 'These things are facts that happen in real life! You don't think so? – Why not? These events are more real than the facts of life!' Andrea, far removed from the conventions of the play, is concerned only with the fact that all men in the theatre are staring at Anna. In their looks, he sees the reflection of his own sexual desire for her. From this moment on, through the two main characters' feelings and actions, the film evolves according to the narrative genres on which it is structured, i.e., the *sceneggiata* and the serial tinged with melodrama. Anna's life, from this point on, will evolve like the *mise en scène* of the play, and Andrea's actions will be closer to those of the male seducer in the *romanzo d'appendice*. When the play ends, Anna and Andrea walk through the narrow streets of Naples, down the steep and winding stairs[11] towards the harbour. Their stopping to exchange kisses and sweet words are the re-enactment of the theatrical *mise en scène* previously seen.

At the end of the walk, as in the serial, Andrea swears that he will return to marry her. After his boarding, Anna, just like the poor girl of a *sceneggiata*, has to find a job without compromising her beauty. She has to endure male harassment and is seduced by a man who proves to be the opposite of what his last name suggests (Dr Illuminato). True to the popular narrative clichés, she is overcome by guilt and tries to kill herself. Scorned by her neighbours, she moves away to spare her family further embarrassment. As in the serial, the lost woman cannot expect to marry a young, handsome man, so Anna accepts Don Antonio's offer. She is fortunate to have found a man who wants to marry her despite the fact that she is no longer a virgin. At this point, the director's progressive intentions begin to come through and start to break out of the narrative clichés to challenge the conformist social message. Anna breaks the engagement and chooses to live in poverty instead of marrying a man who wants to buy and possess her beautiful body. After he takes her out to eat and shows her the new house he is having built for them, he wants to have intercourse since he is going to marry a woman who is no longer a virgin. Anna is learning that life is different from the sentimentality of the *sceneggiata* which she believed to be truer than life. Forced by necessity, she finds a job as an archer in an amusement park for men. Again she is shown as a Venus but, unlike in the bathing scene, now she is inside a large cage surrounded by gaping men who desire her. To make a living, Anna has consented to being an object of the male gaze. It is coincidence that Andrea happens to be among of the gazers. They go out together again and once more they go to see a *sceneggiata*. Anna is more liberated now than during their first encounter and invites Andrea to stay the night. Unlike the female of the *sceneggiata*, she shows her sexual desires. Anna's hopes are revived, but Andrea, the quintessential male, cannot trust her, wondering if she sleeps with everyone. He admits to being like his own father and the rest of the men around them, operating with a sexual double standard. In the last scene showing Andrea and Anna together before they separate forever, he is behind a low wall topped with steel bars, a symbol of the prejudices and the division between the genders. By presenting three different male protagonists – Andrea, Dr Illuminato, and Don Antonio – from various parts of Italy and different social classes, the film makes sure that the audience understands that male chauvinism is a national and not a Neapolitan phenomenon. When Anna slaps the man who wants to comfort her, that violent reaction represents a growth in self-esteem for Anna, who is no longer the passive sexual object depicted in the opening scene at the outdoor market, where she displayed her beauty. No longer an object, but a subject, she can go on with her life without a man or a husband. Life is worth living for a woman, despite male prejudice.

Un marito per Anna Zaccheo is a woman's movie, exploring the issue of being an attractive woman in a society that objectifies beauty and offers women no function beyond service as wives and mothers, deprived of sexual desires or choices.

The slow rhythm of the film, shot for the most part from middle distance, with close-ups reserved exclusively for moments of great crisis (for instance, the lovers' meetings and quarrels), is appropriate for a story concerned with observing how men react to female beauty. The static *mise en scène* that characterizes the film is not a flaw; rather, as Farassino[12] has stated, it symbolically represents the immobility that surrounds Anna's life. De Santis deliberately chose to do away with the grand camera movements he employed in *Caccia tragica* and in *Riso amaro* in order to make the form of the film suit its content. A modest story about a female social issue required a less flamboyant form. Unfortunately, the Italian critics of the 1950s were blinded by their political interpretations and could not see that Anna Zaccheo's problems were generic and not personal.

The film must be considered one of the first to address female objectification in Italy. By adopting the narrative clichés of the *sceneggiata* and the *romanzo d'appendice* as its narrative modes, and then breaking their conservative and conformist social messages, De Santis continued his project to create a national cinema for the masses – a cinema that could both entertain and shape a progressive social consciousness.

In 1953 other important films were produced, such as *Noi donne* (Us Women); *Amore in città* (Love in the City); *Gelosia* (Jealousy); *Villa Borghese*; *Pane, amore e fantasia* (Bread, Love, and Fantasy); and *La passeggiata* (The Walk). These films are important not only because they were made by some of the most acclaimed directors of Italian cinema, ranging from Rossellini, to Antonioni, Visconti, Zampa, Germi, De Sica, Lattuada, and Zavattini, or new emerging directors, such as Risi and Rascel, but also mainly because they put into focus certain critical arguments related to Neorealism. Among these films, for example, *Noi donne* and *Amore in città* attempt to present simple urban news items and to re-create actual events using the people concerned as actors and faithfully re-enacting events. This cold chronological presentation of events shows the vulnerability of the Zavattinian Neorealistic theory which state that facts speak for themselves. For De Santis, taking the camera into the streets could not reveal the history, the past, or the origins of the problems, or help change conservative views and social customs. Objective presentation could neither reveal the problems nor present a deeper insight into characters. *Un marito per Anna Zaccheo* marks the director's effort to move towards a deeper psychological rendering of characters at a time when the Italian national cinema was either trying to vary its aesthetics, by combining comic and realist strategies, as in the so-called Rosy Realism, or faithfully undertaking the re-enactment of actual events, as in *Amore in città*.

9

Honeymoon on a Bicycle: *Giorni d'amore* (1954)

... sollecitateci nelle nostre responsabilità di artisti, ma fateci anche divertire col nostro lavoro, e abbiate fiducia che non ci saremo mai divertiti abbastanza quando saremo arrivati alla fine della nostra vita di artisti.

... urge us to assume our responsibilities as artists, but let us also have fun with our work, and you may be sure that we still won't have amused ourselves enough when we reach the end of our artistic career.

Giuseppe De Santis

In the conformist atmosphere generated by the growing power of a centrist Christian Democrat government, artistic freedom of expression was restricted. State control of funding placed a damper on creative activities and led to self-imposed censorship. Italian cinema was living through the most difficult years since the fall of Fascism.[1] In this period of overall artistic decline, so-called Rosy Neorealism, which institutional-ized optimism along with cheerful misery and political escapism, domi-nated the collective imagination of the national audience. Most of the leading personalities of early Neorealism were paying their dues to the general state of artistic regression. The theoretician Umberto Barbaro had left the country. De Santis, ostracized by the government, was unable to film his story about the peasants' rebellion for land reform in the South. Professor Luigi Chiarini had been fired from the editorial board of the journal *Bianco e nero*. De Sica had returned to acting and had stopped his collaboration with Zavattini, who was writing minor stories for comedies. By the end of the 1950s, the list would be even longer.[2] It appeared that every director had to bow to the industry's demand for light comedy, as this statement by Carlo Ponti confirms: 'Today, everyone intending to produce a film has to cross a minefield of compromise, intimidation and all kinds of pressure ... If a producer is brave enough, he can take a risk, but only once. The second time, he prefers to invest his money in films of pure entertainment, from which he is sure to get a return and which invariably bring him a subsidy for exceptional quality.'[3]

Neorealism, understood as a movement for social protest and investigation, appeared to have concluded its brief journey through the annals of Italian cinema. De Santis sought to create new possibilities for expression and to preserve his commitment to an engaged national cinema with a less political film, *Giorni d'amore* (Days of Love),[4] whose title ironically reflects its time.

In spite of the title and the genre, this peasant tale of the 1950s is a programmatic film, whose content and form reveal no inclination on the part of the director to continue or resuscitate the earlier chronicles and documentaries that idealized poor characters and their milieu. By attempting to use different narrative modes and a less dramatic approach to reality, *Giorni d'amore* makes a definitive break with those schemes. In defence of his new approach, De Santis wrote:

We wanted to fight, particularly within ourselves, the old documentaristic conceptions of realism that were still around, in order to achieve a tone and a style that were more fantastic, more poetic, and freer. We wanted to emphasize how important it was for Italian cinema, which was struggling against a period of regression, to find a tie with the great Italian narrative. We wanted to achieve the optimistic sense of reality of Boccaccio, the kindness and the open-mindedness of Goldoni, the ironic wit of our famous dialectal poets, the wise tolerance of Manzoni, and the sorrow of Verga.[5]

The new aesthetic called for a fantastic and poetic approach to reality that would not stray into the realm of comedy, as did, for example, Renato Castellani's *Due soldi di speranza* (Two Cents' Worth of Hope), made in 1953, and Alessandro Comencini's 'Bread, Love, and Fantasy' series and Dino Risi's *Pane, amore, e ...* (Bread, Love, and ...).' These films, typical of Rosy Neorealism, imitated the Neorealist approach, but infused it with comedy. In this genre, contrived storyline and insistence upon a happy ending pandered to the public desire for cinematic escape and facile solutions to the social problems that the stories explored. De

Santis's strategy was to examine the inner dynamics and colliding forces of time-honoured social custom without alienating the public. In *Giorni d'amore*, ancient southern customs and prejudices preserved by poverty and ignorance came under attack. To better achieve his project, the director chose as models the Goldonian popular dialectal theatre, for example, *Le Baruffe chiozzotte*,[6] the farce, the popular southern *cantastorie*[7] tradition, and the romantic genre. The amorous wanderings of Angela and Pasquale through the countryside (typical of the romantic genre) are intertwined and paralleled with farcical scenes that take place in town. During the exposition of the young couple's nomadic honeymoon, the film achieves its explicit objective of fully exploring characterization, something that De Santis had not done in his other peasant story, *Non c'è pace tra gli ulivi* (No Peace under the Olives). The character development in *Giorni d'amore* is also part of the strategy the director mentioned in his defence of the film – to forge a bond with the great Italian narrative.[8] A close examination of the film story and of how it was elaborated will provide a fair assessment of the strategy's success.

Giorni d'amore tells the story of how two young southern peasants, Angela (Marina Vlady) and Pasquale (Marcello Mastroianni), get married. Pasquale has just finished military service and wants to marry his long-time fiancée, Angela. Angela dreams of a beautiful wedding dress with a long white veil, and a reception with all the relatives and friends. She also would like new bedroom furniture, and possibly a train trip for her honeymoon. Like many other girls, she wants her wedding day to be a memorable occasion. Unfortunately the two families are poor, and to complicate matters the annual harvest has been scanty. Angela and Pasquale desperately try to save money, but they just don't have enough. The wedding as planned would cost them 50,000 lire. Rather than postpone the marriage another year, Pasquale resorts to an ancient southern custom. To save the two families the expense of an official, public wedding, he stages a prearranged kidnapping. Once the marriage is consummated, he will then be 'forced' to marry the dishonoured Angela in a simple ceremony. During the kidnapping, the two families will stage a phony public fight to make sure that the town knows they are not involved in the elopement. Unfortunately, the staged spat blows up into a true argument that almost destroys the entire plan. Angela's father, in the heat of the quarrel, invokes the help of the *carabinieri*, and the parish priest to rescue his abducted daughter. The entire town gets involved in a fruitless and half-hearted search for the young couple. Upon their return, Angela and Pasquale are met by two bitterly feuding families, who disapprove of their union. Angela's family vents their rage by abducting Pasquale, but Angela liberates him, and together they rush to the church for a hasty ceremony. When they come out of the church, they find the two reconciled families lined up on either side of the front steps to greet them.

Like the films of Rosy Neorealism, *Giorni d'amore* is set in a poor southern village and features characters who have modest origins. Most of the shooting was done on location, the script was inspired by actual events, the issues are tackled from the point of view of the common people, and some of the actors were non-professionals. For De Santis, however, these were only peripheral elements, more typical of Zavattini's personal poetics than of a general Neorealist theory.[9] *Giorni d'amore* does not anticipate the political satire of the 1970s or the social-comedy genre that dominated Italian commercial production of the late 1950s and 1960s. It is a farce, narrated with wit and humour, which also shows De Santis's love for his native Fondi.

The film is composed of two stories. The first, told in a mixture of various forms taken from the popular theatre, is the story of the intrigues between the two families. The second story concerns the aspirations and frustrations of a young couple and their consequent elopement, which carries them through a series of idyllic natural settings associated with the romantic genre. In the course of their wanderings, many situations arise, highlighting the disparity between the dreams of a young peasant girl and the hard facts of poverty. In presenting the difficulties that Italian women face in marrying and courtship, De Santis returns to a theme previously developed in *Un marito per Anna Zaccheo*, a topic that, in *Giorni d'amore*, also allows him to contrast the male and female psyche of a rustic milieu.

The first story is set in a small town re-created with the collaboration of the painter Domenico Purificato[10] in a theatrical and picturesque way. Purificato, a childhood friend of Giuseppe De Santis, worked on all the scenes and the costumes and was also consulted for the application of the colours. For Purificato, this experience was the realization of a long-standing dream and of a long artistic meditation on the relation between cinema and painting. During his collaboration with the journal *Cinema*, Purificato had developed his theories on the application of colour to single frames and on their principles of composition. In practice, Purificato studied the movements of figures in single frames and tried to apply the tones and shades of various colours in the empty spaces in order to find a correlation between painting and cinematic language.

Because *Giorni d'amore* marks De Santis's first experience with colour, the input of his photography director was considerable, but it was Purificato who added special, significant details, such as using gelatin on the lenses to give the images a special patina. To carry out his experiments, Purificato turned an unfinished storage room into a studio, where he worked on the colour effects and contrasts later used to re-create the internal atmosphere of the two families' houses. The painter's main concern was to tone down the brightness of the blue, which was the prevailing feature of the Ferrania colour film stock used by Otello Martelli, the photography director. Purificato even touched up trees, walls, and clothes to give a chromatic balance to the scenes. For instance, in the scene where the elopers arrive at the country cottage, Purificato provides a visual counterpart to Angela's red hairbow by hanging a wreath of red tomatoes on the wall. The theatrical *mise en scène* of *Giorni d'amore* is also evident in Purificato's reconstruction of the alley where the two families live and where most of the town scenes take place. Pasquale's and Angela's houses are placed opposite each other in order to enhance the spectacle of verbal exchange between the two families when the kidnapping is publicly announced. Here, Purificato applies his theory that film settings should emulate Italian architectural masterpieces. The façade of one house was reconstructed in a concave curvilinear, similar to Francesco Borromini's Oratory of Saint Filippo in the New Church of Rome. The other house, to allow equal visibility from both ends of the street, is constructed with a curve that is the mirror image of the house on the opposite side. This village ambience is further embellished by the bright colours of the exterior walls and the colourful housewares hanging from them. The windows of the respective houses have printed window shades, depicting a sailor for Pasquale and a mermaid for Angela. The window shades are rolled up and down to announce the entrances and exits of the protagonists. During the public quarrel the members of the two families behave in a marionette-like fashion. Their body and hand gestures are controlled and unnatural, their verbal remarks stilted rather than spontaneous. The dialogue is interspersed with a lively, malicious commentary and witticisms coming from the street, which serves as a sort of parterre. In this sequence, De Santis takes full advantage of a southern Italian tendency to make a spectacle out of quarrels.

The contenders take pleasure in and are excited by seeing the increasing number of onlookers. This is how the script envisions the scene:

The balloon man approaches the (*lupini*) vendor and together, both surprised at the same time, they look up at the two windows ... The dwarf, Saverio, with consternation on his face, looks out of his store. From the barber shop, clients, their faces slathered with soap, look out. Three girls with their church books have become curious and stop.[11]

The onlookers are assembling and slowly begin to get involved in the action, stirring up the reluctant arguers, who, carried away by the (general) excitement of the moment, end up insulting each other intentionally. This part of the script is written as a *didascalia* (stage direction):

Inside Pasquale's house – behind the lowered blinds, Grandma Filomena is looking outside.
FILOMENA: But when are they going to start? Perhaps they have forgotten. We
    had to stage a comedy ...

Inside Angela's house
FRANCESCO [the father]: Nunzia [his young daughter] Start!
NUNZIATA: I don't want to get involved in your business ... (*Sadly*) I'm already
    upset about my own problems.
GRANDPÀ PIETRO: You must start, Francì, you are the father!
FRANCESCO: But the mother is more appropriate.
CONCETTA [the oldest daughter]: I have never quarrelled with anyone in my life
    ... What if the police come?
GRANDPÀ PIETRO (*moving closer to the window, as he is getting ready to pull up the
    blinds*): It is better that way. It will look like a real quarrel!

The script describes the two fathers, afraid to start, who must be pushed by the other members of the families. Once they begin, they are incapable of completing their sentences. For example, after Angela's father has just called out Pasquale's father, he cannot finish saying what Pasquale is accused of.

Their reluctance is used by De Santis as a device to get the onlookers involved. As soon as the improvised fight is in motion, as in *commedia dell'arte*,[12] the actors will act out their unprepared parts and will be stirred up by the onlookers. They, complying with a southern social convention, become the audience, and at the same time an integral part of the show. For instance, they form a search party to bring back the two lovers. Rather than the tense and tragic pursuit organized by the cooperative of Emilia–Romagna in De Santis's first film, Fondi's peasants put together a colourful, raucous procession consisting of all the town's most comical characters. We see a dwarf, a short stocky *carabiniere* marshal, a pot-bellied seminarian on vacation. There is even a reporter on the trail of a sensational scandal.

As the elaborate family quarrel is getting under way, the honeymoon voyage of Angela and Pasquale is evolving in a way that neither of them had anticipated.

The buffoonish spirit that characterizes the first part of the film continues in the second part, during the young couple's 'Days of Love.' At this point of the film, the two families, the lovers, and even the townspeople, have accepted the convention of the public spectacle. The role of social custom is overwhelming and is dictating everyone's behaviour. The public willingly suspends its condemnation of or disbelief in the kidnapping and accepts the need of the two families to squabble and shout publicly in order to convince the townspeople of their disapproval of the elopement. In return, the townspeople accept the temporary illegality of the young couple's situation, and in order to preserve appearances they are even willing to play a part in the drama by pursuing the lovers. Only two events in this peasants' farce are unplanned: the misunderstanding between the two families and Angela's refusal to have sex with Pasquale before an official and legal ceremony. Yet, even the latter is in conformity with social convention, since the girl cannot properly give herself without a ring on her finger and without having worn a wreath of orange blossoms on her head. As we will see in the following explanation, a custom / convention is retained that is truer than the actual facts. Since Angela has spent a night with Pasquale, the town considers her dishonoured, even if sexual intercourse had not taken place between them. Therefore, Angela has to pursue Pasquale and seduce him in order to conform to the townspeople's suspicion.

The elopement starts out on the wrong foot. When Angela leaves the house, she takes the wrong turn, which leads her in the opposite direction of the pre-established meeting-place. To reach her, Pasquale has to make his way through a group of youngsters. The youngsters, dogging his steps and taunting him with a popular tune about making love on the sly, serve as a kind of mocking chorus. When Pasquale finally reaches Angela, she feels ashamed and does not want to be seen crossing the centre of town with him. At last, Pasquale convinces her to sit on the bicycle's handlebars, and they set out on their honeymoon across the Fondi Valley. The obstacles they will encounter reveal hidden facets of their personalities. The multifaceted characterization of the lovers' personalities is one of the elements of the Italian narrative tradition which De Santis sought to imitate in making this film out of a peasant love story.

Angela shows her deep religiosity mixed with peasant prejudice and superstition. She also shows her aggressiveness, stubbornness, intelligence, vivacity, and most of all her sensitivity. Pasquale, on the other hand, is more attached to the land and his work, less romantic, more concrete, often selfish and insensitive to Angela's femininity, age, and modesty. When they arrive at the family hut, Pasquale is eager to consummate his sexual passion. Angela is bashful and unwilling. Pasquale reaches out for her and kisses her, but she pulls back at the sight of the animals all around them. From this point on, the film systematically destroys the young girl's dreams of a beautiful, memorable marriage. Looking at the animals, Angela says: 'Pasquà, these [animals] can see ... The animals are like people ...' The audience that, in town, applauded their families' quarrel is now composed of all sorts of barnyard creatures that stare at them and accompany Pasquale's love effusions with various animal sounds. Pasquale launches at Angela, who defends herself, saying: 'Let's go ... They disapprove.' And later adds: 'If we had had a real wedding now, instead of straw, we would have sheets ... and we would be in a hotel like the rich.' She walks out not knowing which way to turn.

Two events, the phony quarrel between the two families and this pitiful attempt to make love, hold the key to the film's message. In a farcical but polemical manner, *Giorni d'amore* criticizes a society that negates even the simplest aspirations. When Angela says that the animals disapprove, using a dialectal expression, characteristic of the South, which refers to them as 'Christians,' she is unconsciously criticizing her family, who have forced her to run away without a wedding. The barnyard animals, in Angela's eyes, are creatures with more feelings than her family. This criticism, repeated throughout the couple's bicycle voyage, is most explicitly expressed in the evening, as the lovers pass a citrus grove. Angela, as if dreaming, exclaims: 'Look, so many orange blossoms ... Smell the perfume ... If you take away a wedding with orange blossoms, what is left for a poor girl?'

Under a starry sky brightened by the moon, Pasquale makes a small wreath of flowers to crown Angela. As a bashful Angela runs to pick lemons from the trees, a shot rings out. The girl's hip has been grazed by a salt bullet. The farce has taken over again, and their *amore* is halted. Over and over, Pasquale tries to overcome Angela's modesty and reluctance, but she does not trust him. She wants a wedding band on her finger. When at last she seems about to give in, more interference spoils the moment. First, a rowdy band of gypsies arrives and distracts the young Angela. Later, at the barn, they perceive the noises of the approaching search party, which Pasquale mistakes for the owner of the stolen lemons. The couple runs away and takes a boat ride on the lake. In this tranquil place, they appreciate, for the first time, the beauty of nature, and Angela shows the innocence of her age, with candid remarks such as 'Do clouds get wet when it rains?' and 'It feels nice to live like the rich.'

But Pasquale is always on the alert to catch the right moment to seduce her. The peaceful interlude goes on until Pasquale, tired of being rejected, leaves after an outburst of rage. Left alone, Angela meets a group of women, who tell her to run after Pasquale because no one would ever believe that she is still a virgin. Now it is Angela's turn to seduce Pasquale, whom she finds playing dead on the beach. Angela brings him back to his senses with tender caresses. Faced with his stubborn resistance, Angela slowly takes off her dress and, clad only in her petticoat, runs into the water. When she comes out of the water looking like Venus, Pasquale is conquered.

In this see-saw of sad and humorous events narrated in a farcical mode, De Santis captured the customs, the superstitions, and the prejudices of his native town. *Giorni d'amore* is a film which demonstrates that the ways to show the authenticity of a social situation are infinite. Even a comical and farcical film with apparently no sociopolitical pretenses was able to carry the director's project for a national cinema. Without being populist, De Santis was able to capture the psychology, the mentality, of the characters and to enter into their world. Unlike the much more highly acclaimed *Due soldi di speranza,* the 'Bread, Love, and Fantasy' series, and many other Italian-style comedies, *Giorni d'amore* is inspired by the fundamental Gramscian indications of how to create popular literature in Italy. According to this Marxist intellectual, in order that art be popular, it had to sink its roots 'inside the humus of the popular culture, with its preferences, its tendencies ... With its morals and intellectual world, even if backward or conventional.'[13] De Santis and his collaborators, in *Giorni d'amore*, applied Gramsci's suggestions to portray a social condition that they knew well in order to expose its backward, conventional, and moral essence.

10

A Fable of 'I Lupari,' a Vanished Breed: *Uomini e lupi* (1957)

'Uomini e lupi' continua 'Riso amaro' e 'Un marito per Anna Zaccheo.' Non c'è dubbio però che in questo film l'osservazione e l'approfondimento di certi problemi siano stati sentiti maggiormente. Il mondo è quello popolare, come nei miei precedenti lavori. E popolare sono i personaggi, che affondano ancora oggi le loro radici nella fantasia di migliaia di persone.

Uomini e lupi carries forward *Riso amaro* and *Un marito per Anna Zaccheo*. However, without a doubt, this film favours the examination and the investigation of certain problems. The world is that of the common people, as in my previous films. The characters, who still live on, today, in the imagination of thousands of people, belong to the common people as well.

Giuseppe De Santis

In the late 1950s, Giuseppe De Santis was unable to find financial backing for his new film on the life of the communist union leader Giuseppe Di Vittorio,[1] one of the forces behind land-reform strikes in the South, and was forced to continue filming minor stories which, under different social, cultural, and economic conditions, he would never have made. The financial situation was so bleak that the Italian film industry could not afford to take risks on politically controversial films. In November 1955, producer Renato Gualino announced his intention to withdraw Lux Film Studios from film production. On 2 May 1955, Minerva Film declared bankruptcy. On 16 February 1957, Ente Nazionale Industrie Cinematografiche e Affini (ENICA), one of the most important para-state agencies which coordinated subsidies for film production and distribution, was threatened with liquidation. To stay in business, the agency was obliged to sign an agreement with Eric Johnston's Motion Picture Association of America (MPAA), which gave Hollywood direct access to the seventy-three ENICA-owned movie theatres, located in major Italian cities.[2]

The film historian Carlo Lizzani[3] reports that, for the year 1956, Italian film production had fallen to 104 films, from 200 in 1954. The crisis was global. In fact, Lizzani[4] also states that, in 1956, total box-office earnings in the United States had decreased to $740 billion, from $1.050 billion in 1948. The Italian cinema industry suffered another setback when legislation regarding censorship, government financing, and production intended to offset market domination of American films was postponed on 31 December 1957 until the end of the coming year.[5]

In the midst of the crisis, the already difficult relationship between De Santis and the film industry was exacerbated by the director's statements made just before the public release of his new film *Uomini e lupi* (Men and Wolves). On 1 February 1957, in an interview reported by the daily newspaper *L'Unità*,[6] the director dissociated himself from the new film, accusing Titanus's director, Goffredo Lombardi, of violating his artistic rights of expression. As if to underscore these claims, the producer proceeded to complete the final dubbing, synchronization, and mixing without consulting the director. De Santis was furious over the cut of 500 metres of film from the original 3,300 metres, a decision which reduced the release print to 2,800 metres. In spite of the pending lawsuit and charges of tampering, the final cut was released by Titanus–Columbia, bearing De Santis's name as director. The director made the following comment on the controversy: 'From that moment on [the lawsuit and the public denunciation], not only Titanus but every producer member of the ENICA shrank from having any kind of working relationship with a director such as myself who had dared to protest against what they [the producers] considered normal working procedures.'[7]

The film debut was also mired by the futile last-minute attempt of an unknown documentarist from Ascoli Piceno to prevent the release by bringing a plagiarism suit against the film's authors.[8] Despite all the controversy surrounding the final edition of the film and the cuts imposed by the producer, *Uomini e lupi* is still clearly a De Santis work, by virtue of its style, subject-matter, composition, development, setting, sensationalism, and melodramatic conclusion.

The film story was written by De Santis with Tonino Guerra and Elio Petri, who had spent months in the Abruzzo region collecting information on the *lupari* (wolf hunters) and on the local peasants. The script was prepared by the above-mentioned artists with the help of De Santis's long-time friends Gianni Puccini and Ugo Pirro, and with the collaboration of Ivo Perilli, who, according to the director, was chosen by the producer. All the outdoor scenes were shot in Abruzzo during the winter of 1956. Since the native wolves of the region were nearly extinct, wolves were imported from Siberia but, according to the director,[9] these all died after the first month. The indoor scenes were done in Rome, in the Titanus Studios, where the town of Vischio was re-created with the help of Ottavio Scotti.

The film opens with a view of the little town Vischio, 1,200 metres above sea level, in the Apennines. The small village is buried beneath the snow and seems deserted. After this long, introductory, establishing shot, the camera moves in slowly on the town. A truck stops at the village's entrance, and a man descends and walks to the back of the truck to inform his wife of their arrival. She has a little boy sleeping on her lap, clasped in a protective and loving manner that denotes her maternal qualities. The opening scene is clearly a typical De Santis overture but differs from the opening scenes of previous films such as *Riso amaro* (Bitter Rice) and *Caccia tragica* (Tragic Pursuit), where the protagonists are immediately linked (by a slow movement of the camera mounted on a crane) to other human beings in similar situations, thus creating a bond. In *Uomini e lupi* the small family remains set apart from the inhabitants of the village. The sense of isolation that emanates from the scene introduces one of the film's main themes: solitude. This is the story of a lonely and obsolete trade, that of the the *luparo* (wolf hunter), set in the suggestive and fascinating mountains of Abruzzo. It is a tale in which time and place are irrelevant. The psychological development of the characters becomes more important than the social and political concerns espoused by De Santis in his former films. Unable to film the stories he wanted, such as the peasant rebellion, the life of Di Vittorio, or the events that took place in Andria after the war, De Santis returns in this film to a society similar to the one of his third film, *Non c'è pace tra gli ulivi* (No Peace under the Olives), but nowhere does he attempt to preach political unity and collaboration to overcome usurpation and exploitation. *Uomini e lupi* is a film about a world that no longer interests the Italian mainstream culture of the 1950s, which was engaged instead with the debate raised about Neorealism, realism, and the fate of the Italian novel, after Vasco Pratolini's *Metello* in 1955. In film criticism, Luchino Visconti's *Senso* was at the centre of the polemics concerning the representation of reality. Both works led to intense, bitter, and thought-provoking arguments about the importance of character development relative to that of immediacy and objectivity in the recording of news events. Cesare Zavattini, principal defender of the immediacy of Neorealism, criticized *Senso*'s retreat into the historical past. The best counterargument was offered by the critic Guido Aristarco, who claimed that Visconti's film represented an evolution of Neorealism towards historical realism.[10]

Faithful to his vision and understanding of realism as a cinema genre geared towards a popular audience, De Santis, in *Uomini e lupi*, tells the story of an obscure and almost extinct breed, the *luparo* (wolf hunter), depicting his struggle against nature, and his passion, rivalry, and jealousy. The world of *Uomini e lupi* has an insularity similar to the world of peasant folk-tales. The peasants of Vischio live outside the lure of modern consumerism, the influences of the new modes of communication, the stimulation of American culture, and the new forms of entertainment that played such an important role in De Santis's previous films. In his seventh film, De Santis abandons even his iconographic trademark – tempting, beautiful, buxom women, often shown in provocative poses to expose their sensuality. In his new film, De Santis also forgoes the daily news event, which he had formerly used to polemicize against current injustices, choosing instead a primordial world inhabited by archetypes. As a result, his investigation brings to life an environment peopled by unique individuals with distinct personalities, a treatment of character with a humanity never before seen on the Italian big screen. The director is able to achieve his goal by establishing the boundaries for this elemental story of men pitted against savage, cunning animals in primordial nature.

Contrary to what many critics have written, *Uomini e lupi* is not an Italian Western set in Abruzzo, but De Santis's version of a peasant tale rewritten for his medium – cinema. The story presents the director with the many mythological realities of an ancient world – the wolf, the wolf hunter, and the mountain village where peasants live out the winter in fear of being attacked by packs of hungry wolves. The landscape becomes a metaphorical symbol of the unknown and the unexpected, and the traditions and customs become conventions that enhance and penetrate the psychology of the people who live them. De Santis's project in this film was to render, through images, a reality lived and felt in a mythical dimension.

The wolf is a mythical figure in peasant culture. He represents the natural forces of evil, darkness, and even sensuality and sexual temptation. In Italian culture, the wolf figures in many tales and lullabies, and goes as far back as the legend of the Roman she-wolf – the symbol of the city of Siena. The wolf hunter is a real figure, but in the minds of the mountain people has also acquired mythical stature for his courage. In the collective imagination, he keeps evil at bay, protecting the flock and the herd from the wolves. In De Santis's film the eternal struggle against the wolves is carried on by two completely different *lupari*, Giovanni (Pedro Armendariz) and Ricuccio (Yves Montand).

The opening scene introduces Giovanni, a wolf hunter by choice and tradition, whose father had also been an able *luparo*. When Don Pietro wants to hire him to protect his animals from the wolves, Giovanni replies: 'Independence is the only nice thing about my trade. One follows his own mind and lives in the open air. Animals, unlike men, don't ever disappoint anyone. My father used to say: 'Nature is my only master' ... I don't want to have a master.' Giovanni is a traditional and old-fashioned man, with an individualistic mentality that exalts independence and freedom. He is not sensitive to the needs of others, and particularly not to the needs of his wife and child. He is never tender or loving to his wife, Teresa, unless he wants sex. During one of their arguments she remarks, exasperated: 'If your son and I were wolves you would care about us more.' He follows his instincts and physical needs, and in many ways is like the wolves he hunts. During a conversation with his wife, Giovanni replies to her comment on his inability to work with others: 'I don't trust anyone. Can't you see what kind of world we live in?'

His rival, Ricuccio, is a handsome, younger man who has never held a steady job. He is a vagabond, more interested in women and an easy life than in fighting wolves. More modern and sensitive, his personality is more complex. He is a man caught between the old, established values and the new, unstable ones, and this constant tension makes him appear, at the beginning of the film, to be a liar, a womanizer, and an exploiter. However, soon we discover that he is more empathic than Giovanni and has a sense of human solidarity that Giovanni does not possess. Ricuccio's growth in character and humanity is one of the most interesting and well-done aspects of the film.

The dramatic action of the film is based on by the antagonism between Giovanni and his rival, Ricuccio. In the first half of the film,

Ricuccio finds a job as Don Pietro's animal guard. Everything seems to go well for him until he tries to pass a dead German shepherd off as a killed wolf, to cover up for his negligence during a wolf attack on Don Pietro's livestock. The fraud is unmasked by a stern Giovanni, who denounces Ricuccio in front of a laughing crowd gathered in the town square. The film's second half starts with a reversal of roles of the two rivals. The unemployed Ricuccio has taken Giovanni's place at the shack of Nazareno (Bianca's father). Giovanni, on the other hand, on his wife's initiative, has become Don Pietro's hired hand. By the end of the film, Ricuccio wins, not only the admiration of the town by capturing a wolf alive, but also Teresa's heart.

The different methods the two *lupari* employ in hunting wolves display their contrasting temperaments and characters. Giovanni refuses to be employed by Don Pietro, the richest land and stock owner of the area. He prefers his meager independence to a secure job with a boss. Ricuccio accepts the job and immediately starts to court Bianca, Don Pietro's young daughter. Giovanni uses traps and dead sheep as bait to lure the wolves. Ricuccio, on the other hand, uses Don Pietro's herd to tempt the animals so he can then shoot them with a rifle. Giovanni's dream is to catch a she-wolf alive with his bare hands, the ultimate test of his bravery and skill as a *luparo*. Giovanni is as ill-tempered, stubborn, introverted, and self-sufficient as Ricuccio is easy-going, witty, and funny. The younger man enjoys singing and dancing. Giovanni's pride and exaggerated sense of self-sufficiency make him refuse Ricuccio's suggestion that they cooperate in a shared effort to capture wolves. Giovanni's disposition will carry him to his death. When a she-wolf is caught in one of traps, Giovanni engages in one-on-one combat with the beast, rather than waiting for his wife to return with help. Giovanni overcomes the animal with the aid of a net but is killed by a pack of wolves that arrives to aid their mate. After Giovanni's death, Ricuccio's character undergoes a slow and complex transformation that will lead him, first, to become a real *luparo* and, later, to take Giovanni's place as Teresa's companion.

The two major female characters reconfirm De Santis's predilection for strong and determined women in his films. Teresa (Silvana Mangano), who made her first film with De Santis in the role of Silvana in *Riso amaro* (Bitter Rice), plays a very different role in this film. In *Uomini e lupi*, Teresa does not personify the new sex symbol of Italian cinema, but plays the traditional wife / mother who, for the good of the family, endures hardships and renunciations. The psychological portrait of Teresa is complex and penetrating. At first she defers to her husband's strong personality and his chosen work. She is almost like a beast, forced to follow him throughout his nomadic existence. She sadly remarks: 'Real satisfaction, in life, is felt in always having the same house.' Only after Giovanni's death, when Teresa is confronted with Ricuccio's thirst for life and exuberance, does her repressed vitality start to emerge. She slowly envisions a different life, but is held back by her affection for her dead husband. She hides her love for Ricuccio, revealing it only through glances, half-smiles, and small gestures. Unselfishly she advises Ricuccio to marry the rich Bianca. She is a loving woman, but also a caring mother, ready to do anything for her son. The most touching and revealing examples of her endurance and staunchness occur after Giovanni's death. Left alone to provide for herself and her son, Pasqualino (Giovanni Matta), Teresa accepts Ricuccio's tribute of a dead wolf and, with dignity and courage, undertakes the long journey through the snow, collecting gifts from the peasants, that is part of ancient local tradition. Ricuccio aids Teresa during her journey and, in the course of their wandering, becomes fond of Pasqualino and falls in love with Teresa. Teresa maintains her reserve and conceals her true feelings for Ricuccio. Teresa's behaviour as a wife, mother, and loving woman made her one of the most complete and most successful Italian populist female characters of the 1950s.

The other main female character, Bianca (Irene Cefaro), is younger than Teresa. She is the victim of an avaricious father who, reluctant to divide his estate between his two children, seeks to prevent Bianca's marriage to a man poorer than she. Bianca's lot is typical of many in rural, traditional patriarchal societies, where women are considered tokens for barter. She lives a very limited existence of hard work, repression, and family exploitation. Her father's morbid attachment to possessions and power has forced her to repress the expression of her true feelings and sexuality. Bianca falls in love with Ricuccio, but when she finally decides to run away with him, realizing that love is worth the sacrifice, it is too late.

Another important character in the film is the young boy Pasqualino. De Santis uses the child character here in a completely different way from that adopted by other major Neorealist directors. In fact, his approach tends to render one of the accusations levelled against Neorealism less convincing. In general, critics have seen in the Neorealist's depiction of reality a propensity towards despair and suffering, compounded by an insistence on using children as the catalyst for evoking an emotional reasponse in the audience. According to the critic Eric Rhode, children are used by Neorealist directors to avoid certain political and social responsibilities. When the spectators identify with the suffering child, the Neorealist director manoeuvres the audience into a state of passive and helpless contemplation instead of offering a solution to the problems. This criticism does not hold in reference to Pasqualino in *Uomini e lupi*. Pasqualino is used by De Santis to show how many Italian children are forced to leave school to accompany their parents on a search for work. In one sequence, Teresa sadly remarks to her husband, after Pasqualino has fallen asleep, that the child has potential but has stopped learning the alphabet at the letter 'm.' This is just one example of Teresa's frequent remarks to Giovanni concerning Pasqualino's need to have a normal life and education.

The boy also plays an important role in the plot's development by serving as a mediator between Ricuccio and Teresa. In order to make the relationship between Teresa and Ricuccio flow more smoothly, the director stressed the fondness the boy has for his father's rival. When Ricuccio first encounters Giovanni and his family and is rejected by his harsh demeanour and words, Pasqualino is attracted to the younger man's gentle and easy-going manner. Their liking will develop into a strong relationship when Pasqualino benefits from Ricuccio's generous offer to share the gifts he has been given for killing the wolf and to accompany Teresa and her child on their journey through the snow to collect their gifts. During their journey in which the peasants pay tribute for the killed wolf, Pasqualino helps Ricuccio regain his confidence after he is rejected and thrown out of the cart by an angry Teresa.

The landscape plays a very prominent role in the film. With the help of Piero Portalupi, one of the most skilled cameramen and director of photography of the time, De Santis achieves an image that put nature itself in the foreground, making it a protagonist in its own right. Cinemascope, used for the first time in a De Santis film, helps to enlarge the depth of field as the Eastman colour film stock enhances the contrasts between the snow, the dark clothing of the people, and the grey of the houses and the silhouettes of bare trees and shadows. In certain scenes the wintery landscape serves to accentuate or becomes an extension of the characters' state of mind. For example, during the cemetery sequence, the barren snow-bound landscape seems to encloak the black-clad Teresa and her son, Pasqualino, as they place flowers on Giovanni's tomb, thereby bringing out the hidden anguish and the despair of the small family.

The landscape devoid of people is often presented in very long takes in order to give a sense of the unknown and the unexpected. This effect is perhaps most notable during a very slow-moving sequence in which a herd of cattle mills around nervously in an empty field, uttering long and deep cries as it senses the presence of the wolves. The long moments of silence are pierced, at times, by eerie wolf howls, which remind the villagers of the imminent threat. These extended silent scenes are fraught with a pending sense of danger, fear, and tragedy that explodes during the wolves' nocturnal attack on the village. The camera work during this sequence is inspired. A very long take shows the forest around the village. Then the wolves appear, hungry and marauding. The attack is presented in a rapid, dramatic, short montage, and its impact is reflected in the faces of the villagers counterpoised with the attacking wolves.

A long take of empty space is also used in another sequence, with very different intentions and results. During their journey, Teresa, Pasqualino, and Ricuccio come upon a deserted little town, abandoned after an earthquake by the frightened population. The three protagonists react to the empty village in a revealing manner. Ricuccio assumes a clownish stance that mocks the political authorities, and makes a speech encouraging the population to hope for better days. Pasqualino finds a way to amuse himself in the empty houses and is overjoyed at the illusion of possessing a house as big as the one owned by Don Pietro. Teresa, after a moment of silence and bewilderment, is reassured and plays in the snow with her son and Ricuccio. In an uninhabited place, where there are no social conventions, she can show her true nature, elsewhere suppressed by hardship and sorrow.

11

De Santis's Conception of
Cinematic Realism:
Cesta Duga Godinu Dana/
La strada lunga un anno (1958)

Come in tutti i miei film, anche nella pellicola che per la prima volta dirigerò in Jugoslavia, per la cinematografia iugoslava, il tema principale sarà l'illustrazione della lotta dell'uomo per il lavoro. Per lo scenario ci siamo ispirati a tipiche esperienze italiane. Ma siccome penso che esse sono generali, umane, allora sono dell'opinione che si possano adattare a tutti i paesi. La località immaginaria può andare bene per ogni Paese, che, secondo le sue condizioni, combatte per la propria esistenza.

In all my works, as in the film that I am about to direct for the first time in Yugoslavia, for the Yugoslav film industry, the main theme is the human struggle for work. For the setting we [the script writers] have drawn upon typical Italian experiences. Since these experiences are typically human, I am of the opinion that they can be applied to different countries struggling according to their own socio-economic conditions for existence.

Giuseppe De Santis

The treatment, written in 1954, was originally called 'Chiaravalle va in pianura' (Chiaravalle Goes to the Valley), but was later changed to 'La strada nella valle' (The Road in the Valley). The script was finished during the same year but filming did not begin for another four years. It was finally shot (in Ultrascope) in Istria, a region in the former Yugoslavia (now Croatia), with the financing of Jadran Film of Zagreb[1] and Avala Film of Belgrade and was produced by Ivo Vrhovec. The film was released with the Serbo-Croatian title *Cesta Duga Godinu Dana* (The

One-Year-Long Road) and was presented at the Pola International Yugo-slav Film Festival, where it was awarded a prize.

In 1954, De Santis, unable to find a producer in Italy willing to pro-vide full financial backing for the film (at that time, the film would have cost 400 million lire), had put together an international co-production, with the Italian producer Forges Davanzati and the Austrian Wien Film Studio as sponsors for the project. To his disbelief and disappointment, the Advising Committee of the Italian Direzione Generale della Cinema-tografia (a state-controlled agency) gave an unfavourable report to the lending bank, stating that the proposal was financially unsound and the planned film would be unmarketable. The government's ostracism of De Santis's film was reaffirmed in 1958 when it refused to admit the film at the annual Venice International Film Festival. The government an-tagonism towards leftist films and filmmakers in the 1950s is well known and documented.[2] The nation's motion-picture censorship sys-tem attempted to justify stringent political and administrative control of the cinema, while at the same time proclaiming and accepting demo-cratic principles of free expression.

The system of motion-picture censorship that emerged between the 1948 and the 1953 national elections could be described as anti-commu-nist, or extremely conservative at best, in part in response to the tremen-dous political pressure facing the Christian Democratic government during the international cold war of the 1950s. During the immediate postwar period, Premier Alcide De Gasperi relied heavily upon the Marshall Plan to strengthen Italy's economy and to counter pressures from the Left. The American films that flooded the Italian market were seen by the conservative government as propaganda vehicles for promot-ing the Western way of life over communist ideas. One fact that cannot be overlooked is the use made by the American Motion Picture Export Association of the Marshall Plan as a lever in trade negotiations with the Italian film industry. Many of the politically or socially committed films of the period were also subjected to severe extra-legal censorship by the Centro Cattolico Cinematografico (Cinematographic Catholic Centre), local politicians, and court rulings.

For example, in his study on the role played by censorship in Italy, Maurizio Cesari[3] states that the democratic right to be informed and to inform was severely curtailed by the common practice of incriminating intellectuals for defamation and public vilification. The incrimination was mostly used to reduce anti-government criticism and transgression.

Cesari writes that, in 1954, prosecutions for public obscenity increased by 10 per cent and for defamation and vilification by 50 per cent. He also adds that, in order to make a case of incrimination for vilification, one must look back at the 1914 national annals of law. Cesari's research agrees with that of critics George Huaco, Carlo Lizzani, Guido Aristarco, Casare Zavattini, and Georges Sadoul, who conclude that the decline and downfall of Italian films whose purpose was to denounce, or at least protest against, the sociopolitical shortcomings of the postwar period were closely related to the rise of political censorship during the early 1950s.

In another well-documented study, by Mino Argentieri and Ivano Cipriani,[4] experts on national film censorship, ample evidence is brought to uphold that assertion. According to their findings, the fact that the initiation of a constitutional court was postponed from 1948 to 1956 gave local courts and De Gasperi's ministry the freedom to regulate film according to their own interpretation of the new constitution. Although the effects of this situation are speculative, the same cannot be said of the decisive moves by then prime minister Alcide De Gasperi in forming the Cinema Bureau under his auspices and in appointing as its head a conservative Christian Democrat, Paolo Cappa. According to Argentieri and Cipriani, Cappa rehired all the officials who had held posts and honours under the Fascist regime. At the time of his appointment, Cappa's power was nominal. For example, on 7 October 1946, Cappa wrote a letter to the then president of the Italian Association of Film Industry denouncing the immorality and anti-nationalism seen in the films produced by the association. The powerless Mr Cappa could only invite the association's president, Alfredo Proia, to promote nobler themes than of the immoral, sexual, and morbid ones seen in films that he declared condemnable.

The government made sure that the controls became tighter on 29 December 1949, when a new law (n. 958) established that all films whose scripts had been preapproved by the Cinema Bureau could receive a contribution equal to the 10 per cent of the gross revenue from public showings in the four years following the films' national premieres. This newly established credit system, created to support and finance national film production, can be regarded as an upgraded restoration of the Fascist system established in 1923, which prevented the production of political, moral, and religious films by not approving the scripts.[5]

In the 1950s, the centrist government rarely censored scripts. The newly established credit system discouraged producers from financing films considered negative or detrimental to the image of Italy abroad. The Banca Nazionale del Lavoro, from which producers had to borrow the money at low interest rates, was a semi-official agent of the government. Argentieri and Cipriani describe the new system this way:

Control was exercised in a number of ways: by evaluating the subject before filming, by granting or refusing credit through the monopoly held by the Banca Nazionale del Lavoro, by 'advice' during filming and, only in extreme cases, by pure censorship. And the last was the least important: the real acts of censorship took place beforehand, independent of the legal bodies, on the basis of personal relationships, nourishing fear and worry and thereby self-censorship, which became more severe than official censorship. Censorship was effected by a bureaucrat from the Ministry acting as the basis of all sorts of contingencies – generally political – accompanied by flimsies and memos, by representations and pressures of various kinds which went beyond the provisions of the Fascist law of 1923.'[6]

The already rigid control became even stiffer with the nomination of Giulio Andreotti as under-secretary of public entertainment; he inaugurated a system to control the exportation of Italian films as well. Andreotti's claim that, under his surveillance, Vittorio De Sica's *Sciuscià* (1946; Shoeshine) would have never left Italy, is well known. In fact, his office had the right to ban the export of a film that might have given an erroneous view of the nature of Italy. It is well known that Andreotti felt that Neorealist films were rendering bad service to the country by making people throughout the world think that Italy was run by an inefficient government, indifferent to the problems of a beleaguered population. On 10 December 1948, Giulio Andreotti defended his policies, stating that Italian films had to present the good aspects of national reality along with a healthy and constructive optimism. The taboos proscribed by the government for the film industry were numerous, but the most improper and unacceptable included adultery, divorce, the family unit as an institution, the Church, sexuality, nudity, sensuality, and suicide. De Santis's favoured themes – for example, poverty, unemployment, strikes, poor living conditions, sensuality, sexuality, and the struggle for land reform in the impoverished South – were among the topics most feared by the censors. There was a general atmosphere of fear and defeat among the cineaste.

If artistic freedom of expression in the cinema was at its lowest point, in the political arena the situation was not much better. The centrist government of Mario Scelba, supported by the Liberal party and the newly formed Social Democratic party of Giuseppe Saragat, had started a harsh political campaign against the opposition. Its prime goal was to crush any initiative coming either from the Communist party or from the leftist labour union. De Santis's affiliation with the Communist party made him the target of ostracism, antagonism, and direct attacks in the conservative press.[7]

The fact that he had started various lawsuits against the major studios to defend his films and his artist freedom of expression from the censors' cuts and the producers' interference had also made him an undesirable director to work with. For example, De Santis had tried in vain to remove his name from the final version of *Uomini e lupi* (1956; Men and Wolves). He had also fought to keep the original length of *Giorni d'amore* (1954; Days of Love) and had been involved in a long and costly dispute with Excelsia Film to salvage from the censors the scene of the return home of the prostitute in *Roma, Ore 11* (1952; Rome, 11 O'Clock).

In his monograph on De Santis, Stefano Masi[8] reports that, during one meeting of Ente Nazionale Industrie Cinematografiche e Affini (ENICA; the Italian national association of producers), one of the members suggested the compilation of a black list, with De Santis's name at the top. The idea of the list was reminiscent of the McCarthy purge of leftist Hollywood directors, which had already prompted Rome's conservative newspaper, *Il Messaggero*, to denounce publicly Neorealist filmmakers considered anti-Italian for their unpatriotic films. Commenting on the deplorable situation in which laic and leftist directors had to work, De Santis stated:

Censorship and the producers' mercantilistic mentality are blocking our way. We will never open a breach (and what has been happening during these last years attests to it) if we will keep on fighting singlehanded. The responsibility for the present situation must not be found only in the intransigent policies of the clerical government or in the producers' mentality. The responsibility lies with us as well. It is also ours. The leftist forces that have not succeeded in creating the right means to oppose edulcorate filmmaking, both on the productive level as well as in the cultural and ideological spheres. Contemporary Italian democratic filmmaking should have its own production, its own distribution, and its own chain of theatres. One must not forget that democratic filmmaking has its own potential public that too often is left at the mercy and in the power of the soporific poisons of standardized cinema.[9]

Further evidence of the government's ostracism of De Santis is apparent, not only in the previously mentioned decision to exclude *Cesta Duga Godinu Dana* from the International Venice Film Festival, but in the government's refusal also to distribute the Italian version of the film (*La strada lunga un anno*) in Italy, despite the fact that the film had received favourable reviews from French and American critics. In the United States, De Santis's film was nominated for an Oscar for best foreign film (the Golden Globe was awarded to the French film *Mon Oncle*) and had also been named best picture by the Hollywood Foreign Press Association at Coconut Grove on 5 March 1959. Massimo Girotti had also been awarded first prize for his role as Chiacchiera at the San Francisco Film Festival that same year. A shorter version of the film in Italian (the Yugoslavian version is over three hours long; the version I saw on video-cassette is one hour and thirty minutes long), with the same title as the original Italian script title *La strada lunga un anno*, was released by Cino Del Duca, a French–Italian producer, in 1959.

In Italy, the film was boycotted by all the major theatres and was screened mainly under the sponsorship of the Communist party in the second-run provincial theatres of Emilia–Romagna, a region mostly under Communist administration, and by private film clubs. For example, as late as February 1960, the film had not been distributed in Rome or in the South. In Milan, it was shown in one major first-run theatre for only two nights. Today, it is still almost impossible to find a copy of the film in Italy. The National Film Archive in Rome (Cineteca Nazionale) has an inflammable copy that cannot be rented. The only available copy for viewing is at the film school of the University of Padua. The unavailability of the film is confirmed by Antonio Parisi's[10] omission of it in his monograph on De Santis.

Commenting on the difficulties experienced in finding producers and distributors for his film in Italy, De Santis said:

I have always found more problems and hostility in finding producers and distributors after 'Roma, Ore 11' for the very fact that I wanted to bring to the large screen specific themes. I wanted to work in a certain manner, under certain working conditions. I must also admit that by temperament I do not have a submissive nature. Apart from my personality, I have done nothing else but defend my honour, my dignity, and my professional decorum. It was too bad that the rest of my fellow film directors did not do likewise. In that period [the 1950s] my colleagues never protested. Vittorio De Scia, for example, allowed, without protesting, the removal of the funeral sequence from his film

'L'oro di Napoli' [1954; Naples's Gold]. He did not even raise a finger, because he knew that protesting for artistic freedom of expression meant the loss of future work.'[11]

Although ostracized and expatriated, De Santis, with the help of the Italian Communist party, was finally able to film his symbolic story of a road construction, in Yugoslavia. There, he worked relatively free from commercial constraints on the film. The film's realization was not only the fulfilment of a dream, but also a personal revenge against the Italian film industry and the centrist government of the Christian Democrats.[12] However, despite being given the opportunity to make the film according to his own artistic and cultural point of view, on the other side of the Adriatic Sea, De Santis felt like an exile from the Italian film industry. In an attempt to make the film more authentic, De Santis attempted to find areas in Istria that resembled the location he had originally selected to film and to find faces whose features resembled those of southern Italian peasants. In spite of all the difficulties involved, such as working through translators and in a country where the film industry was in its infancy and few professional or well-trained set designers were available, *La strada lunga un anno* is De Santis's best film in terms of theme, structural development and realization. In it, all his cinematic motifs, themes, and stylistic elements come together and are harmoniously connected, joining the choral and the personal, resulting in a popular cinematic epic. The film's metaphoric elements do not reduce the strength or the bite of De Santis's political comments; rather, the skilfully developed metaphor of road construction enhances the message.

The story was written by De Santis with the help of Elio Petri and his long-time friend Gianni Puccini; Maurizio Ferrara, Tonino Guerra, and Mario Socrate joined them in writing the final script. Originally, De Santis planned to shoot the film in his native Ciociaria, where his third film, *Non c'è pace tra gli ulivi* (No Peace under the Olives'), was set. As the first draft's title – 'Chiaravalle va in pianura' (Chiaravalle Goes to the Valley) – suggests, the location of 'Quercie,' a hilltop mountain village in Ciociaria, would have been the ideal place for the construction of the road that would have linked the little town to the plain of Fondi, De Santis's birthplace.

The script depicted the period (1954) when, in the South, the reverse-strike technique (*sciopero al rovescio*) was being widely adopted. The method consisted in occupying and cultivating the land of large land-owners. It was the opposite of what we know as a strike since the peasants did not have jobs. The end of feudalism in 1812 had little impact on the land system in the South in 1954. The existing land system paralysed southern peasantry, making it impossible for labourers to receive a fair reward for their work. Since the peasantry was never able to buy land, the land was still in the hands of a few large – mostly absentee – landlords, whose fields were cultivated by tenant farmers or were left for grazing ground. To counteract this ancient custom, the leftist labour union advised and spurred the peasants to cultivate and plant the land in order to force the government to legislate land reform. The best-known cases in which *sciopero al rovescio* was applied success-fully are the construction of the Vomano Dam in the region of Abruzzo and of the Cormor Canal in the impoverished region of Friuli. *Sciopero al rovescio* was also a way for the labour union to find work for the unemployed. By occupying the land, the peasants would have caused a state of social unrest; in the long run, the occupation might have drawn the attention of the media and gained public support; for the most part, the public rallied in favour of the unemployed peasants who were forced to leave the land they had cultivated.

The original script reflects closely this state of affairs in the South. When De Santis was finally able to film his script, during the winter of 1957–8, in Yugoslavia, the story became more abstract and less localized. The fablist tone and atmosphere, less prominent in 1954, became more pronounced. This characteristic is also attributable to the request of the Yugoslav producer to keep the identity of the village and its inhabitants as symbolic as possible. The fact that the script was originally written in 1954 in part explains the film's prominent stylistic, thematic, ideological, and political differences, which set it apart from the other important Italian films made in the late 1950s. *La strada lunga un anno*, for in-stance, is very different from Federico Fellini's *La dolce vita* (1959), Michelangelo Antonioni's *L'avventura* (1959) and even Luchino Viscon-ti's *Rocco e i suoi fratelli* also released that year.

De Santis's *La strada lunga un anno* could have been, together with his never-filmed 'Noi che facciamo crescere il grano' and 'La vita di Giuseppe Di Vittorio,' the conclusion of his saga on the southern post-war problems during the reconstruction period.[13] In all probability, had these been filmed, De Santis's subsequent filmography would have progressed differently. His cinematic development was hindered by his inability to make the films he wanted at a specific historical time. During the 1950s, his artistic quest moved in two opposite directions. His scripts reveal his poetic vision and strong political commitment;

whereas, the films *Uomini e lupi* and *Un marito per Anna Zaccheo* reflect his poetic world but not his most strongly felt political themes. When *La strada lunga un anno* was made in 1957–8, it had lost the ability to have an impact on the national level, both as a cinematic work and as a political work of art. Cinematically, the film still remains one of De Santis's best, but one could say that its importance in the history of national cinema would have been much greater in 1954, when its political content and its artistic structure would have excited more interest and critical attention. In an interview given after the release of the film in Italy, the director painfully commented: 'I feel the mortification of he who cannot harvest the fruits of his labour. The film removed from the public for which it was originally conceived loses its intent to stimulate a democratic consciousness and assumes a platonic value. It becomes as a manuscript in a bottle left to rest in silence at the bottom of the sea.'[4]

In the stories written in the 1950s but never filmed, De Santis wanted to probe deeper in the southern peasant culture – that rural world that was about to lose its identity with the economical miracle that brought about the peasants' exodus to the North and the first symptoms of consumerism and economical progress. In the world of national cinema, these changes gave rise to a new type of film that would later be known as 'Comedy Italian-Style.' The new demographic, anthropological, and social transformations are also explored in different cinematic forms by Visconti, in *Rocco e i suoi fratelli*, a saga on the problem of integration and assimilation in the aftermath of the internal migration; by Fellini, in *La dolce vita*, a fresco on spiritual decadence and on the quest for purpose in life by Marcello, a reporter still fresh from the provinces; and by Antonioni, whose middle-class characters search for new meaning and stimulation in the affluence and opulence of the recent economic boom. Meanwhile, De Santis continued to explore popular themes and the labour struggle, even in Yugoslavia amid all the difficulties and problems connected with working in an unfamiliar setting.

La strada lunga un anno is a choral fresco and a symbolic depiction of the human struggle for work and dignity in a society that denies many of its members the right to earn a living. The film is an effort on De Santis's part to return to his militant commitment to educate the masses by presenting an elaborate cinematic fable that is both stylistically and visually lavish. Again, in this film, he defies the aesthetic strictures of Zavattinian Neorealism and broadens a style that pressures from the critics and the political regime were driving inceasingly inward, towards purity. In making *La strada lunga un anno*, De Santis reaffirmed his disagreement with the critics; he felt that dissecting a film into infinitesimal particles lost or overlooked what, according to the director's personal aesthetic, constituted the most urgent meaning of a film – its human and poetic value, as portrayed in its message and content. The film serves also to reaffirm the director's dissension with the trend in films of the time to focus on middle-class protagonists. De Santis faulted the films of Fellini and Antonioni, and those Rossellini made during his marriage to Bergman, for dealing with a limited dimension of Italian reality. For De Santis, the newly acclaimed films presented the world from a narrow bourgeois point of view. By following the mode of French films and certain American comedies, the director maintained, the new Italian cinema had lost the collective national inspiration that distinguished and animated its postwar films. In a 1960 interview, given after his return from Yugoslavia, the director stated:

When an artist pretends to immerse his finger in the Italian reality, it must be presented in its totality, which includes its negative and positive sides. Instead, and this is a fact, with only rare exceptions, the picture is always one-dimensional. It is totally black. It lacks the antithesis which is at the very root of every work of art – an antithesis meant, not as a redemption, but as a dialectical investigation of the situation. In these last years, Italian cinema has only accentuated the flaws that undermined the Neorealist experience. Our cinema has not been able to look at reality as a whole. It stopped at the partial aspect of it, touching on either this or that situation without capturing its entirety.[15]

From this statement one can conclude that De Santis is not only voicing his dissent with the new emerging cinema but reaffirming his commitment to a cinema that offers a solution to the problems presented, as he does in *La strada lunga un anno*.

In Yugoslavia, for the first time in his career, De Santis was able to work without studio concern about the marketability of the product. At last he could make a film that would come close to his conception of a cinematic novel (*romanzo*). In *La strada lunga un anno*, many single episodes intertwine into a harmonious whole that explains and clarifies the main event. This film is the realization of a choral story which, in form, narrative structure, and unity, must be considered as the fulfilment of the cinematic version of the Verghian choral and impersonal novel. The *Cinema* group had adopted these novels as models to promote a new and more realist type of national cinema during the stagnant years of the Fascist regime.

Unlike the other films of the period, De Santis's cinematic fable indicates a way out of misery, pessimism, and unemployment – namely, collective work and collaboration. In *La strada lunga un anno*, the plot is based on the continuous interplay between the selfish attitudes of the protagonists and the collective spirit, symbolized by the common effort involved in the road construction. The film alternates between the road construction and the personal events of the workers who are involved with the project. It is characterized by a constant tension that is kept alive by the never-ending personal problems and social conflicts.

An analysis of the film's structure shows how the personal and the social are interwoven to unite the collective with the single lives of the people involved.

The film is divided in four major blocks that follow the changes of seasons, starting in autumn and returning to the same season of the following year. The four major episodes are preceded by an introduction and an epilogue which serve to identify the moral of the fable. The protagonists, the inhabitants of a smal town, are couples, family units, or single individuals who come out of the group briefly to assume pro-tagonist roles and are later reabsorbed by the group as others become prominent. This structural device is enhanced by the camera work, a movement from panoramic and group shots to medium and close shots, following the movements of individuals and the group, as in a folk dance.

The main story is preceded by an introduction that serves as a link to the film discourse. As the protagonists' names appear on the screen, two one-horse carriages coming from opposite sides cannot continue their courses on the only narrow road that links the remote village to the valley. The two drivers get down from their coaches and start a bitter argument over who has the right of way. As they argue, a passenger steps off and nonchalantly walks home. The message is clear: the road is too narrow, but the inhabitants, instead of collaborating to widen it, get lost in bitter and personal confrontation. The bystanders do not care, but the victims of government inefficiency must collaborate to better their lives. This film will teach us how to overcome this inertia and resignation.

In the middle of autumn, in an isolated village situated on top of a rocky, arid hill, a few unemployed men wait eagerly for the return of spring so that they can go search for work elsewhere. One day, as they engage in small talk and keep busy making tobacco from the falling autumn leaves, Guglielmo (Bert Sotlar), one of the many unemployed, along with his wife, Agnese, his daughter, Ginetta, and his ten-year-old son, Giovanni, start to work on widening the only road that links the isolated village to the coast in the valley. The camera moves from a full shot to a medium one of the men on the terrace overlooking the valley, and later rises in a crane shot, followed by a long panoramic view of the valley, as if indicating their repressed desire to reach the coast. Their inertia is fuelled by the general opinion that there are no funds available for the work that would open the village to the markets down in the coastal area. Guglielmo, taking advantage of the mayor's absence, leads everyone to believe that the long-awaited permit to start the road construction has finally arrived. It seems that their ancient isolation and perennial unemployment are finally over. The rest of the townspeople, at first surprised and sceptical, join in the widening of the old road. The happy event is followed by an evening of celebration made possible by the credit granted by the shop owners to the local families. The celebration serves as a transition that allows the story to introduce and define the characters and the ambience. During this interlude the spectator learns about the impoverished state of the day labourers and is exposed to the intimate and personal lives of the townspeople. For example, one sees the other side of Chiacchiera (Massimo Girotti). During the day he seems a sort of anarchist – single and care-free, and with a passion for wine, women, and song. During the evening festivities his weakness for drinking and fun is followed by loneliness and frustration over his inability to find real love.

The pause in the action is followed by the mayor's return, which sets the stage for the confrontation with Guglielmo. Fearing that violence, reprisal, and social unrest will result in the long run if he does not take immediate action, the mayor declares that the municipal administration has not authorized the repairs and will never pay for the work. The infuriated people want to abandon the work, but Guglielmo tries to convince them to continue and finish the road. He plans to use the technique of reverse striking (*sciopero al rovescio*) – in other words, to continue working in spite of the authorities and without pay. Guglielmo hopes that, in the long run, their perseverance will force the authorities to recognize their effort and come up with the money to pay for their labour. His reasoning persuades almost everyone, including a newlywed couple, Pasquale (Niksa Stefani) and Angela (Gordana Miletic), who will emigrate to America if Guglielmo's plan fails.

The work is hard, and the people start to feel discouraged and want to give up. A fight breaks out among the men, and during the commotion

Guglielmo's little boy, Giovanni, is seriously injured, falling into a ravine after being pushed unintentionally by Chiacchiera. Guglielmo is forced to leave so that he can take his son to a distant hospital. Chiacchiera, in order to expiate his guilt, takes over the leadership on the road construction. His new vigour serves as an example to the disheartened population. Soon, the work is interrupted by the refusal of the landowners to allow the road to be built on their land, in fear that the government will never compensate them. Chiacchiera avoids the dangerous confrontation by convincing them that the road completion will also work to their advantage by expanding their business possibilities. The work is resumed but, after a kilometre, comes to another stop in front of an old house, which is the sole possession of a young woman who is a single parent. Her husband has never returned or written from America. The woman, who has a proud, stubborn, and skittish temperament, is almost unapproachable. This time Chiacchiera is able to convince her by letting her stay at his house until the authorities reimburse her loss.

The mining and the consequent explosion of the old home is an excuse for the well-to-do to call the police, who, in turn, arrest many workers on the charge of using dynamite in public without a permit. The work comes to an end. However, the triumph of the nobles is short-lived. To their surprise, the women and the children take over the work the arrested men and, at the same time, put pressure on the local priest to intercede in order to have the complaint withdrawn. The arrested men are released, but the work is interrupted again when the town council baulks at paying them. In protest, the workers go on a hunger strike and lock themselves inside a basement. At this point the local schoolteacher, Del Prà, who until then had opposed the unauthorized construction, joins the strikers. The old man is upset with the selfish and greedy nobles, who want to gain from the road without paying for it. Del Prà, faced with the injustices and saddened by the hardship faced by his former pupils, sees his ideal world, based on law and order, shattered. He decides to take the workers' side and to mediate with the well-to-do. He uses his authority and influence to persuade them to pay the overdue taxes in order to recompense the workers.

Unlike other Neorealist films, *La strada lunga un anno* presents the middle class, in the character of Del Prà, as able to overcome his lot. The schoolmaster is a seventy-year-old man attached to the old traditions. He is an old sentimentalist and a romantic egalitarian who still believes in the old principles of honesty, integrity, and obedience. When the struggle between the authorities and the old conservative ruling class, on one side, and the workers, on the other, reaches its peak, the old schoolmaster is able to overcome his education and culture to align himself on the side of the workers. After his personal victory, the old man, in a very melodramatic scene, dies of fatigue and exhaustion. His death comes at the moment when the workers have achieved a collective consciousness and do not need him any more. Here, De Santis is applying Antonio Gramsci's ideas on the role of the intellectuals.[16] The old intelligentsia will be replaced by the new one, which will be an integral part of the new constituted society. One could say that De Santis himself is an example of the new intellectual, on the side of the workers, making symbolic films to promote a new democratic order based on social and class collaboration.

After Del Prà's death, the road construction has to overcome one last obstacle: the road must pass over a river. As with the other obstacles, the bridge will also serve to reintegrate individuals with the rest of the community. Chiacchiera counts on Davide, a former bridge builder now involved in the black market, to help. Davide wants to use the opportunity to kill Lorenzo, his wife's lover, but at the crucial moment, when he is about to carry out his vendetta, his personal feelings are overcome by the commitment he has with the other workers and their cause. The successful completion of the bridge restores confidence in him and helps him regain his dignity in front of his people and family. The bridge has also given a sense of accomplishment and self-esteem to the rest of the workers. The reunification between Davide and his friends is completed by his reconciliation with his wife, who will follow him to his new job in the city.

The year-long road is finally finished. It took four seasons and a long struggle to accomplish what had never been done before by workers alone. The people of this metaphorical town have now gained a new outlook on life, in general, and on their own lives. There are many other roads to be built or that need repairs, and the government will pay once the work is done. Their new outlook on life is symbolized by the birth of a baby, who needs to be fed. His parents, Pasquale and Angelina, do not dream of emigrating to America any more, but instead put up a sign in which the start of a new road is announced. Guglielmo, who had started the road construction, will be elected major to help the people and to make sure that the nobles pay their taxes. By working together on the road, the townspeople have learned how to collaborate and make gains in overcoming misery and finding work.

In sum, *La strada lunga un anno*, through a narrative structure comparable to a folk dance, intertwines the movements of the group and the single protagonist. During its broader moments, the narrative becomes an epic mixed with buffoonish, dramatic, and pathetic individual episodes. The tension is sustained by the continuous interplay between social and class-related conflicts. Typical of De Santis's poetic world, the lower-class people and the workers are depicted not only as representatives of a social class, with all its distinctive characteristics, but also as individuals, for whom the director has a deep and caring love. This love is manifested in the meticulous representation of celebration as well as in the precise portrayal of eating, washing clothes, and going to bed. The working class in De Santis's cinematic world is the underdog, the victim of the well-to-do and the oppressors. Only through solidarity can the workers and the peasants overcome their subordination and state of deprivation. The happy ending of the story is unlike that of an ordinary commercial film. It derives from the director's dialectical approach to social reality and from his unwavering trust in the power of humanity to better itself. In this film, De Santis again shows his faith in man's ability to achieve a moral and political consciousness. He also shows his faith in human ability to rebel and overcome hardship in hostile circumstances. In the struggle against injustice, the underprivileged can find dignity only in collaboration, and through collaboration they can overcome the obstacles to their emancipation. It is also important to note that the metaphorical road is achieved by democratic means. The greatest victory for the workers of the imaginary village of Zagora is in having forced the other social classes to collaborate and share some of their privileges. Therefore, the road is also a journey to democracy and progress. This democratic and humanistic lesson went unheard in the bitterly divided Italy of the 1950s, where the film was never widely distributed.

12

The End of the Bourgeois Family or Repugnance for a Transformed Society?
La Garçonnière (1960)

Dalla 'Dolce Vita' (1960) in poi, la borghesia entra nel cinema italiano. Io non ho trovato lavoro a vele spiegate perché i miei personaggi continuavano sia pure, mutando le strutture, sia pur all'interno dei boom economici, ad essere quelli che erano ... Questa gente non era scomparsa come mi si diceva per rifiutarmi lavoro.

From *La dolce vita* on, the bourgeoisie enters Italian cinema. I was not able to find work in full sail because my characters, even if within changing structures and economic booms, continued to remain as they were ... These people had not disappeared, as they would tell me to refuse me work.

Giuseppe De Santis

De Santis's return to Italy after *Cesta Duga Godinu Dana* (1958; The One-Year-Long Road) was met with professional adversity and ostracism. In spite of the international recognition it received, his Yugoslavian film was never seriously distributed in Italy, and consequently was never reviewed by film critics.[1]

To make things even worse, De Santis's new project never materialized. With the collaboration of the nationally known Neapolitan writer Carlo Bernari, his disciple Elio Petri, Ugo Pirro, and Tonino Guerra, De Santis had written a story which subsequently became a script about Pettotondo (Round Breast), the legendary Apulian prostitute who never wanted to make more money from her profession than was necessary to satisfy her immediate needs. De Santis was inspired by a well-known folk song of the Apulian peasants.[2] The film had found a producer in

Roberto Amoroso. Previously, the Amoroso family had been involved in producing low-budget films mainly for the local Neapolitan market, but after the successes of *Due soldi di felicità* (1956; Two Pennies' Worth of Happiness) and *Addio per sempre* (1957; Goodbye Forever), Roberto Amoroso was ready to try the national market. De Santis's name, especially after the Oscar[3] nomination in 1960, was considered a desirable springboard for Amoroso's big jump in film quality. Speaking of Pettotondo, De Santis recalls that he had even shot a fifteen-minute-long screen test with the then young and unknown Claudia Cardinale, who had been chosen for the leading role. Under heavy pressure from the lending bank, which was afraid of losing future government film subsidies, Amoroso backed out of the project and was sentenced to compensate Cardinale for breaking the contract. But he salvaged a deal with De Santis and, instead of the film on the round-breasted Apulian prostitute, they collaborated on *La Garçonnière* (The Love-Nest), a film which shows De Santis's contempt for the new Italy of the economic miracle of the late 1950s.[4]

The story of *La Garçonnière* takes place in Rome, where the middle-aged engineer Alberto Fiorini (Raf Vallone) lives with his family in an exclusive section of the city. Giulia (Eleonora Rossi Drago), his wife, has dedicated herself totally to the family's needs. She is very insecure, and emotionally dependent on her husband, despite the fact that she is rich and was brought up in a wealthy upper-middle-class milieu. Alberto, an aging Casanova, keeps a *pied-à-terre* in a working-class section of the city, away from the eyes of his social class and his family. The flat is kept up by the concierge, whose young nephew from Fondi (the director's home town), Vincenzino (Nino Castelnuovo) – a kind of young De Santis alter ego – uses the flat in the engineer's absence. One day, Giulia, who has always suspected her husband, is prompted by her friend Pupa (Marisa Merlini), one of Alberto's former lovers, to follow Alberto to the *pied-à-terre*. Hiding in her car, Giulia sees Alberto walk in and, after a short while, a beautiful young girl, Laura (Gordana Miletic) arrives. Giulia recognizes her as a model from the shop she often visits with Alberto. Giulia gets out of her car and confronts the girl, who insults Giulia before entering the building. Laura does not mention the encounter with his wife to Alberto. Shortly afterwards, Alberto receives a telephone call from his administrator, who informs him of pending financial difficulties. Alberto calls on his wife for financial assistance. Giulia says nothing to him about his sexual affair with the young Laura, but, after their conversation, she asks her two children to join her for a ride and drives to the *pied-à-terre*. Then, she parks the car and turns on the car's alarm system. Alberto, warned by Laura, who has seen everything from the window, decides to go down to the street to see what is going on. Meanwhile, Giulia and the children have decided to go see *La grande guerra* (The Great War),[5] a film playing at the neighbourhood theatre. By pure chance, they run into Alberto, and Giulia unsuccessfully tries to stop him from returning to his young lover. Alberto does return to Laura, but a series of interruptions take place that stop them from consummating their affair. During a conversation, Laura reveals that she has had a previous lover, her former dance partner, and Alberto's illusions of recapturing his youth through pure virginal love are shattered. Disappointed, Alberto falls asleep, and Laura leaves the flat. In the morning, Alberto is surprised to find Giulia sitting in his car. She had spent a sleepless night waiting for him. Reconciled, they drive home, but Alberto cannot promise that he will ever change.

The critics harshly attacked the film. For example, Castello[6] remarked that the human metaphor of an ageing man who, after a long series of sexual affairs, suddenly tries to find new meaning in life through love is not very convincing. Alberto is very ambivalent, and the audience is never sure if he loves Laura or if he suffers from some pathological neurotic condition.[7] Lanocita, commenting[8] on the film's attempt to advance reasons for the legalization of divorce in Italy, remarked that the progressive views of the film were hampered by the depiction of a womanizer who hopes to be the first lover of a young virgin.

De Santis's biographers were not much kinder. For Stefano Masi,[9] *La Garçonnière* is a triumph of the *mise en scène* and the artistic baroque. He saw the film as the culmination of De Santis's taste for accumulation of details, which are visible even in the exaggerated acting. Alberto Farassino[10] has defined the film as perhaps De Santis's ugliest movie. According to the critic, *La Garçonnière* is unbalanced, indefensible, and even pathetic. Antonio Parisi[11] has placed the film outside of De Santis's style and populist thematic by comparing the film's classic unity of time, space, and action to the German *Kammerspiel*.

More than a condemnation of a single social class, or the psychological drama of an ageing man and the end of the bourgeois family, *La Garçonnière* is the beginning of De Santis's distancing from the new demographics of Italian society at the end of the 1950s. At that historical moment, the existing well-defined cultural differences between the various social classes were becoming less visible under the influences of consumerism and the mass media. The rapid cultural changes were also accompanied by an exodus from the country and a consequent decline of peasant culture. Reflecting on these cultural changes De Santis said in 1987: 'Maybe I experienced the cultural changes more slowly and with greater grief than the rest of my colleagues. All these changes took place following a natural course of events in which heroic phases are followed by moments of reflection and stasis. During them, everyone goes through a stage of reflection and self-analysis. These transformations occurred also in me, but more slowly than in others [filmmakers].'[12]

La Garçonnière is set in the city, a locus De Santis saw as capable only of individual dehumanization, corruption, and degradation. In contrast to the rural community, where evil can be overcome, eradicated, or expelled from the social body, the city is a place damned by social fragmentation and detribalization. In urban settings, De Santis's characters are always enclosed or boxed in by narrow, gloomy spaces meticulously elaborated in studio reconstructions. De Santis's city characters, forced to live in disharmony with the environment, cannot fully express or enjoy a healthy sexuality. Sexuality outside of the country can only turn into perversion, degradation, unhappiness or even criminality. In *Roma, Ore 11* (Rome, 11 O'Clock), the city was presented as an evil place. In *Un marito per Anna Zaccheo* (A Husband for Anna Zaccheo), emerging consumerism had created (through new public billboards and advertising) amusement parks for men, and new forms of sexist exploitation that existed only in the cities during the period in which the film was made. All of these motifs of urban disaster are even more marked in *La Garçonnière* because the story deals with an upper-middle-class psychological and existential drama set in the so-called Italian economic boom. *La Garçonnière* is a film that shows De Santis's contempt for the new cultural consequences of the economic miracle.[13] A comparison of this film with *L'Avventura* and *La dolce vita*, both released around the same time (1959–60), makes De Santis's attitude even clearer.

In *L'Avventura*, as Liehm wrote, 'the strictly individual human experience is not tainted by any historical or social factor. The fact that Antonioni chose an upper-middle-class milieu had nothing to do with the attempt to make this particular kind of emotional adventure the privilege (or vice) of one social class.'[14] In *La dolce vita* Fellini depicts a decadent international world. Marcello's search for meaning in life evades him because, in the cynical, loveless, fruitless modern world in which he lives, it is unfindable. Unlike the two contemporaneous films mentioned above, *La Garçonnière* is evidence that the already existing evils which had characterized De Santis's earlier urban films have, by the late 1950s, worsened to the point of having corrupted every social class. The animated street life shown in the opening scene of the Largo Circense neighbourhood before the tragic staircase collapse in *Roma, Ore 11* is missing from *La Garçonnière*. The working-class urban district where the *pied-à-terre* is located has become an urban slum in the wake of 'progress.' The social investigation that has always distinguished De Santis's films is different in *La Garçonnière*. The fact that no harsh contrast is established between the cultural world of Alberto's class and that of the people who live around the *pied-à-terre*, which was seen by some critics[15] as a shortcoming of the film, can be explained by the director's pessimistic outlook on the future of the working class. The world around the flat is turning into an extension of the world inside the apartment. Standardization and consumerism are causing a cultural homogenization of the classes. The working class of *La Garçonnière* does not serve as a counterpart to the sentimental and existential conflict of the upper-class protagonists. The images of the film are less revealing of the concrete financial problems of the working people than of their cultural contamination. If we take into consideration that the working class is seen through the bedroom windows of the *pied-à-terre* or through the eyes of the upper-middle-class protagonists, the message is that the Italian economic miracle of the late 1950s was accompanied by profound contradictions rooted in the general conditions of the postwar restoration. In the film, however, as in the Italian national sphere, where the contradictions go unnoticed, the chorus of the social discomfort of the unemployed and the underemployed is not even seen or heard by Alberto and his circle.

In the main plot, the characters are locked in the traditional triangle: he, she, and the other. Through their conflict, the film not only focuses on the marital crisis of the middle class but also shows the degradation of the family institution and society at large. For instance, Laura, the other, is a young girl from a working-class family who now works as a model. She is a social climber. Laura, with her coy look and her nylon baby-doll outfit, appears to be the vulgarization of the strong independent single women seen in De Santis's previous films: Francesca in *Riso amaro* (Bitter Rice), who, in a personal vendetta, kills Walter, the gangster, who had used her; Anna Zaccheo, who struggles against the sexism of a macho society and finds enough strength to refuse Don Antonio's offer of a loveless but wealthy marriage; Lucia, in *Non c'è pace tra gli ulivi* (No Peace under the Olives), who breaks an ancient custom that uses women as barter goods for their families' enrichment by running to the mountains in search of her besieged lover and risking her own life. And, one of the strongest of De Santis's heroines, Maria Grazia, in *Non c'è pace tra gli ulivi*, who, after having experienced the violence and the humiliation of Bonfiglio's rape, at the young age of seventeen finds the courage to face the town's scorn and publicly denounce him and, at the end of the film, even finds the inner strength to attempt an escape before Bonfiglio kills her.

The debasement is also shown in the behaviour of Giulia, the wife. She has always closed her eyes to her husband's infidelity, but now, threatened by Laura's beauty and youth, she wants to confront him with what she has always known. Her stubborn desire to discover the truth turns into panic. She does not have the courage to carry through her plan to break with Alberto, since the disruption of the marriage would have revealed the emptiness of her existence. She can only go as far as admitting that marital love cannot last forever if it is not supported by strong friendship and mutual understanding. The upper middle class is not the only target of the director's attacks. The concierge is a procuress; Clementina, a young girl in the neighbourhood, is a prostitute; and Pupa, Giulia's friend, is married to a man twenty years her elder, thereby ensuring her financial security but also dooming her to dream about younger men and remember her youthful days, when she used to make love with strong muscular men in the grassy fields.

The youngsters of the neighbourhood are bullies on motorcycles and spend their time in bars and shooting pool. They are violent and have no respect for anyone, as the beating of Alberto attests. On the rare occasions in which the protagonists look out the windows of the *pied-à-terre*, De Santis makes sure that what they see is degradation. In one scene, Laura looks out and sees teenagers dancing in a bar, while in a nearby house two old women watch a commercial on television. The statement is clear: in the new age of consumerism, the elders are confined to their homes and their TV sets and are segregated from the youngsters, who are unemployed. In another scene, as Alberto looks out the window a forward zoom shot shows us what he sees: a plaque commemorating a Resistance victim. Suddenly, Alberto leaves the window and closes it. This scene marks De Santis's first use of a zoom shot in a film. In spite of what some critics have written,[16] De Santis was not adopting the current trend, which was characterized by an overuse and abuse of the technique, but used the shot to convey, through the zoom's fleeting movement and rapidity, that the Resistance was a bleak memory.[17] The Resistance's lost and forgotten ideals are referred to again in

the sequence in which an elderly lady, forced to leave her neighbourhood, cries in front of the plaque dedicated to her son, killed by the
Nazi-Fascists.[18]

The degradation is evident in that almost no one in the neighbourhood feels the comradeship, the solidarity, and the humanity that the
masses felt and shared in De Santis's previous films. The only positive
character is Vincenzino, the medical student from De Santis's native
Fondi. This provincial young man makes love to the local prostitute,
Clementina, in a room that he has strewn with straw to replicate the
fields of his native region. His naïve sensibility is mistaken for homo-
sexuality by the hardened youths of the city. Vincenzino is also attracted
to Laura and wants to save her from the engineer, without understanding that she is also using him. The scene in which Laura leaves the flat
and kisses the wide-eyed Vincenzino before riding off in a taxi, waving
goodbye from the rear window, is meant as a tribute to innocence.

The greatest artistic merits of the film lie in the composition of
scenes and sequences, which confirms De Santis's artistry and mastery
of the visual. Notable for its visual beauty, the scene in which Laura
plays with the hoola-hoop can also be seen as a further comment on the
extent to which Alberto's and Laura's lives consist of illusions. Laura is
playing a little girl's game and, at the same time, is trying to be erotic
and seductive. Her face reflected in the mirror is the image of innocence and provocation as she tries to stimulate Alberto.[19] He, on the
other hand, is disillusioned and, having discovered that Laura is not a
virgin, has fallen into indifference, as is revealed by his gloomy and
distant expression. Through the erotic involvement with Laura, Alberto
had deluded himself that he could recapture his fleeting virility. Indeed,
in the following sequence, Alberto looks out over the courtyard and ima-
gines himself younger, dressed in working clothes, and accompanying
on the trombone Laura's graceful dance. The restlessness and dissatisfaction he exhibits in this oneiric sequence reflect Alberto's dilemma.
He is torn between the stringent reality of his age and the need for
transfiguration through illusion. The film ends with what is perhaps its
most beautiful sequence, rich in the analogical power of representation.
Alberto and his wife, Giulia, are driving home together in the early
morning hours. As they candidly discuss the emptiness of their loveless
marriage, the car slides silently through the vast and empty Villa
Borghese Park, reminding the audience of the emptiness of their long
union and of their words.

In *La Garçonnière*, De Santis condemns everything associated with the

new lifestyle of the economic boom and the levelling of cultural differences in the wake of consumerism and appeal to the masses. His
exposition of the homogenization of the classes and the degradation of
the new Italian society occurred at a historical moment when the
national cinema was embarking on one of its richest decades – a sign of
De Santis's separation from the new emerging cinematic approaches
and artistic visions. De Santis has affirmed that 1960 is a turning-point
for Italian cinema,[20] because, from that moment on, under the influence
of Fellini and Antonioni, the focus would be on the middle and upper
middle classes' existential and neurotic problems. The characteristic
fishermen, minor artisans, and clerks disappeared to make room for the
middle and the upper-middle class. Ever since *La dolce vita* was released,
the whole of Italian cinema has done nothing but mull over the themes
and problematics that relate to these classes, forgetting all other aspects
of Italian life. The director's migration to the Soviet Union to film his
next work, *Italiani brava gente* (*Italiano brava gente*; Attack and Retreat),
the story of peasants forced to fight a war against their will, is a further
indication that, in the Italian market of the time, saturated by the new
Italo-American mythological genre, comedy Italian-style, and the new
directors, there was little space or money left for De Santis's peasant
stories. The peasants' world filmed by De Santis will reappear in a
different guise in the cinematic epic of Bertolucci's *Novecento* and
Olmi's nostalgic *L'albero degli zoccoli* in the late 1970s. In the words of
Alberto, the engineer of *La Garçonnière* – 'I want to make mistakes, I
want to pass as naïve ... even ridiculous ... Is it possible that today even
what is dramatic becomes ridiculous?' – can be read as De Santis's
epitaph for the new cultural situation and as the underlying message of
the film.

13

March On or Die:
Italiani brava gente (1964)

Noi abbiamo avuto il torto di ispirarci alle momorie e testimonianze e alle decine di libri, che hanno voluto lasciarci tutti coloro che la Campagna di Russia l'hanno vissuta sul fronte di battaglia, nelle trincee, al gelo e alla fame. Quei memoriali parlano tutti, non uno escluso, sia pure ad un diverso livello, a seconda della sensibilità politica e storica dei singoli autori, degli stessi fatti e delle stesse cose da noi raccontati nel film.

We can be blamed for having closely followed the memories and the testimonies and the numerous books that all those who lived through the Russian campaign in the front lines, dogged in the trenches, exposed to frost and hunger, wanted to leave us. All these memorials, without exception, attest, if only according to the political and historical awareness of the individual authors, to the same events and the same things narrated in our film.

Giuseppe De Santis

In the 1960s, Italian cinema witnessed a widely acclaimed revival of historical themes. The box-office success of two films in particular – Mario Monicelli's controversial comedy *La grande guerra* (1959; The Great War) and Luigi Comencini's *Tutti a casa* (1960; Everybody Home!) spurred on this new cinematic movement. Monicelli's *La grande guerra*, is a controversial film that explores the role of the ordinary man in the First World War. Luigi Comencini's film also deals with a historical event; however, it treats the occasion in a tragicomic manner. These war films and tragicomic films dealing with past and recent historical events appealed to the public. They comically diminished the horrors of war and criticized an inept and inefficient establishment that had sent men to die for a cause they neither understood nor believed in.

Generally, by presenting working-class soldiers as anti-heroes, these films glorified a way of life exalted by the masses. One has only to think of Vittorio Gassman as Giovanni Busacca and Alberto Sordi as Oreste Jacovacci in *La grande guerra* or as Lieutenant Innocenzi in *Tutti a casa*. All of these characters are masters of the *arte di arrangiarsi* (the art of getting by). The audiences identified with the antihero protagonists, who, for the most part, tried their best to avoid dangerous situations but, when confronted by the unavoidable, rejected the coward's path and rose to the occasion, dying with honour. Because these films immortalized such antiheroes, they avoided censorship by reaffirming and saving Italian national honour. For example, Roberto Rossellini's acclaimed 1959 film *Il generale Della Rovere* (General Della Rovere) belongs to this new genre of film. The film's protagonist, Emanuele Bardone (Vittorio De Sica), is a petty criminal who makes a living by pretending to help save Italians arrested by the Gestapo, under the name 'Colonel Grimaldi.' He is arrested by the Germans, who force him to pose as General Della Rovere, in order to ferret out the Resistance leader Fabrizio. Bardone, rather than providing the name sought by the Gestapo, faces the firing squad, leaving the incredulous Germans with a message for the wife of the real Generale Della Rovere: 'My last thoughts were of you. Long live Italy.'[1] The message shows that he, too, redeems himself.

Many other films, such as Nanni Loy's *Una giornata da leoni* (1961; One Day as a Lion), can be included as well in the new cinematic tred. While most of the films of the period simply demystify Italy's controversial role in the Second World War, a few do much more. Giuseppe De Santis's *Italiani brava gente* (Italiano brava gente; Italians, Good People)[2] challenges the conservative position (mainly held by the military and conservative political forces) that sought to use the death of thousands of Italian soldiers as a basis for rhetorical commemorations and for hagiographic historiography. It openly confronts the fact that, by allying itself with Nazism, Italy became an accomplice in the aggression throughout Europe and Africa during the Second World War.

Italiani brava gente, though imbued with conventions characteristic of the war films of the 1960s – comic gags, controversial historical issues, and antiheroic characters – stands out, not only for its artistic merit, but, above all, as a democratic and honest attempt to bring to the screen a memorable and previously untouched page of Italian history. This representation of the war in Russia condemns warfare without recourse to victimism or rhetorical nationalism, but as the antithesis of life and humanity. The film depicts with historical accuracy the unfortunate events of Mussolini's aggression in the Soviet Union, Italy's most disastrous military defeat, sustained under the most adverse conditions. This senseless expedition, involving 250,000 soldiers, was ordered by 'Il Duce' between 1941 and 1943 against the advice of his own generals and his main ally, Adolf Hitler.[3] Even though other films of the war genre were critical of war and the ineptitude of upper-class officers, the shift from hero to antihero led to contrived conclusions, reaffirming the heroism of simple working-class Italians, whose sacrifices sanctified Italian national honour as well as military values. The antiheroes became admirable figures, worthy of national praise and admiration. On the other hand, De Santis's film is not only a denunciation of the Fascist regime, with its needless sacrifice of tens of thousands of Italian servicemen in Russia to empty words and false ideals, but, most of all, a glorification of solidarity and humanity against war, destruction, militarism, and imperialism.[4]

For years, Giuseppe De Santis had been planning and working on a film on the Armir (Armata italiana in Russia/Italian armada in Russia), as Mussolini's military forces in the Eastern Front are known in Italian. Many elements of that project the director found stimulating. First, there was the overwhelming human drama of the military catastrophe that left an indelible impression on the imagination of every Italian. Add to this, images of the vast reaches of Russian territory where the two revolutions of the twentieth century, the Nazi-Fascist and the Bolshevik, faced each other to determine the victor and, perhaps, the destiny of mankind. In the private sphere, the war on the Eastern Front had left unforgettable scars on many families whose dear ones were among the missing. During the second defensive battle on the Don River, between December 1942 and January 1943, 229,005 Italian soldiers fought to stop the advancing Red Army. Of these, 84,830 died, and 29,690 were taken prisoner. These numbers by themselves attest to the magnitude of the loss and its effect on Italian public opinion and historiography. In the ideological and philosophical realms, De Santis saw the conflict as proof of the triumph of communism over Fascism. As a record of the military catastrophe, the film also served as a historical lesson to those Italians who followed Mussolini's orders blindly and without political awareness.

For at least ten years, Italian producers and filmmakers had been considering the adaptation of the many stories, novels, and memoirs left by the survivors. In 1964, the date of De Santis's film *Italiani brava gente*, forty-seven books had already been published on the war in Russia. In the world of cinema, there were rumours of an adaptation of Rigori Stern's novel *Un sergente nella neve*, of Giulio Bedeschi's *Centomila gavette di ghiaccio*, of Nuto Revelli's *Mai tardi*, of Fidia Gambetti's *I morti e i vivi*, and of the more moving account by Don Carlo Gnocchi, *Cristo fra gli alpini*. De Santis had an original story, written in collaboration with Ennio De Concini, based on the reconstruction of the many accounts written by historians and servicemen who had survived the war on the Eastern Front. De Santis was finally able to carry out his project by putting together the first major Italian–Russian co-production with direct financial support from the American producer, Joseph Levine.[5] The final screenplay was written by Ennio De Concini, Augusto Frassinetti, Gian Domenico Giagni, Serghei Smirnov, and De Santis. The film was also made possible by the new spirit of collaboration between the two superpowers as a result of the thawing of the bitter cold war of the 1950s. *Italiani brava gente* was shot entirely in the Soviet Union, on location, with a few studio reconstructions done in the Mosfilm Studios. The Russians provided all the extras, and the military equipment, which was remanufactured expressly for the film. It took eight months of shooting, four in the harsh Russian winter, to finish the film. The final cost was 1.5 billion lire. Before the final agreement was signed, the Italian producer had to consent that Russian historians, specialists on the Second World War, would review and collaborate on the final version of the screenplay.[6] According to De Santis and his collaborators, the film had to be an accurate historical account of the campaign, based on the verifiable accounts of the participants, who, on the Italian side, for the most part, had been uprooted from their everyday tasks and lives to fight a war of aggression on behalf of and ordered by 'Il Duce.'

Unlike Roberto Rossellini's 1943 film *L'uomo della croce* (Man with the Cross), which depicted Russians as barbaric, uncivilized thugs without faith (as the dedication at the film's conclusion attests), *Italiani brava gente* showed the innate humanity of the Italian working-class soldiers who went to fight a war with no understanding of its causes.[7] They were mostly poor devils, badly dressed, carrying out a task that had nothing in common with their everyday lives. The original title reflects the film's intentions and motivations: 'Italiano brava gente' is the literal translation of the colloquial expression used by the Russian people to address Italian soldiers during the conflict – 'Italiano Karascio.' However, politically, and ideologically, the title assumes another meaning, which is more closely related to Italian culture under Fascism. During the regime, loyal, macho, obedient individuals full of nationalist pride were called 'Bravo Italiano.' One of the cultural goals of Fascism was to forge a new type of man. The education of the young was vitally important for a government which boasted of upsetting all the conventional standards of morality, justice and civilization. Official policy laid down that Italians must be brought up to be more warlike and tough, less artistic and less "nice," and to be always "desperately serious,"' writes historian Denis M. Smith.[8] According to philosopher Giovanni Gentile, Fascism was a style more than a body of doctrine; a manner of acting more than a deed.

The official face of Fascist Italy was martial. Its leaders were heroic individuals, such as aviation aces Italo Balbo and Francesco De Pinedo. Inspired by them, and Il Duce, men had to be strong, virile, warrior-like, athletic, and loyal to both state and family. Il Duce's favourite motto was: 'Better to live one day as a lion than a hundred years as a sheep.' The film's authors wanted to disprove those Fascist ideals, and to show that it was the façade of an ideology that had not changed or cured the many problems still faced by the people. Social reality was more vulgar, and Fascist policies less sensitive towards the very serious problems that remained – above all, poverty and corruption. The new leaders that Fascism had brought to power were, despite the pretentious façade and the propaganda, mostly parvenus and middle-class provincials who used official rhetoric to bolster their position. To this group of people belong the controversial figures of Major Ferro Maria Ferri and the Fascist Unit of the Arditi,[9] depicted in De Santis's film.

For the screenplay's authors, the soldiers from the working class were not the warriors Mussolini had hoped for and had wanted to believe in, but average individuals, incapable, in the main, of killing or harming the enemy.[10] They were not cruel, as the Germans were, but shared a human solidarity which was mostly based on their peasant culture.[11] According to the authors, they had more in common with their enemy, the Russians, than with their German allies. The director wanted to create a popular cinematic epic according to the tenets of realist popular art, for the consumption of the 'seconda visione' houses which attracted a predominately working-class audience. They could share the same antagonistic feelings towards the regime felt by the soldiers killed in the war. It was the director's intention to present the Italian soldiers without the pseudo-patriotic clichés of officialdom. In order to carry out the project, the authors of the screenplay adopted a form that intersperses individual stories with the collective and chronological events of the major campaign battles. Official history is mixed with the minor, personal dramas of the soldiers. Their accounts, filmed in close-up, mirror their anxieties, dreams, and expectations, and are contrasted with the battle scenes, filmed in long and medium shots, in order to match content with style. The final message of the film, on a personal level, is that, despite war and its horrors, the working-class soldiers involved were able to find and live moments of shared humanity.

The film opens in summer 1941, as a train loaded with Italian soldiers of various divisions (Torino, Tagliamento, and Cuneo) rolls through the endless fields of Ukraine on the way to the Eastern Front. The troops are happy; morale is high. The war has been going well, as their German allies have been thrusting ahead with a mighty military offensive. The audience meets the protagonists as the train moves along. Through the various intonations and accents of their speech, the soldiers reveal their backgrounds and the regions they come from. They are from Rome, Catania, Naples, Milan, Florence, and Cerignola, to mention only a few. From their conversations it is clear that they don't know anything about the enemy. 'What does *kolkhoz* [collective farm] mean?' one soldier asks a superior. The other responds: 'I'm not sure. I think it means that the Russians share everything they have, including their wives; therefore, they must all be cuckolded.'

Suddenly the train stops; Russian partisans have sabotaged the railway track. Although the interruption is brief, the panic of the soldiers demonstrates their lack of preparation for the war. As they jump out of the train, confused and unarmed, the camera rises in a crane shot (De Santis's trademark) to establish the locale in which the story will unfold. During the stop one of the soldiers, Loris Bazzocchi, runs through the sunflower fields. The camera moves closer. He is framed in medium shot as we hear him, in voice-over, tell how he died in a similar place without even the pleasure of knowing who won the war. This voice-over is an extract from one of Bazzocchi's letters to his father back in Italy. The artistic expedient is a literary convention, a reminder of De Santis's literary background, but at the same time adds a dramatic and surrealistic feeling to the sequence. It seems as if Bazzocchi is still reproaching the Italian leaders for his fate. The film structure has also introduced a narrative device that will allow the audience to enter into particular past episodes in the life of each of the film's protagonists, all of whom will be killed. The device is of the utmost importance in the rhapsodic construction of the film, which is based on interspersed personal events and reconstructed choral scenes of the battles and civilian society on the Russian Front between 1941 and 1943.

After the brief stop, the journey resumes. In the next major episode, at the edge of a forest, the troops meet a large group of Russian civilians escorted by their German captors. This is the first glimpse of the enemy and the arrogant allies. The Italian soldiers stop, and a spontaneous feeling of human solidarity develops between the prisoners and the Italian soldiers. Giuseppe Sanna (Riccardo Cucciolla), a soldier from the southern town of Cerignola in the region of Apulia, offers half of his loaf of bread to a Russian civilian, causing a violent reaction from a German soldier, who tries to wrest the bread away from the man. Sanna intervenes and starts a brawl with the German. As the other soldiers try to separate them, several Russian prisoners attempt to flee. A young woman and a young wounded man escape and take refuge in a desecrated church full of wheat. The two are later arrested by Sergeant Manfredonia (Nino Vingeli), after two other Italian soldiers, Libero Gabrielli (Raffaele Pisu) and Loris Bazzocchi (Lev Prygunov), leave the church, willfully overlooking them. The young Russian is killed by the Germans as he steps out of the church.

These first episodes serve to introduce not only the protagonists but also one of the film's major themes. The Russians are victims as much as most of the Italian soldiers. They are strong, unbending, determined to fight back, as the choral singing of 'The International' attests. The Germans force the captive Russians to sing 'The International,' hoping thereby to shame them. At first, the prisoners refuse, saying that they don't know the anthem, but when one of the men stands up and proudly starts to sing, the rest follow, in a crescendo that surprises the invaders. This characterization follows the line of the official rhetoric of Stalinist propaganda. The Russians are beautiful, strong, and proud, while the Germans are cruel, insensitive robots who blindly follow orders. Physically they are big, overweight, and not too smart, and don't have a high opinion of their Italian allies. When Gabrielli first meets a German, he is told that Italians are not good fighters but excel as singers and mandolin players. The characterization of the Italians is less schematic than that of the Germans, and the Italians are depicted as being more articulate. The various personalities introduced represent a broad range of people from different regions of Italy. Their personalities also represent the various outlooks on life and politics in Fascist Italy. For instance, the Roman Libero Gabrielli (Pisu) is an average sort of man, quick to flee danger and to save his own skin. Sergeant Manfredonia represents the Fascist ideology, as his servile attitude towards the Germans confirms. He believes in the war and its mission against the Bolshevik enemy, and in the final victory to be shared with the German allies. Sanna's behaviour towards the Russians and his dislike for the Germans can be attributed to his Christian ideals, paralleling the socialist ideals of fraternity and solidarity between men. Bazzocchi is the young, naïve peasant from Emilia, the region with the strongest labour-union traditions and ties to the land. Colonel Sermonti (Andrea Chec-chi) is against the campaign and Fascist imperialism but follows orders as a good military man must do.

After the presentation of the individual protagonists, the next episode is choral and presents a credible reconstruction of a battle for a bridge and the control of a town. After the early skirmishes, the war explodes. The Italian infantry is engaged in a hard fight for the control of a little town across the Bug River, where an important factory is situated. The regiment, under the command of Colonel Sermonti, conquers the town after a fierce and costly battle, but the Russian partisans thwart their efforts by blowing up the factory. The German allies, in charge of the entire operation, round up a number of local people and demand that the Italian army execute them. Among them is a young girl, Katja (Gianna Prokhorenko), whom Gabrielli and Bazzocchi had saved from captivity by letting her hide in the church. At the moment of the execution, the firing squad spares the girl, who runs away in terror. Young Bazzocchi instinctively runs after her across a vast field of sunflowers. When he finally catches up to her, he has only enough time to gaze for a brief moment into her eyes before he is killed by random fire from a plane overhead. The sequence ends in a beautiful and powerful scene, with the girl running towards the approaching Red Army which tramples the motionless body of Bazzocchi as it passes.

In the next sequence, a long take introduces the onset of winter. The regiment of Colonel Sermonti leaves the front lines, to be replaced by fresh troops. The Arditi (shock troops) under the command of Major Ferro Maria Ferri (Arthur Kennedy) arrive at the headquarters. Ferri is the prototype of the Fascist man. His shaved head and black leather gloves are fetishes of Fascist power and masculinity. He shows off the mutilation of his left hand, lost during the Spanish Civil War in 1937, at Guadalajara. His mannerisms, speech patterns, and love of violence satirize the new militarism and nationalism envisioned and promoted by the Fascist authorities. During the final retreat after the battle of Stalingrad, Major Ferri takes over a truck and, in order to be able to steer at high speed, removes the black leather glove, revealing that his mutilation was as much a swindle as were his bravery and toughness. He had deceived his soldiers in the same way that the rulers of Italy had misled the country. This episode produced a wave of protest from the military forces, who questioned its realism and historical accuracy. Even though the episode actually took place in Albania, one must recognize that the transportation to a different place and time of a true event gives a welcome 'ideological timeliness' to De Santis's attack on Fascist militarism and machismo, and also provides the director with another chance to exhibit his talent for grotesque humour.

In the next film episode, the first winter of war has passed. Spring will bring welcome relief to the Italian soldiers, who have withstood sub-zero temperatures without adequate equipment. The same regiment that we saw at the beginning of the film is now camped in a mining town, and must constantly guard against partisan attack. One night they receive an unexpected visit from three partisans in need of a doctor to treat one of their comrades. The leader of the group is convinced that the Italians, because they are 'brava gente' (good people), will provide help. He offers himself as hostage, to be hanged at dawn if the doctor has not returned unharmed by that time. The doctor is a spoiled Neapolitan dandy, who has enjoyed an easy life under the protection of a rich and influential father. Dr Mario Salvioni (Peter Falk) accepts, to prove that he is not a coward. After having saved the wounded Russian, he is killed in a German ambush on the way back to the camp. At dawn at the Italian camp, the soldiers, with regret, hang the Russian hostage with whom they had socialized and fraternized. These touching personal stories of two brave victims of the war are followed by the plundering of a village by the Arditi. By using Pudovkin's ideas on contrasting, the two episodes highlight the difference between the regular Italian soldiers and the Black Shirts. On one hand, we see innocent victims; on the other, the vicious criminals who enjoy violence and use war to satisfy their animalistic instincts, as is seen during the rape of defenceless women.

Another season has passed and winter is approaching as the Russians prepare a massive counter-attack on the Don River. Dug deep in their trenches, the Italians begin to hear snatches of Russian melodies as the Red Army moves in. Before the general retreat, the film shows another episode in which the possibility of sportsmanship ends in tragedy for the two armies. A wild rabbit crosses the empty terrain between the trenches. It is shot after a race between a Russian soldier and an Italian, each starting from his respective position. The spontaneous, friendly game is interrupted by Sergeant Manfredonia, who kills the Russian, thus inadvertently causing the death of the Italian runner. This interlude in the fighting is followed by the final catastrophe.

The Germans have lost the battle for Stalingrad. On the Italian side, friction between the regular troops and the Fascist units of the Black Shirts has now exploded in frequent and brutal confrontations. It is midwinter and the Russians are on the offensive. The regiment of Colonel Semanti, dwindled now to a thousand poorly equipped men, is ordered to slow down the offensive. The order from the commander-in-chief is to resist until the last man is dead.[12] The entire Italian army, left without fuel supplies and cut off from German assistance, is abandoned to its own destiny. Once the retreat starts, every man is on his own. The frames are filled with starving soldiers on foot, trudging on without a clear destination, spurred on by the bleak hope of surviving the deadly cold and the enemy. The troops, blinded by the blizzard and frost-bitten, are slowly decimated. It is a full rout. The few motorized vehicles still operating are taken over by the Fascist units, which, in their desperate attempt to survive, overrun their own soldiers. Sanna and Gabrielli join forces in the retreat. The Russian land, seen as cultivated and rich in the opening sequence of the film, has now become an endless, icy grave-yard. Sanna decides to let himself be taken prisoner and, whistling 'The International,' is killed by the Red Army as he marches towards their lines.[13] Gabrielli, the common man without political ideals, continues doggedly on. First, he takes refuge inside an abandoned tank, where he meets Sonja (Tatiana Samoilova), a Russian who has prostituted herself with the Germans and is now in hiding in fear of reprisals. The following day they move on together towards a village that will never be reached. The exhausted woman is left behind by Gabrielli, who moves on until he, too, drops from exhaustion in a snowstorm. At this point the camera pulls back, as if to close on the Armir's drama. The film's funnel-shaped structure is carried to its logical conclusion: from the opening sequence of the train carrying the army to the front, we have progressed, after a year of hardship, to the army's last man.

The film premiered in Rome on 9 April 1964, at the Corso Theatre. Right-wing newspapers were offended by the anti-nationalistic and anti-Italian propaganda they perceived in its content. They were also offended by the film's favourable presentation of the Russians. Egidio Sterpa,[14] writing for *La tribuna del Mezzogiorno*, interviewed Giulio Bedeschi, Egisto Corradi, and Ottobono Terzi, three writers who had survived the war on the Russian Front, to discredit the accuracy of the film. Mr Corradi complained that the film had left out the heroic defence undertaken by the Alpine division 'Julia' during winter 1942, which held the Russian offensive for an entire month. Mr Bedeschi denounced the way in which the Italian soldiers were depicted as an offence to the memory of all the war dead. Mr Terzi was so ashamed of the film that he called for a prompt intervention by Giulio Andreotti, then minister of defence, to stop public showing of the film. In another article, published by *La voce repubblicana* on 28 September 1964, Giovanni Calendoli also urged the government to check the accuracy of the episode concerning the hanging of the Russian partisan and to ascertain if a Black Shirt officer had ever simulated a mutilation, as had Major Ferri in De Santis's film. Mr Calendoli concluded his attack by saying that, for the sake of those killed in war and those still living, the line between history and fiction must be clearly observed by an artist and supervised by the authorities.[15] Left-wing publications acclaimed the film's honesty and message but criticized the director's conception of realism. For example, the critic Antonello Trombadori, in reviewing the film for the Communist newspaper *L'Unità* on 28 January 1965, disagreed with De Santis's conception of realism, which he defined as a mixture of symbolism, folklorism, sentimentalism, and an idyllic representation of life. In an unpublished letter to French Marxist critic Marcel Oms, De Santis expressed all his distress over the criticism received:

This film took five years of work and suffering. One year to convince the Soviets to make it and to find an Italian producer willing to invest some money. One year to prepare it and one year to shoot it, to edit it, and to have it approved by the various censors. Plus two more years of trouble for the simple fact that I was the one making the film. The right-wing critics have insulted me. They have accused me of having muddied the honour of Italian soldiers and the left-wing critics have not defended me.[16]

In the 1960s, when artistic works were read with political glasses, it was overlooked that De Santis's film presented a new artistic interpretation of the war on the Russian Front. *Italiani brava gente* was full of cinematic citations from the Russian masters, but it was also a realistic account of the encounter with the Red Army.

In 1947, with *Paisà*, Roberto Rossellini showed the first encounter between the Allies, mainly the American army, and the Italians during the Second World War. The six episodes of the film present the cultural clash which from a beginning marked by total misunderstanding, confounded by the language barrier, reached a state of collaboration and mutual respect in the last episode, where American soldiers in the Po Valley chose to die alongside the partisans. In this sense *Paisà* represents the total reconciliation between two peoples – the Americans and the Italians – previously engaged in war. They show themselves to be capable of overcoming mistrust and political differences in the struggle against Nazism and Fascism. In *Italiani brava gente* the encounter takes place between Russian and Italians. Here, there could be no reconciliation, since the former are defending their freedom from the latter. None the less, De Santis attempts to show how the Italian peasant soldiers shared a common love for the earth and a mutual sense of respect for life. In *Paisà*, Rossellini was fascinated by people's reaction to the American myth personified by the American military forces, which, to the eyes of the Italians, appeared as superior creatures from another planet.

De Santis, on the other hand, presents the myth of Great Mother Russia when the Italian soldiers first set foot on Russian soil. For instance, the young, naïve, Emilian peasant, Loris Bazzocchi, is overwhelmed by the vast plains planted in wheat and cannot understand why the local peasants have not yet harvested it. When he tries to question one of the farmers, he is treated with mistrust. He is confused by an old woman who calls him 'Mussolini.' He tries to laugh it off and reassure her, but to no avail. The myth of Great Mother Russia introduced by the rich and fertile fields reaches its culmination during the heavy storm that welcomes the soldiers at their campsite. The rain storm is portrayed in a beautiful and dramatic sequence enhanced by the chiaroscuro effects of the colours that capture with moving, lyrical power the sudden storm. In spectacular contrasting camera movements between the darkening sky and the awed soldiers, De Santis captures brilliantly the overpowering force of nature. This menace is an omen and a tribute to what Dovzhenko called a 'biological and pantheistic conception of nature.' In fact, cinematically the scenes are tributes to the great Russian film school, to Alexander Dovzhenko's *Arsenal* (1929) and to his 1930 silent masterpiece *Zemlya* (Earth/Soil). *Arsenal* focuses on the Ukrainian struggle against the German invasion of the First World War. The action centres around the sabotage of the railway, the strike, and its ferocious repression. The film ends with a moving execution of the strike leaders, which morally serves as a warning to the oppressors – no repression can ever stop a people from fighting for freedom.

In De Santis's film, the sabotage of the tracks in Ukraine and the execution of the Russian partisans in the first episodes of the film stand as artistic and ideological citations of the great master. The references to Dovzhenko becomes even more explicit during the sequences centred around the Emilian soldier, Bazzocchi. In *Zemlya*, the young peasant, Vasili, returns home from a meeting with his girlfriend. As he closes his eyes to recapture her face, he is hit and killed by a bullet. The assassination goes beyond the limits of a single predicament and becomes part of a larger vision dictated by its dialectic development. Vasili was killed, but his death will serve the cause and will be an example to other young men, as his joyous funeral testifies. In *Zemlya*, the cycles of life and its continuity are symbolized by the rainfall on the crops, the passing clouds, and the reappearance of the sun. In *Italiani brava gente*, the Emilian peasant, Bazzocchi, is killed by random fire, as he finally is able to look into the eyes of the Russian girl. It is as if the invasion has stopped the annual cycle of rebirth, life, love, and peace, leaving only death in its wake. The war will carry on the slow process of dehumanization and the natural disruption indicated by the fact that the peasants have not harvested the new crop. As in *Zemlya*, the plains of *Italiani brava gente* are also covered with sunflowers, but rather than a pleasant meeting-place for boys and girls, they have become the ground where innocent victims of war meet and die. Here, Katja, the peasant girl, who has survived a firing squad, is chased by the Emilian farm boy. After a race through the fields, he dies in her arms, brought down by an ironic twist of fate. War has no regard for love and sentimentalism.

In the second episode of *Paisà*, the Black GI finds himself in a shantytown that reminds him of his own poverty and social background. The sight of the caves in which impoverished Neapolitans live evokes for him the ghetto where his race lives, and he does not have the heart to arrest the little urchin who stole his shoes. Thus, two subcultures within their respective societies have communicated through their suffering. *Italiani brava gente* shows Sanna (Riccardo Cucciolla), the stubborn southern Italian, offering half of his loaf of bread in a spontaneous act of human solidarity to a Russian prisoner held captive by the Germans. When he is reprimanded by his superior, he defends his action, saying that the bread belonged to him and not to Hitler or Mussolini. Likewise, the last episode of *Paisà* marks a reconciliation between two former enemies, the Americans and the Italians, who die together. In *Italiani brava gente* an unarmed Russian partisan visits the Italian camp in search of a doctor to operate on one of their wounded fighters. The

Russian appeals to his enemies, confident of their humanitarianism. The Neapolitan doctor accompanies him voluntarily but is killed by the German allies in an unexpected twist of fate.

With the fall of Stalingrad and the Italian army left to its own devices, the Russian landscape becomes the protagonist. At this point, De Santis's film is infused with the theme of approaching death. The Italian soldiers gradually realize, through the decimation of their numbers and the bitter Russian winter, that death is their only companion, and defeat their only end. The power of Russia's climatic force represented metaphorically by the rainstorm at the beginning of the film now explodes with all its winter might on the retreating army. The slow, excruciating march towards death provides an opportunity to portray realistically the routing of the Italian troops and the absurdity of that expedition, and of war in general. In each episode, the film reveals the horrors of war in endless detail. Anguish for its victims is felt in every step over the frozen plain. Art and information become one. Even the film's most melodramatic moments are, for the most part, followed by reconstructed historical events built on Aristotelian verisimilitude. Watching *Italiani brava gente*, one is struck by the fairness with which the various nationalities are handled. Bravery, cruelty, stupidity, and compassion are dealt out in almost equal measure, although the Germans are treated least sympathetically and their cruelty seems overplayed. Today's audience is accustomed to war films, but in the mid-1960s, De Santis's film stood out for its uncompromising realism; none the less, the film can still move an audience to cry and reflect on a senseless war that caused only tragedy and death.

14

Impotence as a Metaphor of the 1970s' Baffling Reality: *Un apprezzato professionista di sicuro avvenire* (1972)

'Il professionista' è anche il film di un uomo che non lavorava da quasi dieci anni. Quindi è probabile che al suo interno vi sia rabbia, disperazione e delusione per tante cose ... Ma è una disperazione che poi si supera.

Il professionista ... is also the film of a man who had not worked for almost ten years. Therefore, it is probable that among its components are rage, despair, and disappointment about many things ... But it is a desperation that eventually is overcome.

Giuseppe De Santis

In 1971, seven years after making *Italiani brava gente* (Italiano brava gente), De Santis (with the financial collaboration of his friend Giorgio Salvioni) founded a cooperative, Film Nova, to produce a film based on a story they had co-written, 'La giornata di dolore dell'avvocato Arcuri' (The Grievous Day of the Attorney Arcuri). The director expected to complete the film in about two months' time so he could finally start, in Yugoslavia, his long-awaited project on the poet Ovid's exile from ancient Rome.[1] De Santis had spent one year in Romania and two years researching historical documents and reading Ovid's works in order to write the film treatment, which he had started with Sergio Amidei, later worked on with Salvatore Laurani, and finished with Giorgio Salviani.[2] The six years prior to the shooting of *Un apprezzato professionista di sicuro avvenire* (An Esteemed Professional with a Secure Future) had been very frustrating for De Santis. In his fruitless attempts to find a producer, he had also tried to work out a deal with Mosfilm for a co-production on 'Dubrovsky,' based on an adaptation of a Pushkin's story.[3] So, unable to find a producer in Italy for his peasants' stories on land reform, and before embarking on his second professional adventure in Yugoslavia, De Santis tried the experience of independent filmmaking to tell a metaphoric story about impotence. Given the special circumstances that made its production possible, *Un apprezzato professionista di sicuro avvenire* must be read, not as an ironical story about De Santis's own career, but as an effort to regain a voice and express a judgment on the transformed Italian sociopolitical reality of the 1970s. In what is to date De Santis's last film, there is a deliberate attempt to cover all the themes and motifs of his previous films in order to unmask the present cultural degradation. In the film story, a young attorney, Vincenzo Arduni (Lino Capolicchio), son of a station-master, has married the daughter of a rich, vulgar, and corrupted construction entrepreneur who has made his fortune at the expense of the community. The father-in-law wants an heir at any cost, but Arduni is impotent. The son-in-law is an attorney and also the construction alderman, receiving favours from his father-in-law, 'Il Commendatore,' in exchange for his political support for the entrepreneur's project to turn wooded areas protected by a town plan into construction zones. The young attorney under pressure from his father-in-law's demands and worried that his inability to provide an heir will lead to a marriage annulment, devises a Machiavellian stratagem involving Don Marco (Robert Hoffmann), a parish priest and Arduni's childhood friend. Although Marco had a calling, when his friend confesses his impotence and puts the problem in evangelical terms, Don Marco performs an act of compassion and makes love to Vincenzo's wife. The sexual experience and the child lead to Don Marco having a spiritual crisis and wanting to leave the priesthood. His decision threatens Arduni's security. Shaken by the possibility that his friend might disclose the child's real paternity, the attorney strikes Don Marco dead with a candlestick inside the church during a violent confrontation. In order to make the evidence point to Nicola Parella (Riccardo Cucciolla), a poor unemployed man who, for a long time, has been looking for work, Arduni steals the alms box together with the candlestick, and plants the evidence in Nicola's house. The accused proves to be smarter than the attorney. Nicola discovers that Arduni is the true killer but, instead of turning him over to the police, takes the blame in exchange for a deal. The lawyer will pay for his son's education and will also provide for the well-being of his family.

Among the reviews that followed the film's release an article by the critic Angelo Solmi[4] stands out; it provoked a resentful private letter from De Santis[5] in which he accused Solmi of being a weather-vane and said that he could do better without his defence. De Santis concluded the letter by saying that, as an artist, he was not at the end of his career and despite the ostracism that he faced as a director, he was still full of vitality and aspirations. In his letter, De Santis also accused the majority of Italian critics of harbouring prejudices against his films. In fact, he said, the same old criticisms – 'photo-romance,' 'serial,' 'melodrama,' and 'barocchismo' (bad taste) – were used to describe and denigrate *Un apprezzato professionista* ..., but no regard was given to the form or content of his new film. Criticisms apart, the film was blocked by censorship,[6] and charges of decadence, corruption, and immorality were raised. As was the case for all of his previous films, the director was criticized for having created an improbable plot. The critics failed to see that the film emblematically covers all the director's previous themes and develops them within the broader metaphor of impotence. The impotence, here, is not only sexual but is symptomatic of the state of contemporary society, where individual and collective morality and solidarity had been degraded. In today's society, corruption, compromises, and kickbacks undermine the social bases at every human level.

Un apprezzato professionista ... is a difficult film to watch and to follow. It starts as a detective story that often seems to shift into a police procedural. In reality, these two genres are narrative techniques employed by the director as pretexts for a sociopolitical inquiry into building speculation, social-climbing, the political mafia, corrupted administration, unemployment, the homeless, clerical celibacy, pornography, and sexual deviation. In this film, none of the ideological or political mediation that distinguished De Santis's early films is present.

The film's narrative structure, a sequence of flashbacks, allows the social and cultural background of the characters to unfold and permits the audience to compare and evaluate them on the basis of their pasts. The intention behind the non-sequential film plot was to present a baffling reality. On this matter, De Santis commented: 'The story is both the past and the present. There is no need to stress continuity one way or the other ... whoever wants to understand, understands ... it is not necessary for one scene to come before or after ... What is it? It is today? Or yesterday? It does not matter; what matters is the totality of the story's message.'[7]

The slow progression of the film, made up of small puzzles, forces the audience to link together the present with the past. This is a deliberate assault against the social spirit of the *nouveau riche* and the mentality of the urban poor who have lost all sense of class identity and are reduced to selling their personal freedom, as Nicola does, in a society that cannot provide employment. The film's complex form shows no evidence of De Santis's six-year absence from the craft, contrary to the view expressed by some critics. On the contrary, it confirms once more the director's skill with the camera. De Santis makes up for the inactivity on the screen by stylistically assimilating the latest technical developments and cinematic experimentations of the so-called *Cinema civile* (political cinema)[8] made famous by a new generation of filmmakers such as Damiano Damiani, Elio Petri, Gillo Pontecorvo, and Florestano Vancini. Instead of criticizing individual civil institutions, as was characteristically done in *Cinema civile*,' De Santis launches a sharp attack on the new society, sparing no social class.

The film accentuates his criticisms by reproposing old themes, motifs, and even characters now deformed by the new social order. For instance, the earth and the train, symbols first seen in *Caccia tragica* (Tragic Pursuit), and repeated in almost all of De Santis's films, reappear in *Un apprezzato professionista* ... The train, earlier a symbol of progress and reconstruction, returns to highlight the generational conflict in the Arduni family. Arduni's father (Andrea Checchi) is a humble station-master who would rather keep his low-paying job than work for his son's father-in-law. In a flashback of generational and ideological conflicts, we see him disapproving of his son's conduct and marriage. The father's socialist ideas are loathed by the young Arduni, who is proud to be ambitious and well educated, unlike his father, who is content with watching trains go by. The earth appears in another flashback, in the context of a generational conflict between Don Marco and his father. The young Marco, on leave from the seminary, unexpectedly announces to his father his intention to take his vows. His father, in a burst of rage, tells him that he is just like his two other brothers who want to abandon the farm as if the earth were condemned.

In the generational conflicts, Arduni's father-in-law is the only happy and successful elder. He has unscrupulously embraced the new ways of life. He is pushy, arrogant, and intrusive, as a winner should be. He believes in the American way of life and wants a strong, powerful, and large family like the Kennedy clan. The American influence is another theme evoked by De Santis in this film. In *Riso amaro* (Bitter Rice), it was seen as a threatening menace for the naïve and provincial Silvana. The new American way of life, characterized by chewing-gum and the innocent steps of the boogie-woogie, was a lure for the young postwar generation. In the 1970s, according to De Santis, the American influence is a model and a way of life. Using the technique of the flashback, the director shows the triumph of the consumer mentality. During his daughter's wedding with Arduni, 'Il Commendatore' gives as a wedding gift a modern luxury car, only after having pushed Arduni's wrecked car into a ravine.

Women, who had always held a central role in De Santis's cinematic campaign against social injustice (as in *Un marito per Anna Zaccheo* [A Husband for Anna Zaccheo], *Roma, Ore 11* (Rome, 11 O'Clock), *Riso amaro*, and even in *Uomini e lupi* [Men and Wolves], are in *Un apprezzato professionista* ... either pornographic objects of male fantasies (as in the case of Lucietta, Arduni's wife) or entirely dominated by men (as in the case of Lucietta's mother). The mother (played by Yvonne Sanson, the femme fatale of the Italian-style comedy) is now a plain mother controlled and dominated by her husband. She does not measure up to the two peasant mothers of *Non c'è pace tra gli ulivi* (No Peace under the Olives). Lucietta, as her diminutive name indicates, is a minor figure; she has a submissive personality, is vulgarly dressed, and usually has a silly smile on her face and nothing intelligent to say. The sex, physical beauty, and eroticism that made De Santis the most discussed and famous postwar director in the 1950s (a period during which such things were taboos for the big screen) have lost their flashy appeal and exuberance in the 1970s. The provocative and sensual dancing movements of Silvana and Walter in *Riso amaro* and Anna's stride as she walks through the stands in the outdoor market or down the narrow steps are visual memories from a lost past. Lucietta is a pornographic object even denied intercourse by her impotent husband, who reads American porno magazines before performing oral sex. Penetration is replaced by masturbation. Lucietta's passive acceptance of her husband's impotence symbolically represents her state of objectification. This state is further attested to by her willingness and collaboration in letting anyone chosen by her husband (Lucietta never knew the identity of the man) impregnate her while she is in a state of unconsciousness. The only time she has intercourse she completely negates her own sexuality and participation.

Don Marco, the priest, is the most intriguing and complex character in the film. He is defenceless, almost pathetic in his commitment to the cause of the underprivileged. His evangelic devotion is destined to fail in a everyday reality, where the laws of the jungle dominate human relations. Don Marco is touching in his innocence. When his dedication to help leads him to have sex with Lucietta, he undertakes such a venture as an act of love, in order to give joy (in this case, a child) to someone who otherwise could not have it. His most controversial decision after the child's birth is to leave the Church. In my opinion, contrary to what most critics have written,[9] his decision to leave is not the result of his having found the sexual experience overwhelming (although this could be interpreted as the film's comment on Church policy regarding priests' celibacy) but is the result of a broader and more profound realization. The birth of a life opens Don Marco's eyes, and he comes to understand that only outside of the ecclesiastic institution will he be able to give more to others. In his act of love, Don Marco acquires a lay person's outlook on life. This interpretation is enhanced by the background music that accompanies Don Marco's sexual encounter. The music of *Carmina Burana*,[10] here rearranged by a pop musician,[11] is a celebration of love and human joy, with a profound anti-clerical, sexually liberating spirit. In early postwar Italian films, priests were always protagonists, cast alongside the progressive forces that opposed Nazi–Fascism. Given my thesis that, in this film, De Santis is revisiting and revising characters and themes from his previous films and contrasting them with the present-day roles, Don Marco in *Un apprezzato professionista ...*, although cast as a renegade priest, should be compared with the two most famous priests of Neorealism, Don Camillo and Don Pietro, the protagonists in *Il sole sorge ancora* (1946; The Sun Rises Again) and in *Roma città aperta* (1945; Rome, Open City). In the first of these two films, religious feelings blend with political ideas. The film's scriptwriters[12] believed that the rebirth of Italy lay in the unity between the Church and the Left, an ideology symbolized by the priest's death alongside the young partisan killed by the Nazist firing squad. In the second film, Don Pietro dies alone for having helped the Partisans. His character is a symbolic representation of all the priests who worked for the liberation of Italy. However, Don Marco's compliance with his impotent friend must be interpreted as an act of collaboration with the attorney Arduni, a corrupted politician involved in his father-in-law's schemes. Through Don Marco's actions the film comments on the role assumed by the clergy in the 1970s. Arduni, a Christian Democrat politician, will be elected mayor in the next election, undoubtedly with the blessing of the Church and the financial support of his father-in-law. The lack of an heir was the only factor that could have threatened his future. Thanks to a priest's act of love, Arduni has insured himself against that menace.

The story is laid in Latina, a city in Southern Latium, not far from the director's home town of Fondi. The location not only allows the director to set up his characteristic conflict between city and country, but also permits comment on the social and cultural transformation brought about by progress and consumerism. Commenting on these transformations De Santis said:

The consumer civilization is only a façade of apparent modernity, which hides untouched ancient injustices and ancient class privileges that die hard. The same can be said about human feelings and passions. They are expressed in new, supposedly modern terms, but are as ancient as the Middle Ages and the feudal system. Of course, in these past years the purchasing power of the underprivileged has increased. But at the cost of what kind of sacrifices and struggles? No, my poetic world, which has always held the masses at its centre, has not truly changed. And I have been kept unemployed for seven years because of this loyalty.[13]

The social investigation in *Un apprezzato professionista* ... focuses on the lower middle class, which has just raised itself above the working class. Arduni and his father-in-law, 'Il Commendatore,' exemplify the first generation of immigrants transplanted to a city. The flashbacks used in the film reveal their peasant background. The father-in-law makes his money from construction speculation and from the funds allocated by the 'Cassa per il Mezzogiorno.'[14] Progress provides, not only new riches, but also a new class of unemployment. This discourse is particularly pertinent to Nicola, who is Arduni's lackey and exemplifies the new class of unemployed. Nicola is the living example of the rural masses who have left the countryside in search of work only to find despair and marginality. He is from Apulia, as his accent indicates, a Southerner chasing after a dream. He lives in a shanty and has a large family, a pregnant wife, and no job. To make the public aware of his predicament, he has hijacked a public bus and taken a bystander as hostage. He has even staged a peaceful take-over of the church, with no plausible results. He remains unemployed and homeless. His protests meet with general indifference and police hostility. The days shown in De Santis's films, when the workers rallied together to recover stolen funds, when the *mondine* symbolically forgave Silvana by throwing handfuls of rice, or when the shepherds of Ciociaria spread their flocks over the rocky hills to slow down the *carabinieri* in pursuit of Francesco, are over. In a society where there is no solidarity among social classes or between fellow men, the poor become a sub-proletariat. What is left for Nicola besides his peasant cunning and resourcefulness? Nicola and his entire family know that Arduni must be trapped in order to be dealt with. Therefore, he climbs to the top of an unfinished building, from which he threatens to kill himself unless the attorney consents to a meeting.

Arduni reluctantly meets his request.[15] On top of the building, Nicola tells Arduni that he has proof that he has murdered Don Marco. Arduni can be reassured, however, that Nicola proposes to take the blame, confessing to the crime, but in return the attorney has to defend him and must provide for the family. Arduni hesitates. To convince him, Nicola points out that atop the building a spectacle is being staged that could enhance the attorney's mayoral campaign.

'Tomorrow all the newspapers will carry the headline "Young attorney saves a desperate man and his entire family from certain death,"' Nicola tells him. Arduni is convinced and agrees. Together they descend, and Nicola is taken away. In a sign of triumph, Arduni raises his arms and reassures the crowd, which happily applauds. Photographers take pictures and ask questions. Lucietta embraces her husband with tears of joy. The spectacle of a hero for our time is on, and people believe what they see. Once again, perhaps for the last time, De Santis is saying that simply showing a photographic reality is not enough. The artist must show the hidden realities behind the façade. In this film, the poor are not spared the director's attacks. Nicola's decision to let the attorney provide for his family, along with their agreement that his youngster will study to be an attorney so that he too can become an esteemed professional, are clear indications of a pessimistic outlook on what the future promises for Italian politics.

Un apprezzato professionista ... is an angry film made by an artist who wants to be readmitted at any cost to the circuit of communication after seven long years of unemployment. De Santis's adventure behind the camera had begun with the premise of creating a national cinema for everyone's benefit, with the masses as protagonists, and with the goal of forging a new social and civil consciousness. The director has repeated on many occasions: 'The audience that prefers my films is, without a doubt, the type that goes to see films shown outside of the major movie houses. In view of the fact that my films tell stories whose protagonists are from this same group and describe their affections, passions, and customs, they share a natural affinity.'[16]

In the 1970s, De Santis has lost his audience and his protagonists. Without the political mediation which, in his early films, had presented a cinematic reality in conflict with the historical and political situation of the time, the director in this, to date his last film tells a metaphorical story about impotence. Impotent is Vincenzo Arduni, faced with his thirst for success, power, and wealth. Impotent is Don Marco, in his spiritual vocation and in his compromises with corruption. Impotent is the unemployed Nicola, humiliated by selling his personal freedom for the well-being of his family. Impotent is the beautiful Lucietta, reduced to a pornographic object. Impotent also is the director, De Santis, in his attacks on the new political order and in representing a baffling reality, so different from the glorious days of the Resistance and postwar Italy.

PART III
THE WORKING CLASSES DECLASSED

15

On the Margin:
Some Reasons for a
Long, Unbroken Silence

Ho al mio attivo undici film diretti in qualità di regista: un bel magro bilancio, come si vede, per una carriera iniziata a vele spiegate nel 1947 con 'Caccia tragica' proprio nel momento di compiere i trent'anni, in un'epoca felice segnata da grandi speranze e da radiose illusioni per chi aveva creduto in un 'cinema nuovo' radicato nelle realtà degradate e struggenti del primo dopoguerra (e oltre) del nostro paese, e per chi aveva lottato per denunciare con la macchina da presa guasti e ingiustizie antichi e nuovi al fine di contribuire allo sviluppo e al rafforzamento della democrazia italiana.

I have made eleven films, as meager a total as can be seen for a career which began in full sail in 1947, when I was thirty years old, with *Caccia tragica*. My career started during a happy period marked by great hopes and radiant illusions for those who believed in a 'new cinema' that would arise from the degraded and tormenting realities of the Italian postwar. It was also a happy period for those who struggled to expose, with the movie camera, ancient and new injustices in order to participate in the development and strengthening of Italian democracy.

Giuseppe De Santis

The destiny of Giuseppe De Santis as a film director is a strange one. Lauded, first, as a film critic for *Cinema* (especially for reviews of films by Rossellini, Blasetti, and De Sica, and articles that foretell trends in postwar Italian cinema);[1] then, as assistant director to Visconti, Vergano, and Rossellini[2] and, finally, for his directorial debut with *Caccia tragica* (Tragic Pursuit) in 1947. His first film was warmly received by Italian critics, who praised the artistry and masterly technique of the young director. Some young intellectuals, already his collaborators in writing for *Cinema* and *Film d'oggi*, along with the painters Vedova, Turcato, and Pizzuto, put up banners upon his arrival in Venice for the international Festival of 1947.

It wasn't long before obstacles appeared on the path to what then seemed a brilliant future full of successes. Primarily for political reasons, his first film was not distributed. At the beginning of 1948, it was excluded from the major city movie houses and promptly criticized by right-wing critics during the bitter political campaign of April 1948. For example, the critic Angelo Solmi,[3] confusing politics with art, branded De Santis's film 'a propagandistic manifesto' designed to bring votes to the Communists.

After the electoral defeat of the Popular Front, the government at first denied permission for the film to be entered in the Cannes Film Festival. Only after much polemical pressure from leftist journalists was *Caccia tragica* included, whereupon it received praise and favourable reviews from the French press.

This episode is emblematic of what was to be De Santis's future as a director. His films in postwar Italy were never received and reviewed on their own merits but always in light of the political activism of the director; as a result, they were linked to the electoral fortunes and the vacillations in cultural policy of the former Italian Communist party.[4] As is well known, the director was criticized for his deviations: political, artistic, moral, erotic, and Neorealistic.

The critics from the Right considered De Santis the spokesman for the cultural policies of the Partito Comunista Italiano (PCI) and consistently focused on the political messages and social criticism in his films, to the total neglect of the stylistic and formalistic dimensions of his works. The leftist critics complained about his stylistic exuberance and about his formalistic obsession with repetitive background details, both of which they saw as hindering the political message of the films. They also faulted De Santis's inability to represent the class struggle in a specific historical context, and in its totality. The director's love of elaborate camera work, showy and refined *mise en scène*, and depiction of the characters' sexuality, according to the left-wing critics, blurred the political focus.

Ironically, even the re-evaluation of De Santis's films, begun in the 1970s by Martini and Melani,[5] originated from what were seen as De Santis's deviations and further misinterpreted them. The new generations discovered that De Santis's films were conscious that the media could be used as an instrument of mass communication, with its capacity to enchant and to create the needs it meets.

It is no longer necessary to dig deep to discover the political and ideological meaning of the films' symbolism. Tastes have changed. De Santis's films contain ideological and political ideas intended to change the way people perceive their world, and their place in it. Thus, his films have the potential, not just to reflect society (as is the case for other Neorealist films), but to help alter society in a truly democratic way. For example, in *Non c'è pace tra gli ulivi* (No Peace under the Olives), as in *Roma, Ore 11* (Rome, 11 O'clock), injustices are linked to specific social factors, and class solidarity and collaboration among the victims are identified as solutions.

Nevertheless, these explanations do not provide an answer to the question that arises at each mention of the Ciociaro director's name: Why hasn't De Santis made any more films? In recent years, during conversations with the director and in reading his letters, articles, and scripts, this question has become ever more pressing in my mind. Why *wasn't he able* to make more films after the early 1970s? The emphasis is important, as it is not as if he voluntarily stopped making movies, given his unquenched desire to get behind the movie camera again. He ironically defines himself 'un regista dimezzato' (a cloven director) and answers the question by saying that he has been pushed aside by the commercial and political mechanisms implicit in show business. He also adds that he has been excluded because of a conservative plot against progressive directors (as was the case in the postwar years) and that he was singled out for his activism in support of the Communist party.

A careful analysis shows that these circumstances, although impossible to ignore, are only part of the cause of the director's long silence, which dates from 1972. In order to put to rest the clichés that have emerged to explain De Santis's artistic inactivity, I put forward some hypotheses here. Not all of them are analysed separately below, but all are explored in the discussion that follows.

1 De Santis's films after *Riso amaro* (Bitter Rice) were not marketable.
2 The source of his creative inspiration dried up, linked, as it was, to an artistic movement, Neorealism, that dissipated after a brief ten-year span.
3 De Santis was so attached to outdated narrative structures and

styles, that he could no longer assimilate and adopt new techniques. His own personal cinematic culture was restricting since it was linked to a fictional and literary structure in which conflictuality, always simple and elementary, develops in a linear and manichean fashion.

4 He is a polemical, argumentative, and obstinate director, always ready to engage in disputes and discussions with critics or producers. He was always prompt to denounce any tampering with and editing of his films by producers and censors, and was never willing to compromise, even if it meant ditching a project.

5 He was a filmmaker with an artistic and political agenda for making films that would not only reflect society but help alter that society in a truly revolutionary sense. The themes he chose were ill-suited for an industry subject to the law of profit in a market economy. His films bring together in mythical form the sundry affairs of peasant reality and, at the same time, spread (by means of the film medium) a new mythology, both popular and socialist, which De Santis defines as progressive and democratic.

6 He was the victim of an international political climate – the cold war – whose repercussions were felt at the national level.

7 He was victim of his own party's ambiguous policies – a party he had been linked to since his years at the Centro Sperimentale, during which time he became its most prominent representative.

Since this assumption gives rise to growing doubt, one risks succumbing to easy conclusions about De Santis's long inactivity. A distinction must be made between the party's political and cultural policies imposed on De Santis and the personal choices made by the director that coincided with the party line. I am referring, above all, to the 1950s, and in particular to the policies concerning the occupation of the southern farmland. Furthermore, an interpretative key is offered by the polemics raised over a period of time between the director and left-wing critics and intellectuals. One should also read the letters in which the director's resentment towards some of those of the same political faith surface, especially those letters written to the French critics Marcel Oms and Georges Sadoul.[6] It must also be remembered that De Santis did not choose to strike an autonomous course for himself because he felt instinctively linked to the themes, the faces, and the problems of his populist and working-class characters, who were fighting, as he thought and believed, the same battles he was.[7]

8 His own cinematic agenda proved to be inadequate. At the beginning of the 1970s, with the advent of industrialization and the flowering of new themes, existentialism and disintegration of social and civil awareness were unable to find a place. From this cultural and social transformation emerges a new generation of filmmakers who will give birth to the so-called civil cinema. Furthermore, popular entertainment came to be dominated by the Italian-style comedy and new historical, mythological, and erotic genres.

9 The end of any future attempts to mediate the gap that existed between Neorealist films and popular and commercial ones.

10 In order to evaluate these hypotheses, one needs to consider De Santis's unrealized projects as well. The least verifiable of all the possibilities could turn out to be the most pertinent to an understanding of the artist's long inactivity. After the first three entries, De Santis's filmography would have evolved very differently if he had made 'Noi che facciamo crescere il grano' (We Who Grow Grain), a project about events in Melissa, which judging from the script, would have been a splendid choral film with many subplots on the theme of land occupation by peasants in the South.

'Pettotondo' (Round Breast) is a script about an Apulian prostitute who sells herself, not for profit, but just to make ends meet. Another script concerns the adventurous and extraordinary life of an illiterate farmer from Cerignola, Giuseppe Nicassio, who lands in jail but, determined to pursue his studies, finally achieves a high-school diploma, then he dedicates himself to the labour-union struggle, under the name Giuseppe Di Vittorio.

Any discussion of the unmade films of the 1950s must include mention of a project which features *sciopero a rovescio* (the refusal to be without work), a common protest tactic in the South which in Yugoslavia, became *Cesta Duga Godinu Dana* (The One-Year-Long Road). In the 1950s De Santis also wrote 'Il cavallo di lui' (His Horse), a symbolic story about the fate of Mussolini's horse after the end of his regime. Had these films been made, it is evident that De Santis's cinematic legacy would have been quite different, although in what way remains a matter of conjecture. It also seems clear that these projects represented a turning-point for the director. It was their failure to materialize that kept De Santis from finding the most congenial path to his own identity and artistic maturity.

It has often been said that, with the exception of *Riso amaro*, De

Santis had no box-office successes. However, his films were not commercial failures, and they more than measure up when compared with the sophisticated and artistic films of the period. In fact, De Santis's films had a moderate commercial success, especially considering their production costs.

Caccia tragica reaped a profit of 80 million lire in 1947,[8] at the same time that the box-office champion, *Come persi la guerra* (How I Lost the War), by Carlo Borghesio, made 293 million lire. In Italy, *Riso amaro* brought in more than 400 million lire, while *La sepolta viva* by Guido Brigone earned 530 million lire. *Non c'è pace tra gli ulivi* exceeded 400 million lire when *Gli ultimi giorni di Pompei* (The Last Days of Pompeii) by Paolo Moffa and Marcel L. Herbien made 841 million lire. *Roma, Ore 11* made 270 million lire in the period in which *Anna* by Alberto Lattuada, the biggest earner of 1952, made 1.25 billion lire. The failure of *Umberto D* by De Sica and Zavattini in the same year should be kept in mind. *Un marito per Anna Zaccheo* (A Husband for Anna Zaccheo) brought in almost 350 million lire, while the best film of the year, *Pane, amore e fantasia* (Bread, Love, and Fantasy) by Luigi Comencini topped a billion lire. Even the much criticized *Giorni d'amore* (Days of Love) and *Uomini e lupi* (Men and Wolves) together made more than 721 million lire, while *Ulysses* by Mario Camerini, the biggest seller of 1954, and *Belli ma poveri* (Poor but Beautiful) by Dino Risi, the big success of 1956, reached 1.8 billion and 998 million lire, respectively. De Santis's major film, *Italiani brava gente*, earned over half a billion lire only in Italy, while *A Fistful of Dollars* by Sergio Leone, and Giuseppe Colizzi's *Più forte ragazzi* (Harder Boys), record-breaking successes in 1964 and 1972, made 3.18 billion and 4.86 billion lire, respectively. *La Garçonnière*, at 124 million lire, is De Santis's only true commercial disaster. Taking into account that the Ciociaro director made films at production costs far below those of the films mentioned for comparison, by such major directors as De Sica, Visconti, and Rossellini, he was in no way a commercial risk, a charge that is often repeated. Further, these gross figures do not include international gross returns, mainly from the United States, South America, and the Soviet Bloc, the last, a market not available to most of the other films mentioned, many of which were not exported at all.

Another criticism often heard in Italian film business circles is that De Santis was, and continues to be, a difficult director, not wanted by producers because of his absurd demands that he oversee his work in all its details. My research and interviews with the director have brought me to two diverging conclusions. Let me trace briefly the relationships that developed between director and producer and the conflicts that arose with the critics.

During the making of *Caccia tragica*, financed by the Associazione Nazionale Partigiani d'Italia (ANPI; National Association of Italian Partisans), the young director refused to make changes to the script, requested more time and money to carry out the electoral-meeting scene, and sought to employ walk-ons. The producer, Giorgio Agliani, turned to the Communist party for help, and Antonello Trombadori was sent to Rome to convince De Santis to compromise. In *Riso amaro*, the director imposed the inexperienced Silvana Mangano, the American actress Doris Dowling, and an unknown Raf Vallone on Lux Film, the producers. With the completion of the film, a prolonged conflict flared up between De Santis and the critics over his so-called baroque-style decadence and eroticism and his scanty documentation of the practice of rice cultivation and the work of the rice workers.

Non c'è pace tra gli ulivi led to a new problem with the critics, particularly with the director of *Cinema*, Adriano Baracco,[9] who accused De Santis of D'Annunzianism, baroque style, and aestheticism. De Santis didn't give in; on the contrary, stung by these criticisms, he continued to write open letters to left-wing journalists and to trade magazines, accusing the critics of politically biased judgments and of scanty critical acumen.

After his third film, it became increasingly difficult for De Santis to find producers. After long-strained relations with Lux Film, which had refused to produce some of his projects – a modern adaptation of Alessandro Manzoni's *I promessi sposi* (*The Betrothed*) set in Sicily; a film on illiteracy in Italy; and a project about Portella della Ginetra (the 1 May 1947 slaughter of a dozen protesting Sicilian peasants) – De Santis broke his contract with the studio.

In 1952, in the middle of the cold war, with the help of Cesare Zavattini, he managed to convince Paul Graetz to finance *Roma, Ore 11* for Transcontinental Film. In the long run, this film irreparably harmed the director. At its debut, the critics hailed it as outstanding for its content and coherency; however, De Santis's image as a politically involved director led to severe criticism of the film's commercialism, overstructure, and thematic exploration of the political intrigues of the Italian cultural milieu. When the film came out, right-wing critics carried a defamatory campaign against the director as far as parliament, where a representative of their faction proposed an investigation into the presumed revolutionary activities of De Santis and the Communist party. The director was charged with having used state film subsidies for party propaganda, an absurd accusation since the film was financed by French and American funds.

The opening of the film was preceded by an intense legal battle between De Santis and Transcontinental Film, which wanted to cut the scene showing the homecoming of the prostitute, played by Lea Padovani.[10] Cutting the scene was a violation of the contract; therefore, the production company relied on the court testimony of Cesare Zavattini, who expressed his misgivings about the artistic value of the scene and asserted that the director had insisted on including it against the advice of the other scriptwriters, who found it too long and costly. The director won the case but lost a possible source of financial support.

To better understand the atmosphere of those years, it must be remembered that this period (1947–54) was the apogee of the Cold War. In the United States, the House Committee for Un-American Activities had begun the witch-hunt for Hollywood artists suspected of Communist association and anti-American propaganda. A second repressive wave began in 1951.[11] Of all the Italian directors, De Santis was the only one to have written a long article condemning the sentencing of Julius and Ethel Rosenberg to death for treason. He even called for a petition against the Permanent Subcommittee on Investigations, presided over by the Wisconsin senator Joseph R. McCarthy. The hysteria over Communist directors is apparent in the statements of Ayn Rand, who considered *Mission to Moscow*, the film version of a book by the American ambassador to Moscow, commissioned by then president Roosevelt, Communist propaganda.

Perhaps more revealing is the statement by actor Adolphe Menjou warning producers not to entrust screenplays to directors or actors capable of disseminating anti-American propaganda with a glance or a slight vocal inflection. According to Adrian Scott, in an 1955 article entitled 'Hollywood Review,' a total of 214 persons were blacklisted – including 106 screenwriters, 36 actors, and 11 directors.

In Italy, repercussions from these events were felt, and the 1950s are remembered as a period of self-censorship. What many don't remember is that, during this period, De Santis's name was added to the list, along with the infamous comment of the minister Giulio Andreotti: 'the Ciociaro must not make any more films.'

The campaign unleashed against producer Domenico Forges-Davanzati for having given the directorship of *Un marito per Anna Zaccheo* to

De Santis is a case in point. The producer had to defend himself against an accusation of having Communist sympathies by the right-wing press.[12] Another interesting matter concomitant with the opening of this film is the response of *L'Unità*, which ostracized De Santis. The official paper of the Communist party, under the directorship of De Santis's friend of long standing, Pietro Ingrao, published a series of readers' letters accusing the film of sexism. Among these, a letter from the left-wing writer Fausta Cialente[13] stands out. As usual the director defends himself and counterattacks, defining the film as a statement against the mentality of Italian males and about the difficulty of being beautiful and female in a society where machismo is rampant and female virginity is a prerequisite for matrimony.

The criticisms left their mark on the psyche of the director, who felt he had been betrayed, abandoned by his comrades of the old anti-Fascist struggle. The situation grew worse with subsequent films. *Giorni d'amore* should have been 3,300 metres long, but the producers had it cut to 2,999. The next film, *Uomini e lupi*, first envisioned by the director in a long-playing version of 3,300 metres, was shortened by Titanus to less than 2,800. De Santis protested the cuts and abandoned the project. The edit was done without his collaboration. The director then attempted to have his name removed from the final version, but without success.

De Santis became known as a director who sued and carried his protest to the press. He states that he was only defending his work against interference by censors and producers. The fact remains that he had to wait until 1966 to make another film in Italy. His next film, *Cesta Duga Godinu Dana*, was produced in Yugoslavia, and the Yugoslav ambassador had to accept the Golden Globe award on De Santis's behalf, as the director was again denied entrance to the United States. In an ironic twist of fate, his sister, wife of the Italian vice-consulate in Los Angeles (Mario Tedeschi), was present at the ceremony, along with her husband, who had refused to use his influence to procure a visa for his brother-in-law.

La Garçonnière was made possible by a concession on the part of producer Roberto Amoroso, who had signed a contract with De Santis for 'Pettotondo.' When the banks refused to finance the latter, alarmed by its subject – a strange story of a travelling prostitute – it was decided to change the subject-matter and what resulted was *La Garçonnière*. A similar incident had taken place previously. On 9 August 1955, *Arnaldo dello Spettacolo* made note of plans to suspend another one of De Santis's unrealized projects, 'Case aperte' (Open Houses). The ministry prohibited it upon discovering that De Santis was to direct.

La Garçonnière turned to be one of the least costly films but the most highly censored – a total of 5,000 metres were cut. The filming lasted only seven weeks and, because of the small budget, the director used Raf Vallone and his own future wife, Gordana Miletic.

Italiani brava gente, the director's last big film, was a Russian production bolstered by American financial aid. De Santis tells the story of his peasants at war in a cinematic discourse rich with reference to and praise of the Russian masters Eisenstein and Dovzhenko. The film release was held up by the censors, who changed the title. The right-wing press, at the urging of some war veterans, started an active campaign against the director, accusing him of defamation of the army and calling for an inquiry by the defence minister, Giulio Andreotti. The director was absolved of the charges.

Un apprezzato professionista di sicuro avvenire didn't fare any better. It was censored, denigrated, and attacked, even by the Vatican. So concludes a career that had started out with high hopes and a multitude of projects, many of which are still on the director's desk today. The laws of the marketplace and implacable ideological bans explain in part De Santis's silence. However, the possibility that something intrinsic to the structure and the thematic or stylistic elements of his work is responsible should also be explored.

Ever since the days of his association with *Cinema*, De Santis had had a vision which, in the postwar period, became concretized into the need to create populist art that contained all the ambiguities and intuitions about the problems and issues of his time. De Santis's cinematic vision is Neorealism tailored to reach the lower classes. In 1947, he described it as 'a popular art, in the sense of having chosen as protagonists of my films the lower classes, with their hopes, suffering, joy, struggles, and contradictions.'[4]

The director aimed at creating populist cinema that, while respecting the common people's tastes, would also re-elaborate narrative structures and modes handed down from popular tradition. These traditional elements he would fuse in the codified forms of cinematic entertainment, creating a collective mythology that would help rebuild and create a new Italy from the ruins of Fascism and foster a new democratic consciousness. De Santis's idea of cinema becomes more interesting if one considers that he attempted to organize not only the content of his films, but also their audiences' level of awareness and understanding. By situating the content of his films firmly in the rural world of southern peasantry, the world with which he was most familiar, he hoped to create a cinema with a strong moral and civil tension that would make an impact on national reality.

To conclude, De Santis's long silence should make us reflect on and help us to understand some of the dark periods of Italian cultural and civic life – more so, if the simplistic assumption of the PCI's dictatorial cultural hegemony, especially in the world of cinema, is viewed in the light of De Santis's long cinematic inactivity. If such dictatorial hegemony existed, why wasn't De Santis able to film his peasant stories in the 1950s? Clearly, his unfinished project of creating a national popular cinema remains a meaningful and useful instrument for conducting more thorough research into the political intrigues that conditioned Italian postwar cinematic production.

De Santis's project represented a compromise between the cinema's artistic Neorealist experience and its commercialism. The early Neorealist cinema was a refined artistic experience that appealed to a certain stratum of the public, primarily progressive middle-class intellectuals. It was the outgrowth of a humanist and liberal hypothesis whereby cinema would be artistic research and a cultural and political struggle for a better society. It entailed the removal of the structure at the foundation of the film industry. It also superimposed the utopian nineteenth-century concept of naturalistic and non-technological art on the complex emerging problems of cinematic spectacle and its means of communication. De Santis's vision was to create an artistic cinema for the enjoyment and emancipation of the masses without denying established cinematic modes and genres.

Unlike the other major postwar Italian directors, De Santis wanted his films to show a solution to the social and class-related problems of the time. To this end, it is worthwhile mentioning the lecture he gave in 1951 in Florence. On that occasion, the director criticized the pessimistic and sentimental tendency of his fellow directors. Taking as his example De Sica's *Bicycle Thieves*, De Santis pointed out pietism and sentimentalism as the predominant tendencies of Italian Neorealism. He also faulted Pietro Germi's *Il cammino della speranza* (The Path of Hope) for not showing a solution to the publicized problems of the Sicilian miners. According to De Santis, the resignation in accepting the existing injustices and the failure to indicate a way out were the result of a disposition that the other filmmakers had towards historical reality. On this point, De Santis stated: 'The [other directors] did not go to the

trouble of collecting background information on the causes of the problems. In so doing, they ended up, without even realizing it, supporting
the thesis of certain organizations that have an interest in denying a
political solution to the problems."[15] In this statement it is clearly De
Santis's aim to create a committed type of cinema – one that did not
merely focus on the problems but offered a solution. For this very
reason, he wanted to create a national cinema that could reach everyone.
He could never have conceived an intellectual, esoteric type of cinema,
such as Antonioni's or Fellini's. However, it seems obvious that his
program could not have survived as a cultural product within the market
cycles of a profit-driven industry.

16

From the Specific to the General:
Some Concluding Considerations

... la mia ambizione artistica è di creare film con l'intento di gettare le basi, o di riallacciarmi a una tradizione che sia dentro il giusto appello di Gramsci a una visione nazionale-popolare dei contenuti, e del linguaggio con cui questi contenuti devono essere espressi. E allora, a me sembra che è proprio in base a questa ambizione che bisogna giudicarmi. E non lanciare ogni volta contro di me le accuse di 'spettacolarismo,' 'erotismo,' 'dannunzianesimo,' 'cattivo gusto,' 'formalismo,' ed altri 'ismi' del genere, che costituiscono, appunto, il pregiudizio critico e il luogo comune sul mio lavoro.

... my artistic goal is to make films that lay foundations or that hark back to a tradition compatible with Gramsci's timely call for a national-popular art and for a language with which its content can be expressed. Therefore, it seems to me that I must be judged by this ambition and not have flung against me every time accusations of 'sensationalism,' 'eroticism,' 'd'Annunzianism,' 'bad taste,' 'formalism,' and other similar 'isms' which make up, precisely, the critical preconceptions and the clichés used to define my work.

Giuseppe De Santis

De Santis's films, contrary to what the new generation of Italian film critics has written and publicly stated on several occasions, need no rehabilitation or moral and critical reparation.[1] De Santis is a Neorealist auteur, regardless of how the term is applied or defined.[2] Even if they did not always applaud or completely understand his films, the critics of the late 1940s and 1950s generally dealt with his work respectfully, whether with approval or disapproval.[3] He was never excluded from the

Italian postwar cinematic debate on Neorealism. De Santis's films fall within the two main currents of postwar Italian cinema. In one of these trends, the attempt to document everyday life or past events is predominant; in the other, the dominant commitment to showmanship seeks to dramatize reality. Traces of these two major tendencies are to be found in almost all Neorealist films. Although closer to the second strain, De Santis's filmography never relinquishes the idea of cinema as a vehicle and an expression of social and political commitment. His filmography can be understood as a continuous effort to reconcile the traditional canon of story-telling with cinematography within the critical, civil, and democratic investigation of postwar Italian cinema. The *modus operandi* was never a hodgepodge of various styles, genres, and cinematic influences rearranged in schematic or dogmatic cinematic compositions, but a constant re-elaboration of cinematic and narrative structures in a concentrated effort to find new forms of artistic expression and to create a cinema accessible to all. Any attempt to dismiss his films as products of a subcultural populist art, tinged with overtones of 'serial,' 'photo-romance,' and 'erotism,' or as an effort to cater to the lowest popular tastes for the sole purpose of financial gain and commercial exploitation of a purer codified form of Neorealism, must be disregarded as critical approximations that do not take into account all the components and complexities of De Santis's films. The director's artistic ambition was to create cinematic spectacles which would prompt adoption of or propose new forms of social behaviour by denouncing current social injustices. His artistic and social concerns were also tied to the dilemma of how to heighten the artistic awareness of the masses. De Santis's aim is clearly stated in his 'Confessioni di un regista,' where we read:

Cinema interests the artist because it gives him the possibility of speaking to everyone. But this same possibility requires a naturalness, a simplicity, an immediate rendering of the facts that he wants to narrate. I have always tried to develop, even if often in a conventional manner, feelings, simple and linear passions, so that my films could reach the hearts of an ever-growing audience. I did it, not with the intention of inducing the spectators' passive contemplation, but rather to make of them alert protagonists by reawakening their dormant sentiments, long repressed by the viewing of films which often fail to stimulate their better instincts.[4]

De Santis found Italian cinema devoid of any relationship to an authentic narrative tradition. By creating a national cinema that would introduce elements of higher culture in popular contexts, he hoped to fill the cultural vacuum left by previous Italian intellectuals. De Santis expressed his ideas on the matter this way: 'They (the intellectuals) enjoy portraying our people as incapable of creating the beautiful or the ugly, the true or the false ... Italy lacks an authentic popular narrative in the sense of romances, tales, and short stories that touch upon the people's vital problems.'[5] In the same article, referring to the popular films of the day watched by popular audiences, he writes: 'Our poorly made films, the crowd-pleasers, come from American culture ... Did some historical or social factor preordain that the grass roots of Italy, the country's backbone, should deserve no better than this?'[6]

Unlike acclaimed directors, such as Visconti, Rossellini, and De Sica, or less well-known international figures, such as Lattuada, Germi, Zampa, and Castellani, De Santis expressed a profound love for the peasant world, his native Ciociaria, and a clear antithesis between country and city. Within these major motifs, De Santis, like the other Neorealist directors, addresses the discomforts of the lower and upper-middle classes, but, unlike many of his contemporaries, he is more interested in the contradictory changes brought upon the masses by technology, the mass media, economic progress, the Americanization of postwar Italian life, slow democratization, urbanization, and – in his last two films – corruption, degradation, and cultural homogenization.

Perhaps more than any other postwar Italian filmmaker, De Santis documents the slow and painful adjustments of the Italian woman within a changing culture still imbued with old prejudices, stereotypes, taboos, chauvinist customs, and religious dogmas and superstitions. In his films, women are often protagonists, but are not characterized as dedicated, unselfish wives or mothers, as in many films of the period, but rather as modern individuals with much more liberated ideals and aspirations and, most of all, not denied their own sensuality and sexuality. De Santis's world is made of adventures, dramatic action, passion, and well-defined social contrasts. His first films are populated with good and evil characters who either die or redeem themselves. In all his films, passion is the predominant force that shapes the protagonists' fates.

De Santis's aim of creating a national popular cinema for everyone is the result of a realist vocation whose precedents are to be found in the critical articles written during his collaboration with the journal *Cinema*. As a critic for that journal, De Santis played a prominent role in promoting and defining the paths that cinematography and new filmmakers should take in order to revive the stagnant national cinema. He also promoted the reaction against the banality that had for so long dominated Italian films of the Fascist era. In what would be considered an apprenticeship, he slowly progressed from theoretical schemes to concrete projects – first, as a scriptwriter; then, as assistant director to Visconti and Rossellini; later, as co-author of *Il sole sorge ancora* (The Sun Rises Again), and, finally, as the full-fledged director, in 1947, of *Caccia tragica* (Tragic Pursuit). The essays published in *Cinema* reveal some of the themes which would later become characteristic of his films. For example, 'Per un paesaggio italiano' (For an Italian Landscape) foreshadows De Santis's predilection for a fusion of characters, environment, and landscape. The rich locale offered not only a dramatic setting for the events, but also became an integral factor in the narrative by showing characters in their natural, everyday milieu. Well-defined environments added authenticity, humanity, and warmth to De Santis's stories and their protagonists. In all De Santis's films, the physical surroundings assume the role of a protagonist, whether it is in the form of rice fields (*Riso amaro*), vast countryside (*Caccia tragica*), rocky, arid slopes (*Non c'è pace tra gli ulivi*), tranquil and fertile plains (*Giorni d'amore*), a building's staircase and crowded streets (*Roma, Ore 11*), dark and dreary rooms (*La Garçonnière*), or a decadent bedroom (*Un apprezzato professionista di sicuro avvenire*). Often, in rendering these ideas, the films reach excesses, such as overelaborate composition and scenography, packed with the details and extras that speak to De Santis's love for spectacle. The director has never concealed these predilections; on the contrary, he has often referred to them as qualities. Speaking on the subject, De Santis said in 1953: 'In my films dances, songs, ceremonies, and rites serve to substantiate a character, to develop a situation, mainly to create an atmosphere, to reveal the distinguishing features of one region from another with regard to landscape, customs, its very soul, and the virtues and vices of its population.'[7]

De Santis, the director, sought to make film the expression of his ideas. He introduced higher forms of culture in popular contexts and also used popular artistic forms of expression, giving them a new meaning by inverting the conservative and traditional message they earlier conveyed. For instance, the gangster style used in *Caccia tragica*, the photo-romance in *Riso amaro*, the *opera buffa* (farcical comic opera) and popular theatre in *Giorni d'amore*, the Neapolitan theatre (*sceneggiata*) adopted in *Un marito per Anna Zaccheo* – all are examples of popular artistic modes of entertainment which are demystified as De Santis unmasks their conservative messages.

A certain desire to emulate the nineteenth-century novel has always been at work in De Santis's films. It is well known that the director started as a writer, and succeeded in publishing several short stories before enrolling at the Centro Sperimentale. As a critic he made the structure of the nineteenth-century narrative the basis for the rebirth of a national cinema. Critical attacks on the films of Castellani, Poggioli, Chiarini, and Soldati, in which they are declaimed as formalistic and stylized, appeared under De Santis's name in *Cinema* during the 1940s. The future director nevertheless pointed out some redeeming features in these films. He acknowledged their attempt to depict an authentic cultural reality, a major preoccupation characteristic of the novels from which the film stories derived. The article 'Per un paesaggio italiano' (For an Italian Landscape) can be read, along with the other two articles written in collaboration with Mario Alicata, as a manifesto promoting the diffusion of a certain type of literature as a model for better films and a new national cinema. According to De Santis's thesis, filmmaking had passed from a documentary stage into the phase of story-telling and, as a result, was interweaving its destiny ever more closely with narrative art form. This conclusion must not be misunderstood or read as an attempt to undermine the artistic or expressive autonomy of the seventh art, but rather as an authentic insight on the part of Alicata and De Santis into the subtle affinity between the narrative structures of the two art forms. What is perhaps more important is that they saw in *verismo* and in Verga the only types of literary models that could carry on the marriage between cinema and literature. The correctness of their intuition has been confirmed by the numerous films that evolved directly from that type of literature, and by other films that reproduced the same narrative structures.[8] De Santis's own films demonstrate that he was more interested in the second possibility because of an instinctive vocation for naturalism. He is either author or co-author of all the stories and subjects of his films. Even the film titles have a distinct and recognizable literary background.[9] The major difference between De Santis and the other major postwar directors, such as Rossellini and De Sica, lies in the elaboration of the narrative structure in the cinematic discourse. In De Sica–Zavattini's films or in Rossellini's early films, and in Visconti's *La terra trema*, there is an attempt to dissolve the eye of the camera into the reality represented. In every De Santis film, on the other hand, there is a marked narrative structure, and narrative solutions are often used to develop the plots and to weave subplots. For his films, De Santis has drawn from various literary sources. He has taken from the serial, the photo-romance, the popular theatre, and the nineteenth-century novel, always with the intention of creating a great fresco, an epic. De Santis has stated[10] that his films can be divided into novels and short stories. In the first group he has included *Riso amaro*, *Caccia tragica*, *Italiani brava gente*, and *La strada lunga un anno* (The One-Year-Long Road). In the short-story category, he has included *Un marito per Anna Zaccheo*, *Giorni d'amore*, *La Garçonnière*, *Uomini e lupi*, and *Un apprezzato professionista* ... As a critic, I would point out that the structural differences between these two categories of films are in the plot development. The major works, as the director classifies them, are choral stories whose modal structure is closer to that of a naturalistic novel. The conflict between the protagonists, which often extends to entire social classes, or even nations, is clear and well defined, and follows a linear progression. The main plots' development, as well as the subplots, are linear and based on rules of elementary opposition. The minor films contain fewer characters. The conflicts between the antagonists are more complex, and the characters have a more developed and defined psychology. These distinctions and divisions are further proof that, in his attempt to open new avenues to Italian audiences with the creation of a national cinema, Giuseppe De Santis also aspired to become that cinema's story-teller.

Notes

Foreword

1 Parenthetical English titles in roman type are my translations.
2 Gianni Rondolini, *Dizionario del cinema italiano: 1945–1969*, 110.
3 Roy Armes, *Patterns of Realism: A Study of Italian Neorealist Cinema*; Peter Bondanella, *Italian Cinema from Neorealism to the Present*; and Mira Liehm, *Passion and Defiance: Film in Italy from 1942 to the Present*.
4 Millicent Marcus, *Italian Film in the Light of Neorealism*, 14–17.
5 My wife and I corresponded regularly with the De Santises until 10 July 1991, when Lorraine, a lieutenant in the United States Army Reserve, was killed near Dhahran, Saudi Arabia, while on active duty during the Gulf War. She received her PhD posthumously from Purdue University in December 1991 in recognition of her scholarship, as manifested in her publications in English, Italian, and French, and her work in progress on her dissertation, entitled 'Golden Necklace, Leaden Chain: Socio-biological Destiny and the Female Artist,' in which she argued that 'women are torn ... between their biologically and socially influenced urge to create offspring and to nurture, and their desire to express themselves individually outside the confines of the family.' Purdue University has established the Lorraine K. Lawton Award in her memory to encourage and acknowledge research and writing by and about women in Italian literature and/or film presented at the Purdue University Conference on Romance Languages, Literatures, and Film and published in *Romance Languages Annual*. Since Lorraine's death, I have been remiss in many ways.
6 The lecture De Santis presented on 7 October 1989 at the Purdue University Conference on Romance Languages, Literatures, and Film was published in the 1989 *Romance Languages Annual* (*RLA*). Comments made by

De Santis during his week-long stay in Indiana, in particular, those in response to questions asked after his lectures at Purdue University and at Indiana University (10 October 1989), which were not published in the 1989 *RLA*, are identified in the notes as 'PU/IU.'

7 Antonio Gramsci, *An Antonio Gramsci Reader: Selected Writings, 1916–1935*, 300–20.

8 These reflections were originally published as 'UCLA Course Notes' in 1973 and in *Film Criticism* in 1979.

9 Giuseppe De Santis, 'Birth, Development, and Death of Neorealism,' 4.

10 Ibid.

11 Ernest Callenbach, letter to Lorraine and Ben Lawton, dated 13 December 1989.

12 De Santis, 'Birth, Development, and Death of Neorealism,' 4.

13 Ibid.

14 Ibid.

15 Ibid.

16 Mario Verdone, *Il cinema neorealista*, 19.

17 Giuseppe De Santis and Mario Alicata, 'Verità e poesia: Verga e il cinema italiano,' *Cinema*, 10 October 1941, 216–17; cited in Marcus, *Italian Film in the Light of Neorealism*, 14–15.

18 The term 'pedinamento' is usually not translated. Verdone, in *Il cinema neorealista* (p. 19), describes it as 'the very essence of Zavattini's conception of Neorealism, that is, the camera tracks a man in the street, it accompanies him as he wanders around, as he meets people, until it discovers his nature and until it creates the story.'

19 Andrea Martini and Marco Melani, 'De Santis,' 313.

20 André Bazin, *What Is Cinema? II*, 60.

21 One might, of course, argue that Bruno, the child, represents the new, postwar, post-Resistance generation, which, unlike his father's generation, is willing to challenge the status quo. From this perspective, De Santis would, presumably, consider the film Neorealist.

22 This expression might be translated as 'Neorealism viewed through rose-coloured glasses.'

23 The Agnelli family is to Fiat, the major Italian automobile manufacturer, what the Ford family used to be to its eponymous corporation. To understand the importance and power of the Agnelli family in Italy, imagine a Ford family controlling Ford, General Motors, and Chrysler.

24 The *Catalogo Bolaffi del cinema italiano* gives a clear idea of the critical response the film continued to elicit until relatively recent times: 'The desire to communicate his ideas with a vast public, and to present the

social and political problems of postwar Italy in an easy and obvious manner, pushed the director to adopt questionable artistic solutions, to utilize
vulgar means of communication, compromising in the end the seriousness
and the commitment of his ideological discourse, which collapses in a
series of comic-book or dime-novel episodes'(my translation).

25 De Santis, PU/IU.

26 The recent revisionist reviling of Columbus as a genocidal imperialist is
one of the more absurd manifestations of this proclivity. We might as well
criticize him for not having booked a flight on the Concorde. For intelligent correctives of certain of these excesses, see Mario Vargas Llosa, 'The
Children of Columbus,' and Mario B. Mignone, ed., *Columbus: Meeting of
Cultures.*

27 Innumerable Italian films of the past forty-five years have both lampooned
and condemned the chauvinist behaviour towards women displayed by cer-
tain of their countrymen. See, among many others, Federico Fellini's *The
White Sheik* (1953), *La dolce vita* (1960), *Amarcord* (1974), and *Ginger and
Fred* (1989); Pietro Germi's *Divorce Italian Style* (1964); Mario Monicelli's
Big Deal on Madonna Street (1959); and Lina Wertmüller's *Seduction of
Mimi* (1971), *Swept Away* (1974), and *Seven Beauties* (1976). Fellini, in 'The
Fascism within Us,' defines this kind of simple-minded, escapist, maschil-
ist behaviour as the 'psychological, emotional manner of being a fascist'
(Peter Bondanella, ed., *Federico Fellini: Essays in Criticism*, 20–1).

28 Marcus, *Italian Film in the Light of Neorealism.*

29 De Santis, 'Birth, Development, and Death of Neorealism,' 5.

30 Ibid.

31 Ibid.

Preface

1 All translations from the Italian are my own, unless otherwise noted.

2 Ciociaria is a province in the southern part of Latium, with distinctive
cultural and linguistic traits. De Santis, although he moved to Rome, is
always identified with this subculture.

3 An appellation De Santis has categorically rejected, saying: 'Neorealism
never had any fathers, only one great mother, the Resistance': interview
with De Santis conducted by the author on 21 October 1989, at Wake
Forest University in North Carolina.

4 See, for example, Pierre Leprohon, *The Italian Cinema*, 106; Mira Liehm,
Passion and Defiance: Film in Italy from 1942 to the Present, 96; and Alfonso
Canziani, *Gli anni del neorealismo*, 141–6.

5 See Andrea Martini and Marco Melani, 'De Santis.' Starting with the 1974 Pesaro Conference on Neorealism, a major revival of De Santis's work has taken place. The new generation of film critics has seen in De Santis's cinematic discourse a critical reflection on mediology. See for example Alberto Parassino, *Giuseppe De Santis*, and *Cinema e cinema* 9/30 (1982), a special issue on De Santis.

6 Farassino, *Giuseppe De Santis*.

7 The term refers to A.A. Zhdanov, a member of the Soviet leadership under Stalin, after the Second World War. Zhdanov's ideas on socialist realism became a kind of manual for dealing with cultural problems throughout the entire communist movement. In Italy, his writings were published under the title *Politica e ideologia*.

1: De Santis's Early Years

1 See Giuseppe De Santis, 'Ripensando ai tempi di *Cinema* prima serie,' in *Verso il neorealismo*, 36.

2 Giuseppe De Santis, unpublished letter to Giovanni Grazzini, 'Le gouaches di Guttuso per "Riso amaro."'

3 De Libero wrote an article about their encounter. See Libero de Libero, 'Ciociaro come la Ciociaria.'

4 Ruggero Zangrandi, *Il lungo viaggio attraverso il fascismo*.

5 Gianni Puccini (Milan, 1914–Rome, 1968) was one of the best critics and scriptwriters of the Neorealist period. He studied at the University of Rome and at the Centro Sperimentale, and from 1940 to 1943 wrote for the journal *Cinema*. Puccini also wrote scripts for Visconti, De Santis, Lizzani, and Nanni Loy. He directed several films in the realistic style, such as *Il carro armato dell'8 settembre* and *I sette fratelli Cervi*. After Gianni's death, his younger brother, Massimo Mida Puccini, made a film, *Il fratello*, based on their relationship.

6 On Puccini's offer see De Santis, 'Ripensando ai tempi di *Cinema* prima serie,' 33.

7 In the Meridiano de Roma, De Santis published his first short story, 'Paese,' a fictional portrait of his grandfather.

8 Giuseppe De Santis, 'Confessioni di un regista,' 20.

9 On this matter see Massimo Mida, 'Cinema e antifascismo: Testimonianza su una genesi.' The years between 1925 and 1939 saw an increased interest in America, reflected in a number of books such as *America primo amore* (1935; America, First Love) by Mario Soldati, and *America amara* (1939; Bitter America) by Emilio Cecchi, which had a great influence on De

Santis's generation. The America that De Santis saw and came to love was that depicted in Hollywood films. In 1920, 220 Italian films were produced; the number dropped to 12 in 1928, and when the young De Santis started to go to the movies, Italy's more than 3,000 movie theatres were screening mostly imported films. The old-fashioned American cinema had an enormous impact. As De Santis said: 'Personally I was tremendously influenced by American films, but it started with the great admiration I felt for American democracy from 1934 to 1936. For my entire generation, that democracy was the greatest expression and form of freedom. The American films which I saw reinforced my ideal and model of democracy. When I remember what the New Deal did for American cinema, it seems to me that a great engine was in motion, making history. Most of all I loved the films of King Vidor, especially *Hallelujah*, which takes place on a cotton plantation and evolves through the various personal dramas which shape its structure. This particular film influenced me enormously when later I made my own *Riso amaro*': interview with De Santis, conducted by Antonio Vitti on 22 October 1989, at Wake Forest University.

10 It was in collaboration with Gianni Puccini that De Santis wrote a script for Camillo Mastrocinque's film *Don Pasquale* and a script for a film that was never made, 'I figli di Zorro.'

11 Mario Alicata and Giuseppe De Santis, 'Verità e poesia: Verga e il cinema italiano,' 217.

2: A Member of the 'Cinema' Circle

1 The latter article was in response to Fausto Montesanti's criticisms of the former. See Fausto Montesanti, 'Della ispirazione cinematografica.'

2 Sebastiano Martelli, *Il crepuscolo dell'identità*, 14.

3 After 1926 little remained of the anti-Fascist movement in Italy. All political parties had been proscribed by Mussolini, but a skeleton Communist organization continued in secret, perhaps as the only existing party, apart from Fascism itself. In the 1940s, during their collaboration on *Cinema*, Alicata, Ingrao, Gianni Puccini, and others were all members of the clandestine Communist party existing in Rome.

4 On how the *Cinema* group used a codified language to express their political ideas see Pietro Ingrao, 'Lucchino Visconti: L'antifascismo e il cinema.'

5 Mario Alicata, 'Ambiente e società nel racconto cinematografico.'

6 Mario Alicata and Giuseppe De Santis, 'Verità e poesia: Verga e il cinema italiano,' 217.

7 Mario Alicata and Giuseppe De Santis, 'Ancora de Verga e del cinema italiano,' 315.

8 Giuseppe De Santis, 'Ripensando ai tempi di *Cinema* prima serie,' in *Verso il neorealismo*, 35–6.

9 On how *Cinema* started and was later assigned to Vittorio Mussolini see Gianni Puccini, 'I tempi di *Cinema.*'

10 Vittorio Mussolini has always maintained that he was never aware of the anti-Fascist ideas of his subordinates. See Jean A. Gili, *Le Cinéma italien à l'ombre des faisceaux (1922–1945)*, 209–44.

11 For a complete definition of this term see Massimo Mida and Lorenzo Quaglietti, eds., *Dai telefoni bianchi al neorealismo.*

12 Gian Piero Brunetta, *Cinema italiano tra le due guerre: Fascismo e politica cinematografica*, 75.

13 Alessando Pavolini, 'Il rapporto della cinematografia italiana,' in *Dai telefoni bianchi al neorealismo*, eds. Massimo Mida and Lorenzo Quaglietti, 37.

14 On the use of propoganda in films during the Fascist period, see Brunetta, *Cinema italiano tra le due guerre*, 74–81.

15 Peter Bondanella maintains that the criticism directed at the numbers of directors who, between 1940 and 1943, turned to adaptations of late nineteenth- or early twentieth-century naturalistic fiction is unwarranted. He admits that these directors evaded contemporary issues but, at the same time, maintains they gained invaluable training that would prepare them for their contributions to Italian cinema after the war. See Peter Bondanella, *Italian Cinema from Neorealism to the Present*, 21–2.

16 Giuseppe De Santis, 'Un garibaldino al convento,' 118.

17 Giuseppe De Santis, 'Quattro passi fra le nuvole,' 152.

18 Giuseppe De Santis, 'Harlem,' in *Verso il realismo*, 195–8.

19 Giuseppe De Santis, 'Il jazz e le sue danze,' in *Verso il realismo*, 65–8.

20 De Santis has never reviewed this 1935 film but, during our conversations, has often praised it along these lines.

21 To this group also belonged the 'Calligraphers' – a term coined by De Santis to describe those who combined formalistic preoccupation with a retreat to the past, reconstructing it with decor and beauty.

22 Giuseppe De Santis, 'Un colpo di pistola,' in *Verso il neorealismo*, 144.

23 Ibid.

3: A Dream Comes True

1 Giuseppe De Santis, 'Sogni del cineasta.'

2 Giuseppe De Santis, 'Stampe.'

3 Interview with De Santis conducted by Antonio Vitti in April 1991, at De Santis's home in Fiano Romano, Italy.

4 I am referring to Giovanni Verga (1840–1926), who followed the realist tradition in Italian art, focusing mainly, in his short stories, on human passion. Verga's most famous novel, *The House by the Medlar Tree*, depicts the destructive power of ardent passions and rebellion. Luchino Visconti's *La terra trema* (The Earth Trembles) is based on Verga's novel.

5 On the role played by LUCE Institute during the Fascist regime see James Hay, *Popular Film Culture in Fascist Italy*, 201–32.

6 Interview with De Santis conducted by Antonio Vitti in April 1991, at De Santis's home in Fiano Romano, Italy.

7 Giuseppe De Santis, 'Portofino,' in *Verso il neorealismo*, 76.

8 Giuseppe De Santis, 'Per un paesaggio italiano,' in *Dai telefoni bianchi al neorealismo*, eds. Massimo Mida and Lorenzo Quaglietti, 198–201.

9 Stefano Masi, *De Santis*, 24.

10 Millicent Marcus, *Italian Film in the Light of Neorealism*, 15.

11 Giuseppe De Santis, 'Cinema sud e memoria: Il regista Giuseppe De Santis racconta.'

12 Mario Alicata and Giuseppe De Santis, 'Ancora di Verga e del cinema italiano,' 315.

13 Giuseppe De Santis, 'Un pilota ritorna,' in *Dai telefoni bianchi al neorealismo*, eds. Massimo Mida and Lorenzo Quaglietti, 257–60.

14 On the Easter 1940 encounter on the ship bound for Capri see Mira Liehm, *Passion and Defiance: Film in Italy from 1942 to the Present*, 1. This famous encounter is also cited in Alberto Farassino's *Giuseppe De Santis*, 10. Gianni Puccini was the first to write about Visconti's and De Santis's encounter, in 'Il venticinque luglio del cinema italiano.' De Santis told me that, during the trip to Capri, he tried to persuade Visconti to make the film 'Palude/ Ossessione' around Sperlonga and Fondi, where, in 1950, he would shoot *Non c'è pace tra gli ulivi*.

15 Mario Puccini – father of Gianni, Mario, and Dario – was a well-known literary critic and scholar who had known Giovanni Verga personally and worked on *Gramigna*'s script dialogue.

16 Carlo Lizzani, 'Tra due età,' in *L'avventurosa storia del cinema italiano raccontata dai suoi protagonisti, 1935–1959*, eds. Franca Faldini and Goffredo Fofi, 81.

17 Lino Micciché, *Visconti e il neorealismo*, 29–30.

18 On the formation of the 'Cineguf' and its role in promoting new talent for Italian cinema see Philip V. Cannistrato, *La fabbrica del consenso fascismo e mass media*, 301.

19 The writer Alberto Moravia had also worked on the script, but his name was not included in the credits, owing to the racial laws passed in Italy against the Jews in 1938.

20 Giuseppe De Santis, 'E con "Ossessione" osai il primo giro di manovella.'

21 Giuseppe De Santis gave me this information during our talks at his house in Fiano Romano in spring 1991.

22 This information is also confirmed by an unpublished letter written to De Santis by Elli Parvo, from Tagliacozzo, dated 14 September 1945, in which she mentions the work done by De Santis in Rome.

23 Jean A. Gili, *Le cinéma italien à l'ombre des faisceaux (1922–1945)*, 156.

24 Vittorio De Sica, 'Roma, città aperta,' in *L'avventurosa storia del cinema italiano raccontata dai suoi protagonisti, 1935–1959*, eds. Franca Faldini and Goffredo Fofi, 90.

25 Alfonso Canziani, *Gli anni del neorealismo*, 270.

26 Luchino Visconti was arrested by the Germans during the round-up that followed the shooting of 335 Italian hostages at the Fosse Ardeatine, in March 1994. The massacre was carried out by the Germans as a reprisal for the partisans' attacks on their troops stationed in Rome. Visconti, who was sentenced to death, escaped from prison with the aid of the guards and, in 1945, returned to work in the theatre, until an American psychological-warfare group asked him to film the trials and executions of Pietro Koch and Pietro Caruso.

27 Giuseppe De Santis, 'L'ANPI presenta,' in *L'avventurosa storia del cinema italiano raccontata dai suoi protagonisti, 1935–1959*, eds. Franca Faldini and Goffredo Fofi, 118–19.

28 Giuseppe De Santis, quoted by Mira Liehm in *Passion and Defiance: Film in Italy from 1942 to the Present*, 61.

29 De Santis, 'L'ANPI presenta,' 119.

30 Alberto Farassino, *Giuseppe De Santis*, 17.

4: De Santis behind the Camera

1 I'm referring to 'E in crisi il neorealismo?' and 'Confessioni di un regista.'

2 Giuseppe De Santis, 'Conversazione con Giuseppe De Santis: La ricerca realistica come impegno civile.'

3 In *Non c'è pace tra gli ulivi*, De Santis left out eroticism, the American cultural influence, and the influences of the photo-romance, choosing instead to adhere faithfully to the primitive cultural stage of his native region.

4 Besides De Santis's artistic contribution to the film, he also played a central role in getting the ANPI to finance it.

5 Pier Giuseppe Murgia, *Il vento del nord*.
6 The film's title comes from a Chekhov short story, but the plot mechanism is inspired by Fritz Lang's *M* (1931; The Monster of Düsseldorf). In this film, a man-hunt is started to apprehend a child-murderer, who is finally trapped by the denizens of the underworld and condemned to death by their leader. As was De Santis's, the storyline of Lang's film was based on a news item.
7 Alberto Farassino, *Giuseppe De Santis*, 20.
8 Giuseppe De Santis, 'Per un paesaggio italiano,' in *Dai telefoni bianchi al neorealismo*, eds. Massimo Mida and Lorenzo Quaglietti, 198–201.
9 *Caccia tragica* was released in Milan the week before the election, at the six largest theatres, and it shared the bill with Ernst Lubitsch's *Ninotchka*. Lubitsch's 1939 film is a comedy about a Russian woman who chooses the Western style of life over Soviet communism. The historian Giuliano Procacci, recalling the election, writes: 'And the Americans sent parcels of food and clothing which were something more than a welcome gift in those hard times. On the eve of the elections of 18 April 1948 a letter arrived together with the parcel: it asked the recipient to vote against the communists and for the party trusted by America, the Christian democrats. The clergy too were deeply involved in the electoral struggle: votes came even from the nuns of closed orders, from hospital patients and from those in mental asylums. In fact, following a Christian democrat suggestion, the vote had been declared obligatory': *History of the Italian People*, 378.
10 See Angelo Solmi, '"Caccia tragica" non ha portato voti al fronte, il film di Giuseppe De Santis doveva essere l'antidoto di "Ninotchka."' The title of the article speaks for itself: '*Caccia tragica* did not bring votes to the Front: Giuseppe De Santis's film had to be an antidote to *Ninotchka*.'
11 Alberto's acquittal by the peasants ideologically symbolizes the promise of a future socialist reality, where justice will be administered by proletarian trials and not according to the bourgeois code of laws. In 1975, Bertolucci's *Novecento* (1900) stages a similar trial, when Olmo asks the peasants to judge Alfredo Berlinghieri, the master (*padrone*).
12 The peasants' gesture assumes another meaning as well. Alberto saved the earth from the mines' explosion; therefore, the pelting symbolically becomes an act of reconciliation between men and nature after the horrors committed during the war.
13 For an interpretation of the figure of Lilì Marlene as the beginning of the collective aspiration for pleasure which, together with consumerism, lulls and levels national and sociopolitical barriers see Stafano Masi, *De Santis*, 39.

14 Mario Cannella, 'Ideology and Aesthetic Hypothesis in the Criticism of Neorealism.'

15 The Italian critics who reviewed *Caccia tragica* found the children's masked sequence cerebral and unnecesssary. For example, see Lorenzo Quaglietti, 'Situazione del cinema realistico.'

5: And Then Came Silvana

1 On how Silvana Mangano was chosen for the role see Giuseppe De Santis, 'Cinema, sud e memoria: Il regista Giuseppe De Santis racconta,' 19.

2 Guido Aristarco, '"Riso amaro".'

3 Giuseppe De Santis, quoted in Antonio Costa, 'Conversazione con Giuseppe De Santis,' 70.

4 Among the numerous articles on *Riso amaro* from leftist critics that came out immediately after the film's release, the most important are: Anna Gobbi, 'Come abbiamo lavorato per "Riso amaro"'; Renzo Renzi, '"Riso amaro"'; and Pino Baldelli, '"Riso amaro".'

5 The information on Flaiano comes from Costa, 'Conversazione con Giuseppe De Santis,' 70.

6 Peter Bondanella, *Italian Cinema: From Neorealism to the Present*, 85.

7 Giuseppe De Santis, 'Cinema e narrativa.'

8 Giuseppe De Santis, lecture given at Pisa, 18 February 1988.

9 American GIs had affixed a Hayworth pin-up poster to the atomic bomb exploded on Bikini Atoll. The soldiers had named the bomb 'Gilda,' after her best-known role.

10 On how the film production was delayed see Carlo Lizzani, '*Riso amaro*': *Un film diretto da Giuseppe De Santis*, 32.

11 Callisto Cosulich, quoted in Gian Piero Brunetta, *Storia del cinema italiano: Dal neorealismo al miracolo economico*, vol. 3: *1945–1959*.

12 The grossing figures for the two films are taken from Roberto Chiti and Roberto Poppi, eds., *Dizionario del cinema italiano*, 87 and 358.

13 The information on the photo-romance is from Carlo Bordoni and Franco Fassati, *Dal feuilleton al fumetto*.

14 Damiano Damiani, quoted in ibid., 128.

15 De Santis gave me this information during our talks at his house in Fiano Romano, 14 April 1991.

16 De Santis, 'Cinema, sud e memoria,' 19.

17 Lizzani, '*Riso amaro*,' 24.

18 Giuseppe De Santis, quoted in Costa, 'Conversazione con Giuseppe De Santis,' 70.

19 Lux Film even asked Fellini to collaborate, but, according to De Santis, he
   refused after reading the treatment: De Santis, quoted in Lizzani, 'Riso
   amaro, ' 19.
20 Lizzani, ibid., 27.
21 Fiction is one of the thematic concerns of the film. The movie starts with
   the voice-over of a radio announcer describing the departure of a multitude
   of women of all ages and social classes for the rice planting season. The
   next shot consists of a close-up in which the announcer looks straight at
   the camera, as if he were speaking to the audience in reporting on the
   mondine, but the camera pulls back and the audience discovers that the
   announcer is an actor, playing a part in a film, and that he is not speaking
   to them but to a Radio Torino microphone. The director has thus shown
   the first fictitious element in the film and also a medium – radio – inside
   another medium – the film they are watching. In order to authenticate his
   report, the announcer goes on to interview various women selected at
   random about their impressions, needs, and ideals. Then the camera shows
   two men who, from their clothes, appear to be policemen. The announcer's
   voice fades away into the distance, and the audience's suspicion about the
   two men's identity is confirmed. Once again the spectators see the element
   of fiction prevailing over the documentary approach. During these scenes,
   De Santis's conception of filmmaking comes to mind: 'In my opinion, realism does not at all exclude fiction or all the classical cinematographical
   means.' De Santis's reflection on the fictional nature of cinema is present
   throughout the film. As Andrea Martini and Marco Melani have said (see
   'De Santis'), De Santis makes good use of the new semantic possibilities by
   bringing to the foreground everything that in the past had been left in the
   background. They are referring to the role of the chorus and the setting. In
   so doing, the director focuses on the theatrical and the fictional qualities of
   phenomenological appearances. In *Riso amaro*, the list of things that are
   not what they appear to be is long and includes the false embrace between
   Walter and Francesca, used to hide from the police, and the worthless
   necklace that they have stolen, which Walter then uses to lure Silvana to
   his side, presenting it to her as an engagement gift. More than the many
   items shown outside their respective phenomenological appearances, the
   scene in which the arriving soldiers hide behind huge cardboard masks
   confirms De Santis's views on fiction.
22 During the dance sequence with Silvana and Walter, Marco cuts in, as in
   Vidor's films, where Blacks play 'Breakaway,' forming a circle around two
   dancers and interrupting their dance by cutting in.
23 The first fight between Walter and Marco was repeated over and over, and

De Santis made the actors fight for real, according to Italo Calvino, 'Tra i pioppi della risaia la "cinecittà" delle mondine,' 3.

24 Sandro Botticelli's *Pietà*, which more specifically is a lamentation, is now in Munich, at the Alte Pinakothek.

25 Lizzani, 'Riso amaro,' 166.

26 See Giuseppe De Santis, 'Il linguaggio dei rapporti,' in *Dai telefoni bianchi al neorealismo*, eds. Massimo Mida and Lorenzo Quaglietti, 149–51.

27 Giovanna Grignaffini, 'Verità e poesia: Ancora di Silvana e del cinema italiano.'

6: Myth and Reality among the Shepherds of Ciociaria

1 Before the film premièred in Milan on 28 October 1950, De Santis wanted his name removed from the credits because Lux, the distributor, had given in to the censors' request to change the director's off-screen comment from 'You have seen him struggle for his rights even against the law, because he felt in the right' to 'You have seen him struggle because he felt in the right.' The censors felt that the deleted phrase was an instigation to rebellion against the forces of the state. Lux and the censors won the argument, and the second version was chosen over De Santis's objections. On De Santis's comments on the dispute see Ugo Casiraghi, 'Intervista con il regista Giuseppe De Santis.'

2 Gianni Puccini, 'La quercie.'

3 Anna Gobbi, 'Fra i pastori in Ciociaria.'

4 Ennio Flaiani, 'La sinistra e d'Annunzio.'

5 Alberto Moravia, 'Neodannunzianesimo tra i Ciociari.'

6 Adriano Baracco, '"Non c'è pace tra gli ulivi".'

7 Giuseppe De Santis, 'Non c'è pace,' 261–2.

8 During one of our conversations, De Santis said: 'Had it been possible, I, all throughout my career, would have made only films about the South.' On De Santis's relationship with the South see 'Cinema, sud e memoria: Il regista Giuseppe De Santis racconta.'

9 Giuseppe De Santis, quoted in Antonio Parisi, *Il cinema di Giuseppe De Santis*, 73.

10 For example, see Parisi, ibid., 102.

11 For a reading of the final showdown between Francesco and Bonfiglio as an American Western see ibid.

12 All the quotes from the film are taken from De Santis's personal script, which he allowed me to consult during my visit to his home in Fiano Romano, in April 1991.

13 On De Santis's comments about Raf Vallone's (Francesco in the film) straight-on stares into the camera see Andrea Martini, 'Conversazione con Giuseppe De Santis: La ricerca realistica come impegno civile,' 130, and Fernaldo Di Giammatteo, '"Non c'è pace tra gli ulivi".' Di Giammatteo's article uses Eisenstein's essay on acting to criticize Franco Lulli's, Raf Vallone's, and Lucia Bosé's acting, which the critic finds exaggerated and heavily reliant on facial expressions.

14 Before this big cinematic return to peasant culture, De Sita made *Banditi a Orgosolo* (1961; Bandits at Orgosolo), which deals with banditry and sheep rustling in Sardinia.

7: The Stairway of Dreams and Illusions

1 On how De Santis could not find a producer for his film see Vice, 'Pro e contro De Santis,' *Mondo operaio,* 5 January 1954, 23.

2 For example, Tullio Cicciarelli, in *Lavoro-Nuovo,* 29 February 1952, finds *Roma, Ore 11* better than De Sica's *Umberto D.* For other critics the film marks the artistic coming of age of De Santis: see Guido Aristarco, '"Roma, Ore 11",' and Corrado Alvaro, 'Più che neorealismo.' Not all critics agree on the artistic merits of the film; for example, see Mira Liehm, *Passion and Defiance: Film in Italy from 1942 to the Present,* 96, and Nino Ghelli, '"Roma, Ore 11".'

3 On a Bollettino ANSA dated 4 July 1951, from Paris, De Santis, replying to Genina's insinuation of plagiarism, explains how his film is strictly based on the materials collected from a long investigation of the accident.

4 In the 1950s, there were millions of unemployed or underemployed, and for very many people in the South, conditions of life were desperate. Between 1955 and 1971, 9.14 million Italians were involved in interregional migration. For more details see Paul Ginsborg, *Storia d'Italia dal dopoguerra a oggi,* 291.

5 Giuseppe De Santis, 'Ricordo di Elio Petri,' in *Il cinema italiano d'oggi, 1970–1984: Raccontato dai suoi protagonisti,* eds. Franco Faldini and Goffredo Fofi, 291–3.

6 Elio Petri (Rome, 1929–1982), director, journalist, and scriptwriter, began his film career as a scriptwriter for De Santis. He is best known for making films dedicated to exploring the structure of society. Perhaps his best film is *Investigation of a Citizen above Suspicion* (1969).

7 See Aristarco, '"Roma, Ore 11",' 146.

8 After *Roma, Ore 11,* De Santis's name disappeared from the list of major Italian directors. The critic Alberto Farassino writes on the matter: 'De

Santis, at the beginning of the fifties, is already considered a finished author, a former protagonist fallen to the level of an extra': *Giuseppe De Santis*, 35. It is important to remember what happened in the political sphere during those tumultuous years. After the release of *Roma, Ore 11*, De Santis fell victim to the new legislative action adopted by the conservative government of Prime Minister Mario Scelba (January 1954 to June 1955). De Santis's film became the centre of a governmental discussion and inquiry. The government wanted to find out if De Santis's film had received financial support from the Soviet Union or if any of its earnings had supported or financed any activities related to the Italian Communist party (PCI). In January 1954, the government passed a strong resolution against governmental support of, distribution of, or loans to any film, director, or producer connected to or even influenced by the PCI. De Santis's name appeared at the top of the government's black list distributed to the producers. The list was published by ARI (the official press agency), and a press campaign against leftist directors followed. On 22 April 1954, the minister Giuseppe Ermini defended the new measures in an article published by *Il messaggero* (p. 11).

8: Could an Italian Male Marry an Everyman's Woman?

1 This information came up during one of our conversations at Fiano Romano, in spring 1991.
2 In Giannetti and Laurani's story, Anna Zaccheo was a beautiful girl from Perugia who, after a long period spent as a prostitute, married a rich Roman prince, who gave her a crown as a wedding gift; hence, the title of the story, 'A Crown for Anna Zaccheo.' After having agreed to use the story, De Santis convinced the other collaborators to change, not only the title, but also the social message of the film.
3 On the subject, De Santis told the jounalist Luigi Constantini: 'The problem that I deal with in the film is the false position that we insist on imposing on women. This problem belongs to and arises from male prejudices, which unfortunately are well developed in Italy': *Diorama*, March/April 1952, 15.
4 The *sceneggiata* is a Neapolitan popular play whose plot revolves around themes taken from popular and well-known songs in order to make the people participate. In the *sceneggiata*'s relation to cinema see Stefano Masi, 'Il cinema regionale delle sceneggiata.'
5 On the matter De Santis stated: 'Naturally I see Anna Zaccheo's story with eyes that, as always, try to penetrate reality. I foresee the objections and I must confess that this film will seem, to an extent, less problematic than

my other films. I must also add, in this regard, that the Neorealist road has become harder and to come to terms with censorship is not easy. I believe in the constructive language of the Neorealist cinema, but in today's conditions the task is almost desperate': ANSA, *Notiziario cinematografico* 7/825 (16 June 1953), 4.

6 Fausta Terni Cialente, 'Anna Zaccheo ovvero il trionfo delle gambe.'

7 Giuseppe De Santis, 'A proposito di un articolo di Fausta Cialente.'

8 Feraldo Feraldi, '"Un marito per Anna Zaccheo".'

9 On Forges-Davanzati's defence, see ANSA, *Notiziario cinematografico* 9/827 (16 September 1953), 2.

10 'The female question was not able to assume an adequate place in the political programs of the democratic movement, nor did it become a plaguing preoccupation of the intellectuals': Vittorio Spinazzola, *Cinema e pubblico*, 22.

11 For De Santis, the stairway stood for the ups and downs of human existence. For an interpretation of the stairs as related to the American musical see Piera Detassi, 'Anna Zaccheo: Questa donna è di tutti.'

12 Alberto Farassino, *Giuseppe De Santis*.

9: Honeymoon on a Bicycle

1 According to the critic Goffredo Fofi, the political intolerance of the 1950s together with the stronger censorship of those times were the direct result of the Yalta treaty between the superpowers. See Fofi, *Il cinema italiano: Servi e padroni*.

2 For a complete account of Italian cinema in the 1950s see Giorgio Tinazzi, ed., *Il cinema italiano degli anni '50*.

3 Carlo Ponti, quoted in Pierre Leprohon, *The Italian Cinema*, 127.

4 According to De Santis, the film is a fable dedicated to the youngsters. The dedication reads: 'This love fable is dedicated to all those girls and all those guys who, at last, are able to fulfil their dreams of marriage after many painful and extravagant vicissitudes.'

5 Giuseppe De Santis, Gianni Puccini, and Elio Petri, 'La parola agli autori del film "Giorni d'amore".' De Santis also wrote a long letter to Guido Aristarco, defending his film: De Santis, 'De Santis ci scrive.' The director's defence was followed by a long article written by Aristarco in which the critic faults De Santis's understanding of Gramsci's concept of popular culture: Aristarco, '"Giorni d'amore".'

6 Carlo Goldoni (1707–1793), Italian dramatist, is best known for having reformed Italian theatre by replacing the improvisation of an outlined plot in comedy with a fully developed script. Many critics maintain that *Le*

Baruffe chiozzotte, written between 1760 and 1762, is his best play. The story takes place in Chioggia, near Venice, and deals with the sudden spats between the fishermen's women and their lovers, and their reconciliation.

7 The Cantastorie were singers who sang and often recounted in verse peasant stories in public squares during local festivities.

8 De Santis, Puccini, and Petri, 'La parola agli autori del film "Giorni d'amore".'

9 Giuseppe De Santis, 'Confessioni di un regista,' 22.

10 For Purificato's collaboration on the film see Bruna D'Ettore, *Domenico Purificato dalla pittura al cinema*.

11 All of the quoted material is from the unpublished script that De Santis allowed me to consult at his house in Fiano Romano, in April 1991.

12 Commedia dell'arte, Italian popular comedy developed chiefly during the sixteenth to eighteenth century, involved massed entertainers improvising from a plot outline based on themes associated with stock characters and situations.

13 Antonio Gramsci, *Letteratura e vita nazionale*, 67.

10: A Fable of 'I Lupari,' a Vanished Breed

1 Carlo Lizzani, *Il cinema italiano*, 201.

2 Ibid., 200.

3 On the controversy see ibid., 194–202.

4 Ugo Casiraghi, 'Una favola moderna in Cinemascope con "Uomini e lupi" dei monti d'Abruzzo.'

5 Stefano Masi, *Giuseppe De Santis*, 81.

6 Casiraghi, 'Una favola moderna in Cinemascope.'

7 Masi, *Giuseppe De Santis*, 79.

8 On the debate see Cesare Zavattini, 'Una grossa botta in testa al neorealismo,' in *Antologia di 'Cinema nuovo,'* ed. Guido Aristarco, 888–92, and Guido Aristarco, 'Dal neorealismo al realismo: Senso di Visconti,' in *Letteratura e cinema*, ed. Gian Piero Brunetta, 87–96.

9 For example, Antonio Parisi, *Il cinema di Giuseppe De Santis*.

10 Eric Rhode, quoted in Phillip Robert, *The Altering Eye*, 66–7.

11: De Santis's Conception of Cinematic Realism

1 Jadran Film of Zagreb, first involved in the financing of the film, withdrew during the shooting because De Santis took more than the three months stipulated in the original contract.

2 The censorship operated on political matters. There are ample examples of its objectives: Andreotti's famous open letter after the showing of De Sica's *Umberto D*, which served to orient censors, directors, and producers. The censors' interference with the freedom of the cinema reached a climax with the trial of Renzo Renzi and Guido Aristarco, who had written *L'Armata Sagapò*, a script about the Italian war on Greece. They were tried in military court and sentenced to jail terms.

3 Maurizio Cesari, *La censura in Italia oggi (1944–1948)*.

4 Mino Argentieri and Ivano Cipriani, 'Fig Leaves and Politics.'

5 On the new credit system and awards law, and their effects on the industry see Lorenzo Quaglietti, *Storia economico-politica del cinema italiano*.

6 Argentieri and Cipriani, 'Fig Leaves and Politics,' 175.

7 For example, two articles, one in *Sicilia del popolo* (28 November 1959) and the other in *Giornale di Sicilia* (29 June 1959), mentioned that De Santis had taken more time than that stipulated in the contract. They also tried to besmirch the director's political ideas by questioning the high salary he received from the Yugoslav studio for this film. The authors of these articles either were unaware of or chose to ignore the director's statement published in ANSA, *Notiziario cinematografico* 8/285 (27 November 1957), 4, in which De Santis candidly discussed the funding for the film, its losses, and the problems involved in its production.

8 Stefano Masi, *Giuseppe De Santis*, 11.

9 Giuseppe De Santis, quoted in Enzo Muzii, 'La straola di De Santis.'

10 Antonio Parisi, *Il cinema di Giuseppe De Santis*, 166.

11 Giuseppe De Santis provided this information during one of our conversations at Middlebury College, summer 1993. De Santis's never-filmed scripts are discussed in the final chapter of this book.

12 At Middlebury, on 4 July 1993, De Santis remembered how once, from the Yugoslav side of Adriatic Sea, he made an obscene gesture in defiance of Andreotti to relieve his past frustrations.

13 Giuseppe De Santis, quoted in Muzii, 'La strada di De Santis.'

14 Ibid.

15 Giuseppe De Santis, 'Intervista con De Santis,' *L'Unità* 3/18 (1960), 9.

16 On the role of the intellectual see Antonio Gramsci, *Gli intellettuali e l'organizzazione della cultura*.

12: The End of the Bourgeois Family ...

1 Antonio Parisi states that he was not able to see the film in question: *Il cinema di Giuseppe De Santis*, 166. During my research in Italy I discovered

that the Italian film archives in Rome has an inflammable print of the film, which is not available for screening.

2 De Santis had heard Pettotondo's story during his childhood from his mother, Teresa Goduti, who was born in Apulia.

3 *Cesta Duga Godinu Dana* received a Golden Globe for best foreign film, and Massimo Girotti won an Oscar for best actor in a foreign film for his portrayal of Chiacchiera.

4 De Santis provided this information during one of our conversations in Fiano Romano in April 1991.

5 *La grande guerra* (The Great War), Luigi Comencini's 1959 mixture of black humour and anti-militarist rhetoric, is used polemically by De Santis to comment on the type of films that appealed in the late 1950s. The film shared the Lion d'Or with Rossellini's *General Della Rovere* at the Venice International Festival in 1959.

6 Giulio Cesare Castello, '"La Garçonnière".'

7 I am referring to the disorder described by Peter Truchtenberg in *The Casanova Complex*.

8 Arturo Lanocita, '"La Garçonnière".'

9 Stefano Masi, *De Santis*, 89.

10 Alberto Farassino, *Giuseppe De Santis*, 43.

11 Parisi, *Il cinema di Giuseppe De Santis*, 128.

12 Giuseppe De Santis, quoted in *Cinema e Mezzogiorno*, ed Vincenzo Camerino, 127.

13 On the Italian economic miracle see Giuliano Procacci, *History of the Italian People*, 379–83.

14 Mira Liehm, *Passion and Defiance: Film in Italy from 1942 to the Present*, 180.

15 For example, see Giulio Cesare Castello, 'Censura a macchia d'olio.'

16 See Farassino, *Giuseppe De Santis*, 45.

17 Alberto Fiorini's behaviour shows De Santis's critical attitude towards all the middle-aged Italian men who, in the 1950s, had rejected political involvement and were living without political ideals. Intertextually, the choice of the actor Raf Vallone for the part of the engineer Alberto Fiorini is appropriate; in fact, the actor had made his cinematic debut under De Santis's direction in the role of Marco, the positive populist hero, in *Riso amaro*. In 1950, he was also cast in the role of the good shepherd, Francesco Dominici, in *Non c'è pace tra gli ulivi*. In 1960, when De Santis cast him as Alberto Fiorini, Raf Vallone was one of the most famous and most highly paid actors in Italy and was not involved in politics. During the bitter political campaign of 1948, which determined Italy's position in the Western Alliance against the Eastern Bloc, Vallone posed as the father for a

political poster showing the future Italian socialist family. The other members of this family were Carla Del Poggio, who played Giovanna in *Caccia tragica* (and later married director Alberto Lattuada), and the young Luisa De Santis, the director's daughter.

18 The release of *La Garçonnière* was preceded by dissent and harsh polemics between the producer, Roberto Amoroso, and De Santis. The producer wanted the scene in which the mother of the slain partisan calls the Nazi-Fascists 'assassins' removed. Amoroso felt that the scene would impede the film's commercial and artistic success. De Santis's protest led to a lawsuit, which De Santis won, and the scene was retained in the final version of the film.

19 Censorship played a large role in the film's debut in Rome. At the Capranica theatre, on 22 November 1960, before the projectionist ran the film, two agents from public security walked into the projection room and cut the bedroom scene between Laura and Alberto. They were acting on an order from Ferrara's chief of police and in contravention of a government committee order that had given approval for the public release of the film, providing the director would cut 78 of the sequence's 336 frames.

20 Writing about the 1960s, Mira Liehm said: 'A new group of filmmakers eventually emerged out of the growing power of Italian cinema, bringing to life an extremely heterogeneous and shortlived phenomenon sometimes referred to as the New Italian Cinema': *Passion and Defiance: Film in Italy from 1942 to the Present*, 188.

13: March On or Die

1 Rossellini's film shared first prize with Monicelli's *La grande guerra*. Unlike Monicelli's film, which was criticized only by the conservatives, Rossellini's film also earned the approbation of Gino Guermandi and the son of General Roboletti, a general assassinated by the Gestapo's self-declared leftists. This criticism asserted that trying to pass off a coward and Nazi spy, Della Rovere, as a Resistance hero was an insult to the honour and memory of those killed during the Second World War. On the polemics concerning the interpretation of Della Rovere's character see Carlo Lizzani, *Il cinema italiano*, 250–1.

2 'Italiano brava gente,' the original title, was censored by the government. The film was later approved under the new title 'Italiani brava gente.' An English version with the original title is available in the United States. I have also seen, at Middlebury College, a different version with the title 'Attack and Retreat.'

3 On the war in Russia, British historian Denis Mack Smith writes: 'Mussolini had been given only the vaguest intimations of this fatal move and was
caught in the middle of negotiations with Russia for a commercial treaty.
Once again, however, he was completely taken by Hitler's confident assur-
ances of easy victory, and in a gross miscalculation, he insisted on sending
200,000 Italians to the Russian front, again contrary to Hitler's wishes and
without consulting even his own generals ... There Italians in Russia found
themselves faced with an impossible task, and they only learned to hate the
haughtiness and brutality of their German allies': *Italy*, 481.

4 On this subject historian Giuliano Procacci writes: 'With the attack on the
Soviet Union and the intervention of the USA in December 1941 the war,
as is well known, took an increasing turn for the worse for the Axis powers
... The tragedy was sealed by the news from Russia: in December 1942 and
January 1943 the Italian army of 110,000 men had been defeated, and
more than half its men died under enemy fire or from the cold. The few
survivors recount how their "German comrades" had refused them the
means of transport they needed to save themselves': *History of the Italian
People*, 367.

5 In a 1962 interview De Santis told journalist Franco Calderoni that Joe
Levine was involved in the film project and that actors Anthony Perkins
and Ernest Borgnine had been chosen. See Franco Calderoni, 'Dalla coproduzione al primo ciak in gennaio.' Before shooting began, these actors
were replaced by Peter Falk and Arthur Kennedy.

6 On this matter see Calderoni, ibid.

7 Denis Mack Smith writes: 'Italians, whether fascist or antifascist, fought
hard and loyally in their country's defence. Yet many of them felt from the
outset that their cause was wrong, and as visions of a quick and easy
victory weakened the war grew increasingly unpopular': *Italy*, 480.

8 Ibid., 423.

9 The black-shirted Arditi (shock troops) were originally an assault battalion
first formed in 1917, during the First World War. Under Mussolini, they
became more closely associated with Fascism than did the rest of the army.

10 Denis Mack Smith writes: 'Italians were staggered by German cruelty, and
even Mussolini was surprised that his allies could surpass him in brutality
and yet feel no compunction': *Italy*, 478. On Mussolini's disillusionment
with his people Smith writes: 'Mussolini was forced to admit to his foreign
minister ... that he had little faith in the Italian race ... He even said that
the Italians of 1914 were better than those of 1940, despite the fact that
this was a poor commentary on the achievements of fascism. Italians he
now described as a race of sheep': ibid., 480.

11 De Santis explains: 'We [authors] were interested in catching those moments of the war in which cruelty was overcome by dialogue between Russians and Italians. Discussions took place. The Russian civilians made a clear distinction between the Italian army and its German counterpart. The title "Italiani brava gente," despite being a little too patriotic, reflects an undeniable historical reality': Calderoni, 'Dalla coproduzione al primo ciak in gennaio.'

12 To enable his men to escape Sermanti stays behind with a few soldiers. When he receives the signal from his men that they have gotten past the encircling enemy, he starts to bury his fallen soldiers instead of trying to join those who have escaped. De Santis wanted the approaching Russian soldiers to give the honours of war before taking Sermanti and his men prisoner. The Russian producer refused, saying that it would have been too much. De Santis recounted this episode at Middlebury College at the Summer School session in 1993.

13 According to De Santis, the Russian producer did not want this episode in the film. He was able to persuade the Russians by using their disagreements with Chinese Marxists as proof that even communists could kill fellow communists. De Santis related this episode at Middlebury College in 1993.

14 The interview with the three writers appeared in *Tribuna del Mezzogiorno*, 3 September 1964, 13.

15 De Santis defended his film in an open letter he wrote to Giulio Andreotti, Minister of Defence, in which he reaffirmed the historical accuracy of his work, the characterization of the Italians, and the cruelty of the Germans. He mentioned that even Khrushchev had praised the behaviour of the Italian troops, adding that they had also committed base actions and that to conceal that fact would be a grave injustice to truth: 'Lettera aperta del regista De Santis al ministro della difesa Andreotti,' *Paesa sera*, 10 October 1964, 15.

16 Unpublished letter from De Santis to Marcel Oms, 11 April 1965.

14: Impotence as a Metaphor of the 1970s' Baffling Reality

1 The film was never made. De Santis told me that the Yugoslavian government, under pressure from its Romanian counterpart, decided against making the film.

2 De Santis said that he wanted to use Tomi, on the Black Sea, as a location for 'Ovidio, l'arte di amare' (Ovid, the Art of Love), since that was where Ovid died in exile. The Romanian government found the story pornographic and the depiction of local peoples offensive. De Santis maintains that the

Romanian opposition must derive from the representation of Ovid as the Emperor Augustus's political victim. The censors feared that such a characterization stood for freedom of artistic expression against political oppression.

3 De Santis told me that he could not convince the Soviet producers to finance the modern interpretation of Pushkin's story, written by De Santis and Ugo Pirro, and therefore decided against pursuing the project.

4 Angelo Solmi, 'Non sparate sul regista.'

5 I thank De Santis for letting me read his letter of 24 June 1972. Solmi wrote back on 30 June 1972, defending his professional integrity and critical objectivity.

6 The censors requested the deletion of a bedroom scene in Arduni's house in which the actress Fermi Benussi, playing Lucietta, is nude and her husband is about to engage in oral sex.

7 Giuseppe De Santis, quoted in Piera Patat, 'Il cinema di Giuseppe De Santis.'

8 For a definition and account of the *cinema civile* (political cinema) see John Michalczyk, *The Italian Political Filmmakers.*

9 For example see Solmi, 'Non sparate sul regista,' 124.

10 A collection of vocal pieces, essentially of profane inspiration, composed between the eleventh and the early thirteenth century, written primarily in vulgar Latin and occasionally in French and High German. These collections featured love songs, drinking songs, and attacks on the ecclesiastic orders.

11 The pop musician is Maurizio Vandelli, a friend of De Santis's daughter, Luisa, cast in the role of Nicola's wife in *Un apprezzato professionista* ...

12 Guido Aristarco, Giuseppe De Santis, Carlo Lizzani, and Aldo Vergano.

13 Giuseppe De Santis, quoted in Aldo Scagnetti, 'De Santis sette anni dopo; "Non cambio idea".'

14 In 1950 the Cassa per il Mezzogiorno, a special investment board for the South, was set up with substantial finances for building roads, dams, aqueducts, and irrigation works.

15 Vincenzo Arduni's climbing to the top of the building at Nicola's request can be read as the film's comment on his thirst for success, a sarcastic reference to the highest point of his career.

16 Giuseppe De Santis, 'Confessioni di un regista,' 22.

15: On the Margin

1 See Giuseppe De Santis, *Verso il neorealismo: Un critico cinematografico degli anni quaranta.*

2 De Santis worked as assistant director on *Ossessione* (Obsession), *Il sole sorge ancora* (The Sun Rises Again), and the unfinished 'Scalo merci' (Freight Yard).

3 Angelo Solmi, '"Caccia tragica" non ha portato i voti al fronte, il film di Giuseppe De Santis doveva essere l'antidoto di "Ninotchka",' 21.

4 In 1991 the Partito Comunista Italiano (PCI) dissolved and its members split into two new parties, the Partito della Sinistra (PDS) and the more radical Rifondazione Comunista (RC).

5 Andrea Martini and Marco Melani, 'De Santis,' in *Il neorealismo cinematografico italiano*, ed. Lino Miccichè, 307–17.

6 Unpublished letters kept in De Santis's studio at Fiano Romano: to Oms, dated 5 June 1966, and to Sadoul, dated 30 November 1955.

7 De Santis equated his concept of Neorealism and filmmaking with Antonio Gramsci's ideas concerning the creation of a new literature defined as political, historical, popular, and rooted in the people's culture, even if that culture might be conventional and backward.

8 These data are from Umberto Rossi, 'Ha dovuto o lo hanno fatto tacere?'

9 Adriano Baracco, '"Non c'è pace tra gli ulivi".'

10 On 30 November 1954, Excelsa Film SPA requested the cut of the scene that the presidency of the Council of Ministers would later order. The studio also asked that the money used during the five days in which the scene was filmed be reimbursed. A photocopy of the request is in my possession, signed by M. Cavalieri, Excelsa's attorney.

11 The information on the effects of the cold war on Hollywood are from Goffredo Fofi, Morando Morandi, and Gianni Volpi, *Storia del cinema*, vol. 2, 19–21.

12 ANSA, Notiziario cinematografico 6/121 (26 September 1953), 2.

13 Fausta Terni Cialente, 'Anna Zaccheo, ovvero il trionfo delle gambe.'

14 Giuseppe De Santis, 'Confessioni di un regista,' 29.

15 Ibid., 31.

16: From the Specific to the General

1 For example, Alberto Farassino, *Giuseppe De Santis*, or the special De Santis issue of *Cinema e cinema* 9/30 (1982).

2 For a critical definition of Neorealism see Bert Cardullo, *What Is Neorealism? A Critical English-Language Bibliography of Italian Cinematic Neorealism*.

3 I'm referring to the national debate provoked by *Riso amaro*. In October 1948, *L'Unità* protested that Silvana did not represent the typical Italian working woman. The film was also classified 'Forbidden to All Believers' by

the Catholic Film Centre because of its eroticism. In 1954 *Roma, Ore 11* provoked a government debate and was also classified 'Forbidden to All Believers.' *Non c'è pace tra gli ulivi* was reviewed by some the best-known Italian writers and critics of the time, such as Alberto Moravia, Corrado Alvaro, Ennio Flaiano, Ugo Casiraghi, Guido Aristarco, and Georges Sadoul. By the late 1950s, Da Santis's name had ceased to make front-page news. The critical interest that accompanied his films began to diminish with the release of *Un marito per Anna Zaccheo* (1953). Harassed by a government that had moved away from the liberal postwar aims, De Santis soon found himself without producers and financial support for his peasants' stories. He was forced to work in Yugoslavia to make *Cesta Duga Godinu Dana* (1958).

4 Giuseppe De Santis, 'Confessioni di un regista,' 19.

5 Giuseppe De Santis, 'Cinema e narrativa,' 20.

6 Ibid., 21.

7 De Santis, 'Confessioni di un regista,' 20.

8 For the debate on cinema and literature during the postwar period see Giorgio Tinazzi and Marina Zancan, eds., *Cinema e letteratura del neorealismo.*

9 De Santis's long and elaborate film titles have literary or filmic antecedents. For example, *Caccia tragica* (Tragic Pursuit) comes from a work of Chekhov; *Riso amaro* (Bitter Rice) from Emilio Cecchi's 1939 novel *America amara* (Bitter America); and De Santis's story 'Il nostro pane quotidiano,' unfortunately never filmed, from King Vidor's *Our Daily Bread* (1934).

10 On 11 May 1991, at his house in Fiano Romano.

Bibliography

Abruzzese, Alberto. *Forme estetiche e società di massa*. Venice: Marsilio Editori, 1973.
- 'La regola sociale dello spettacolo.' *Rinascita* 40 (October 1977), 25–6.
- '1943–1953: Appunti sullo sfondo economico sociale.' *Politica e cultura nel dopoguerra*. Quaderno informativo 56. X Mostra Internationale del Nuovo Cinema. Pesaro, 1974.
Adorno, Theodor W., and Hans Eisler. *La musica per film*. Rome: Newton Compton Editori, 1975.
Ajello, Nello. *Intellettuali e PCI, 1944–1958*. Rome–Bari: Laterza, 1979.
Albano, Vittorio. 'Il professionista.' [Review of *Un apprezzato professionista di sicuro avvenire*.] *L'Ora*, 29 April 1972, 14.
Alicata, Mario. 'Ambiente e società nel racconto cinematografico.' *Cinema* 135 (10 October 1942), 279–81.
Alicata, Mario, and Giuseppe De Santis. 'Verità e poesia: Verga e il cinema italiano.' *Cinema* 127 (10 October 1941), 216–17.
- 'Ancora di Verga e del cinema italiano.' *Cinema* 130 (25 November 1941), 314–15.
Alvaro, Corrado. 'Più che neorealismo.' *Il mondo*, 15 March 1952, 11.
Antonioni, Michelangelo. 'Per un film sul fiume Po.' *Cinema* 68 (April 1939), 254–7.
Aprà, Adriano. 'Rossellini oltre il neorealismo.' In *Il neorealismo cinematografico italiano*, ed. Lino Miccichè, 288–99. Venice: Marsilio Editori, 1975.
Aprà, Adriano, and Claudio Carabba, eds. *Neorealismo d'appendice – per un dibattito sul cinema popolare: Il caso Matarazzo*. Rimini–Florence: Guaraldi Editori, 1976.
Aprà, Adriano, and Luigi Martelli. 'Premesse sintagmatiche ad un'analisi di Viaggio in Italia.' *Cinema & Film* 2 (1967), 198–207.

Arbasino, Alberto. 'Fantasmi italiani/gli intellettuali, l'impegno, il potere. Pretende la segretaria il nuovo Poeta di Corte.' *La repubblica* 20 (July 1977), 19.

Argentieri, Mino. 'Allarmanti prospettive per il cinema pubblico.' *L'Unità*, 18 October 1974, 20.

– *La censura nel cinema italiano.* Rome: Editori Riuniti, 1974.

– 'Pregi e limiti del nuovo De Santis.' *Rinascita* 20 (1972), 19.

Argentieri, Mino, and Ivano Cipriani. 'Fig Leaves and Politics.' *Film Studies*, November 1961, 172–82.

Aristarco, Guido. *Antologia di cinema nuovo: 1952–1958.* Rimini–Florence: Guaraldi Editori, 1975.

– 'Dal neorelismo al realismo: Senso di Visconti.' In *Letteratura e cinema*, ed. Gian Piero Brunetta, 87–96. Bologna: Zanichelli, 1980.

– '"Giorni d'amore".' *Cinema nuovo* 50 (10 January 1955), 31–3.

– '"Roma, Ore 11".' *Cinema* 82 (15 March 1952), 146–7.

– *Sciolti dal giuramento: Il dibattito critico-ideologico sul cinema negli anni cinquanta.* Bari: Edizioni Dedalo, 1981.

Armes, Roy. *Patterns of Realism: A Study of Italian Neorealist Cinema.* Cranbury, NJ: A.S. Barnes, 1971.

Asor Rosa, Alberto. *Scrittori e popolo.* Rome: Savelli, 1975.

Autera, Leonardo. Review of *Un apprezzato professionista di sicuro avvenire. Corriere della sera*, 18 May 1972, 22.

Baldelli, Pio. *Cinema dell'ambiguità.* Rome: La Nuova Sinistra, 1971.

– 'Cronaca, realtà, poesia.' *Cinema nuova serie* 32 (1950), 70–2.

– '"Riso amaro".' *Cinema* 32 (30 January 1950), 70–2.

Baracco, Adriano. 'Etichette mortali.' *Cinema nuova serie* 48 (1950), 36.

– '"Non c'è pace tra gli ulivi".' *Cinema nuova serie* 48 (1950), 47.

Barbesi, Luigi. Review of *Un apprezzato professionista di sicuro avvenire. L'Arena di Verona*, 4 May 1972, 9.

Bavagnoli, Carlo. 'Via della Passerella.' *Cinema nuova* 47 (1954), 22.

Bazin, André. *Che cosa è il cinema?* Milan: Garzanti, 1973.

– *What Is Cinema? II.* Trans. Hugh Gray. Berkeley: University of California Press, 1971.

Bechelloni, Giovanni. *La macchina culturale in Italia.* Bologna: Il Mulino, 1974.

Bell, Daniel, Dwight Macdonald, Edward Shils, Clement Greenberg, Leo Lowenthal, Paul F. Lazarsfeld, and Robert K. Merton. *L'industria della cultura.* Trans. Adriana Dell'Orto and Annalisa Gersoni Kelly. Milan: Bompiani, 1969.

Bello, Marisa, and Stefano De Matteis. 'La sceneggiata.' *Scena* 1 (1977), 33–4.

Bellour, Raymond. *Il western. Fonti, forme, miti, registi, attori, filmografia*. Milan: Feltrinelli, 1973.

Bettetini, Gianfranco. *L'indice del realismo*. Milan: Bompiani, 1971.

– *Produzione del senso e messa in scena*. Milan: Bompiani, 1975.

– 'Vorrei un chilo di oggetti culturali.' *Il giorno*, 11 July 1977, 12.

Blasetti, Alessandro, and Gianluigi Rondi, eds. *Cinema italiano oggi*. Rome: Carlo Bestetti Edizioni d'Arte, 1950.

Bondanella, Peter. *Italian Cinema*. New York: Ungar, 1994.

– *Italian Cinema from Neorealism to the Present*. New York: Ungar, 1990.

– 'Neorealist Aesthetics and the Fantastic: The Machine to Kill Bad People and Miracles in Milan.' *Film Criticism* 3 (Winter 1979), 24–9.

Bondanella, Peter, ed. *Federico Fellini: Essays in Criticism*. New York: Oxford University Press, 1978.

Borde, Raymonde, and André Bouissy. *Le nouveau cinéma italien*. Lyon: Serdoc, 1963.

Bordoni, Carlo, and Franco Fassati. *Dal feuilleton al fumetto*. Rome: Editori Riuniti, 1985.

Bourget, Jean-Loup. 'Social Implications in the Hollywood Genres.' *Journal of Modern Literature* 13 (1973), 121–5.

Brunetta, Gian Piero. *Cinema italiano tra le due guerre: Fascismo e politica cinematografica*. Milan: Mursia, 1975.

– *Letteratura e cinema*. Bologna: Zanichelli, 1976.

– 'Non hanno pane? Diamogli dei film.' *La repubblica*, 12 October 1977, 19.

– 'Padri "buoni" e verità scomode.' *La repubblica*, 27 October 1976. Reprinted in *Cinema italiano sotto il fascismo*, ed. Riccardo Redi, 261–3. Venice: Marsilio Editori, 1979.

– *Storia del cinema italiano dal 1945 agli anni ottanta*. Rome: Editori Riuniti, 1982.

– *Storia del cinema italiano, 1895–1945*. Rome: Editori Riuniti, 1979.

Bruno, Edoardo. '"Roma, Ore 11".' *Filmcritica* 13 (February 1952), 50–1.

Bruno, Edoardo, ed. *Teorie e prassi del cinema in Italia, 1950–1970*. Milan: Gabriele Mazzotta, 1972.

Buache, Freddy. *Le cinéma italien d'Antonioni a Rosi*. Paris: Maspero, 1969.

– *Le cinéma italien 1945–1979*. Lausanne: Editions l'age d'Homme, 1979.

Buss, Robin. *Italian Films*. New York: Holmes and Meier, 1989.

Calasso, Robert. 'Il guanto di Gilda.' *Panorama* 601 (25 October 1977), 95.

Calderoni, Franco. 'Dalla coproduzione al primo ciak in gennaio.' *Il giorno*, 16 November 1962, 12.

Caldiron, Orio, ed. *Il lungo viaggio del cinema italiano. Antologia di 'Cinema' 1936–1943*. Padua: Marsilio, 1965.

Calvino, Italo. *I sentieri dei nidi di ragno*. Turin: Einaudi, 1967.
- 'Tra i pioppi della risaia la "cinecittà" delle mondine.' *L'Unità*, 14 July 1948, 3.
Camerino, Vincenzo. *Il cinema di Giuseppe De Santis*. Lecce: Elle Edizione, 1982.
Camerino, Vincenzo, ed. *Cinema e Mezzogiorno*. Lecce: Specimen Edizione, 1987.
Campari, Roberto. 'America, cinema e mass-media nel neorealismo italiano.' *Cinema e cinema* 10 (1977), 62–9.
- *I modelli narrativi. Cinema americano 1945–1973*. Parma: La Nazionale, 1974.
Cannella, Mario. 'Ideology and Aesthetic Hypotheses in the Criticism of Neorealism.' *Screen* 14/4 (Winter 1973/4), 5–60.
Cannistrato, Philip V. 'Ideological Continuity and Cultural Coherence.' *Bianco e nero* 36/9–12 (September/December 1975), 14–19.
- *La fabbrica del consenso: Fascismo e mass media*. Rome–Bari: Laterza, 1975.
Canziani, Alfonso. *Gli anni del neorealismo*. Florence: La Nuova Italia 1977.
Canziani, Alfonso, and Cristina Bragaglia, eds. *La stagione neorealista*. Bologna: Cooperativa Libraria Universitaria, 1976.
Cardullo, Bert. *What Is Neorealism? A Critical English-Language Bibliography of Italian Cinematic Neorealism*. New York: University Press of America, 1991.
Carpi, Fabio. *Cinema italiano del dopoguerra*. Milan: Schwarz Editore, 1958.
Casetti, Francesco. *Bertolucci*. Florence: La Nuova Italia, 1975.
- *Dentro lo sguardo. Il film e il suo spettatore*. Milan: Bompiani, 1986.
Casiraghi, Ugo. 'Angela e Pasquale fuggono per coronare i loro "Giorni d'amore".' *L'Unità*, 9 December 1954, 9.
- 'Intervista con il regista Giuseppe De Santis.' *L'Unità*, 4 October 1950, 8.
- '"Non c'è pace tra gli ulivi".' *L'Unità*, 15 October 1950, 9.
- '200 ragazze incontro alla morte per 15.000 lire di stipendio.' *L'Unità*, 28 February 1952, 10.
- 'Una favola moderna in Cinemascope con "Uomini e lupi" dei monti d'Abruzzo.' *L'Unità*, 17 February 1957, 13.
Castello, Giulio Cesare. 'Censura a macchia d'olio.' *Punto d'attualità*, November 1960, 7.
- '"Giorni d'amore".' *Cinema nuova serie* 146/7 (1954), 37.
- *Il cinema neorealistico italiano*. Turin: Edizioni Radio Italiana, 1959.
- '"La Garçonnière".' *Corriere della sera*, 19 April 1961, 27.
Cavicchioli, Luigi. 'Non è il solito prete.' *Domenica del corriere*, 27 April 1972, 95.
Cesari, Maurizio. *La censura in Italia oggi (1944–1948)*. Naples: Liguori Editore, 1982.

Chiaretti, Tommaso. 'Il regista De Santis parla dei suoi film.' *L'Unità*, 17 February 1952, 9.

Chiti, Roberto, and Roberto Poppi, eds. *Dizionario del cinema italiano*. Rome: Gremese Editore, 1991.

Cialente, Fausta Terni. 'Anna Zaccheo, ovvero il trionfo delle gambe.' *L'Unità*, 21 January 1954, 4.

Cinema e cinema 9/30 (1982). Special De Santis issue.

Cirio, Rita. 'Telefoni bianchi pieni di polvere.' *L'Espresso* 5 (November 1977), 61–3.

Cleopazzo, Giampiero. *Il neorealismo di Giuseppe De Santis*. Galantina: Editrice Salentina, 1980.

Codelli, Lorenzo. 'Vivan las cadenas (notes sur *Catene*).' *Positif* 183/4 (1976), 22–5.

Cosulich, Callisto. 'Ho voluto tagliare le gambe di Marina.' *Cinema nuovo* 48 (1954), 18–22.

– Review of *Un apprezzato professionista di sicuro avvenire*. ABC, 5 May 1972, 62.

– '"Ritratto in piedi" per un Ente seduto.' *Paesa sera*, 21 November 1974, 19.

Crocenzi, Luigi. 'Andiamo in processione.' *Il politecnico* 35 (1947), 21–3.

Costa, Antonio. 'Conversazione con Giuseppe De Santis.' *Cinema e cinema* 9/30 (1982), 65–72.

De Libero, Libero. *Ascolta la Ciociaria*. Rome: De Luca, 1953.

– 'Ciociaro come la Ciociaria.' *Milano sera*, 18 October 1950, 19–20.

Dell'Acqua, Gian Piero. 'L'elusiva guerra di De Santis.' *Cinema 60* 46 (1964), 52.

De Sanctis, Filippo M. 'De Santis, Giuseppe.' In *Filmlexicon degli autori e delle opere*, vol. 1, 244–5. Rome: Edizioni di Bianco e Nero, 1958.

De Santis, Giuseppe. 'A proposito di un articolo di Fausta Cialente.' *L'Unità*, 16 February 1954, 5.

– 'Birth, Development, and Death of Neorealism.' Ed. and trans. Lorraine Lawton and Ben Lawton. In *1989 Romance Languages Annual*, ed. Ben Lawton and Anthony Tamburri, 2–6. West Lafayette: Purdue Research Foundation, 1990.

– 'Cinema e narrativa.' *Film d'oggi* 21 (June 1945), 1–16.

– 'Cinema, sud e memoria: Il regista Giuseppe De Santis racconta.' *Paese sera*, 16, 18, 22, 29 July; 1 and 5 August 1981.

– 'Confessioni di un regista.' *La rivista del cinema italiano* 1/2 (January/February 1953), 18–41.

– 'De Santis ci scrive a proposito di "Giorni d'amore".' *Cinema nuovo* 49 (25 December 1954), 427–9.

- 'E in crisi il neorealismo?' *Filmcritica* 4 (March/April 1951), 109–12.
- 'E con "Ossessione" osai il primo giro di manovella.' *Cinema nuovo* 3 (June 1984), 15–19; 4 / 5 (August/October 1984), 26–9.
- ' "Giorni d'amore" e la critica.' *Cinema nuovo* 49 (25 December 1954), 401.
- 'Il linguaggio dei rapporti." In *Dai telefoni bianchi al neorealismo*, eds. Massimo Mida and Lorenzo Quaglietti, 149–51. Rome–Bari: Laterza, 1980.
- 'Malafede nel cinematografo.' *Vie nuove*, 5 November 1950, 29.
- 'Il malessere del cinema italiano: La sinistra ha rinunciato.' In *Cinema e Mezzogiorno*, ed. Vincenzo Camerino, 119–22. Lecce: Specimen Edizione 1987.
- 'Lettera aperta del regista De Santis al ministro della difesa Andreotti.' *Paese sera*, 10 October 1964, 15.
- 'L'ultimo dei Mohicani.'. In *Il cinema italiano d'oggi 1970–1984: Raccontato dai suoi protagonisti*, eds. Franca Faldini and Goffredo Fofi, 504–6. Milan: Mondadori, 1984.
- 'Malafede nel cinematografo.' *Vie nuove*, 5 November 1950, 29.
- 'Non c'è pace.' [Letter to Adriano Baracco.] *Cinema nuova* serie 50 (November 1950), 38.
- 'Per un paesaggio italiano.' In *Dai telefoni bianchi al neorealismo*, eds. Massimo Mida and Lorenzo Quaglietti, 198–201. Rome–Bari: Laterza, 1980.
- 'Quattro passi fra le nuvole.' *Cinema* 157 (10 January 1943), 133–6.
- 'Quel giorno di febbraio a cavallo di una grù.' *Cinema Giovani*, September 1982, 22. Reprinted in *Paese sera*, April 1983, 10.
- 'Relazione al convegno sul realismo.' *Il contemporaneo*, 1959. Reprinted in *Storia del cinema italiano*, ed. Carlo Lizzani, 361–3. Milan: Parenti, 1961.
- 'Scuole. Quelli del "Centro"' and 'Scuole. La rivista di "Vi" Mussolini.' In *L'avventurosa storia del cinema italiano raccontata dai suoi protagonisti, 1935–1959*, eds. Franca Faldini and Goffredo Fofi, 40–1 and 44–8. Milan: Feltrinelli, 1979.
- 'Sogni del cineasta.' *Cinema* 118 (16 June 1941), 451.
- 'Stampe.' *Cinema* 123 (10 August 1941), 449.
- 'Una lettera a Adriano Baracco.' *Cinema nuova* serie 50 (15 November 1950), 38.
- 'Una lettera di De Santis.' *Cinema nuovo* 100 (20 November 1954), 416.
- 'Un garibaldino al convento.' *Cinema* 139 (10 April 1943), 198.
- 'Un pilota ritorna.' In *Dai telefoni bianchi al neorealismo*, eds. Massimo Mida and Lorenzo Quaglietti, 257–60. Rome–Bari: Laterza, 1980.
- *Verso il neorealismo: Un critico cinematografico degli anni quaranta*. Ed. Callisto Cosulich. Rome: Bluzoni, 1982.
- 'Verso un cinema italiano.' *Bianco e nero* , 12 June 1942, 19–20.

- 'Vola ancora l'aereo Zavattini.' *L'Unità*, 13 October 1990, 19.
De Santis, Giuseppe, Corrado Alvaro, and Basilio Franchina. 'Noi che facciamo crescere il grano.' *Cinema nuova* 18 (1 September 1953), 139–42; 20 (1 October 1953), 215–18.
De Santis, Giuseppe, and Gianni Puccini. 'I figli di Zorro.' *Cinema* 103 (10 October 1940), 271–2.
De Santis, Giuseppe, Gianni Puccini, and Elio Petri. 'La parola agli autori del film "Giorni d'amore".' *L'Unità*, 19 December 1954, 10.
De Sica, Vittorio. 'Opinioni sul neorealismo.'. In *L'avventurosa storia del cinema italiano raccontata dai suoi protagonisti, 1935–1959*, eds. Franca Faldini and Goffredo Fofi, 78–81. Milan: Feltrinelli, 1979.
Detassis, Piera. 'Anna Zaccheo: Questa donna è di tutti.' *Cinema e cinema* 9/30 (1982), 54–61.
D'Ettore, Bruna. *Domenico Purificato dalla pittura al cinema.* Rome: Cadmo, 1988.
Di Giammatteo, Fernaldo. 'Cinema italiano 1945–1955: Storia di un'illusione e di un fallimento.' *Il ponte* 4/5 (1955), 682–6.
- '"Non c'è pace tra gli ulivi".' *Bianco e nero* 50 (December 1950), 78–81.
- '"Riso amaro".' *Bianco e nero* 12 (December 1949), 53–6.
Donaggio, Adriano. 'Sono andato a teatro per tre sere (colloquio con Marshall McLuhan).' *L'Espresso* 39 (October 1977), 13.
Dorfles, Gillo. 'Com'è bello, sembra falso.' *Corriere della sera*, 1 August 1977, 13.
Durgnat, Raymond. 'Genre: Populism and Social realism.' *Film Comment*, July/August 1975, 20–9.
Eco, Umberto. *Apocalittici e integrati.* Milan: Bompiani, 1965.
- *Opera aperta.* Milan: Bompiani, 1965.
Escobar, Roberto. 'Il ventennio nero.' *L'Avanti*, 16 October 1976, 19.
Faldini, Franca, and Goffredo Fofi, eds. *L'avventurosa storia del cinema italiano raccontata dai suoi protagonisti,1935–1959.* Milan: Feltrinelli, 1979.
Farassino, Alberto. 'Caro Lizzani, non si combatte a occhi chiusi.' *La repubblica*, 19 October 1976, 19–20. Reprinted in *Cinema italiano sotto il fascismo*, ed. Riccardo Redi, 256–8. Venice: Marsilio Editori, 1979.
- 'E adesso la guerra diventa finzione.' *La repubblica*, 4 March 1977, 19.
- *Giuseppe De Santis.* Milan: Moizzi, 1978.
- 'Trent'anni di commedia all'italiana.' *La repubblica*, 20 and 29 July, 6 August 1977, 13–16, 15–17, 16–18.
Farassino, Alberto, and Sergio Grmek Germani. *Fantascena.* XV Festival Internazionale del Film di Fantascienza. Trieste, 1977.
Ferladi, Feraldo. '"Un marito per Anna Zaccheo".' *Fiera letteraria*, 27 January 1953, 6.

Ferraù, Alessandro, ed. *Annuario del cinema italiano, 1976–1977*. Rome: Centro Studi di Cultura, Promozione e Diffusione del Cinema, 1977.

Ferraù, Alessandro, and Gino Caserta, eds. *Annuario del cinema italiano, 1967–1968*. Rome: Centro Studi di Cultura, Promozione e Diffusione del Cinema, 1969.

Ferraro, Adelio, ed. *Momenti di storia del cinema*. Florence: Centro Studi del Consorzio Toscano Attività Cinematografiche, 1965.

Ferrini, Franco. 'I generi classici del cinema americano.' *Bianco e nero* 3/4 (March/April 1974), 4–109 (special issue).

Filippini, Enrico. 'I "poverissimi" anni cinquanta quando il mondo cambiava stile.' *La repubblica*, 13 October 1977, 14.

Flaiano, Ennio. 'La sinistra e D'Annunzio.' *Il mondo*, 1 July 1950, 10.

Fofi, Goffredo. 'A sud del cinema italiano: Incontro con Giuseppe De Santis." *Scena*, June/July 1981, 34–5.

– *Il cinema italiano: Servi e padroni*. Milan: Peltrinelli, 1977.

– 'La sceneggiata uccisa dalla storia e dai neofiti.' *Scena* I (1977), 12–16.

Fofi, Goffredo, Morando Morandi, and Gianni Volpi, eds. *Storia del cinema*, 4 vols. Milan: Garzanti, 1992.

Fortini, Franco. 'Il realismo italiano nel cinema e nella narrativa.' *Cinema nuovo* 2 (1953), 13, 362–3.

Franco, Mario, ed. *Il cinema popolare italiano negli anni '50: Roberto Amoroso*. Naples: La Cineteca Altro. 1976.

Fratelli, Arnaldo. 'Tra cinema e letteratura.' *Filmcritica* 19 (June 1952), 198–200.

Furno, Mariella, and Renzo Renzi, eds. *Il neorealismo del fascismo: Giuseppe De Santis e la critica cinematografica: 1941–1943*. Bologna: Edizioni della Tipografia Compositori, 1984.

Gallo, Giuliano. 'Erano bianchi o neri?' *Panorama* 551 (9 November 1976), 129–31.

Gambini, Antonio. *Storia del dopoguerra. Dalla liberazione al potere DC*. Rome–Bari: Laterza, 1975.

Ghelli, Nino. '"Giorni d'amore".' *Bianco e nero* 1/2 (1955), 116–17.

– '"Roma, Ore 11".' *Bianco e nero* 1 (April 1954), 84–9.

– '"Roma, Ore 11".' *Bianco e nero* 17 (February 1952), 84–9.

– '"Un marito per Anna Zaccheo".' *Bianco e nero* 1
(March 1954), 84–5.

Gili, Jean A. *Le cinéma italien à l'ombre des faisceaux (1922–1945)*. Paris: Institut Jean Vigo, 1990.

– 'Quattro passi fra le nuvole contro il mito della falsa felicità.' *La repubblica*, 2 November 1976, 15.

Ginsborg, Paul. *Storia d'Italia dal dopoguerra a oggi*. Turin: Einaudi, 1989.

Gobbi, Anna. 'Come abbiamo lavorato per "Riso amaro".' *Cinema nuova serie* 8 (15 February 1949), 243–5.

- 'Fra i pastori in Ciociaria.' *L'Unità*, 12 December 1950, 8.

Goimard, Jacques. 'La rose des genres à Hollywood.' *Positif* 177 (1976), 34–9.

Gramsci, Antonio. *An Antonio Gramsci Reader: Selected Writings, 1916–1935*. Ed. David Forgacs. New York: Schocken, 1988.

- *Gli intellettuali e l'organizzazione della cultura*. Turin: Einaudi, 1966.

- *Letteratura e vita nazionale*. Rome: Editori Riuniti, 1971.

Grignaffini, Giovanna. 'Petri e Rosi: Timeo Danaos et dona ferentes.' *Cinema e cinema* 7/8 (April/September 1976), 100–8.

- 'Verità e poesia: Ancora di Silvana e del cinema italiano.' *Cinema e cinema* 9/30 (1982), 41–6.

Grmek Germani, Sergio. 'Cinema italiano sotto il fascismo: Proposta di periodizzazione.' In *Materiali sul cinema italiano 1929–1943*, quad. inf., 63. Pesaro: Undicesima Mostra Internazionale del Nuovo Cinema, 1975.

Gromo, Mario. *Cinema italiano (1903–1953)*. Milan: Mondadori, 1954.

Guidi, Guidarino, and Luigi Malerba. 'Che cosa pensano del pubblico. (Inchiesta. Riposta de De Santis).' *Cinema N.N.* 78 (1952), 42.

Hay, James. *Popular Film Culture in Fascist Italy: The Passing of the Rex*. Bloomington: Indiana University Press, 1987.

Ingrao, Pietro. 'Lucchino Visconti: L'antifascismo e il cinema.' *Rinascita*, 26 March 1976, 6.

Kaminsky, Stuart M. *American Film Genres: Approaches to a Critical Theory of Popular Film*. New York: Dell, 1977.

Kazev, Ivan. *Giuseppe De Santis*. Moscow: Iskustvu, 1965.

Kezich, Tullio. 'Neorealismo rosa.' *Letteratura* 13/14 (1955), 204–7.

Kolker, Robert Phillip. *The Altering Eye: Contemporary International Cinema*. New York: Oxford University Press, 1983.

Kyrou, Ado. *Amour-érotisme et cinéma*. Paris: Le Terrain Vague, 1957.

Landy, Marcia. *Fascism in Film: The Italian Commercial Cinema, 1931–1943*. Princeton: Princeton University Press, 1986.

Lane, John Francis. 'De Santis and Italian Neo-Realism.' *Sight and Sound* 5/6 (August 1950), 245–7.

Lanocita, Arturo. '"La Garçonnière".' *Corriere della sera*, 19 April 1961, 27.

La Polla, Franco. 'Il genere come sottoprodotto.' *Cinema e cinema* 7/8 (1976), 68–71.

Lawton, Ben. *Italian Cinema: Literary and Political Trends*. Los Angeles: Center for Italian Studies, University of California at Los Angeles, 1975.

- 'Italian Neorealism: A Mirror Construction of Reality.' *Film Criticism* 3 (Winter 1979), 8–23.

Leone, Francesco. 'Una lettera su "Riso amaro".' *L'Unità*, 5 October 1949, 13.

Leprohon, Pierre. *The Italian Cinema*. Trans. Roger Greaves and Oliver Stallybrass. London: Secker and Warburg, 1972.

Liehm, Mira. *Passion and Defiance: Film in Italy from 1942 to the Present*. Berkeley and Los Angeles: University of California Press, 1984.

Lizzani, Carlo. *Il cinema italiano*, 3d ed. Rome: Editori Riuniti, 1992.

– *Il cinema italiano, 1895–1979*. Rome: Editori Riuniti, 1979.

– 'Questi borghesucci erano prefascisti.' *La repubblica*, 16 October 1976, 3–4. Reprinted in *Cinema italiano sotto il fascismo*, ed. Riccardo Redi, 253–5. Venice: Marsilio Editori, 1979.

– *'Riso amaro': Un film diretto da Giuseppe De Santis*. Rome: Officina Edizioni, 1978.

Lizzani, Carlo.'Mondine e pastori.' In *L'avventurosa storia del cinema italiano raccontata dai suoi protagonisti, 1935–1959*, eds. Franca Faldini and Goffredo Fofi, 153–7. Milan: Feltrinelli, 1979.

Luperini, Romano. *Marxismo e intellettuali*. Venice: Marsilio Editori, 1974.

Lutzemberger, Maria G., and Sergio Bernardi, eds. *Cultura, comunicazioni, lotta di classe*. Roma: Savelli, 1976.

Mack Smith, Denis. *Italy: A Modern History*. Ann Arbor: University of Michigan Press, 1959.

McLuhan, Marshall. *Understanding Media*. New York: McGraw-Hill, 1964.

Mancini, Elaine. 'Giuseppe De Santis.' In *The International Dictionary of Films and Filmmakers*. Vol. 2, *Directors and Filmmakers*, ed. Christopher Lyon, 131–2. Chicago: St James Press, 1984.

– *Struggles of the Italian Film Industry during Fascism, 1930–1935*. Ann Arbor: University of Michigan Research Press, 1985.

Marcus, Millicent. 'De Santis's "Bitter Rice": A Neorealist Hybrid.' In *Italian Film in the Light of Neorealism*, 76–95. Princeton, NJ: Princeton University Press.

– *Italian Film in the Light of Neorealism*. Princeton, NJ: Princeton University Press, 1986.

Marmori, Giancarlo. 'Cinefilo 1e e la sua piramide.' *L'Espresso*, 5 October 1977, 17.

Marotta, Giuseppe. 'Noi che facciamo crescere il grano.' *Cinema nuovo* 18 (November 1953), 139–42.

– 'San Gennaro pensaci tu.' *Cinema nuova serie* 18 (1 September 1953), 137–8.

Martelli, Sebastiano. *Il crepuscolo dell'identità*. Salerno: La Veglia Editore, 1988.

Martini, Andrea. 'Conversazione con Giuseppe De Santis: La ricerca realistica come impegno civile.' In *Cinema e Mezzogiorno*, ed. Vincenzo Camerino, 123–31. Lecce: Specimen Edizioni, 1987.

Martini, Andrea, and Marco Melani. 'De Santis.' In *Il neorealismo cinematografico italiano*, ed. Lino Miccichè, 307–17. Venice: Marsilio Editori, 1975.

Martini, Stelio. 'Viaggio di nozza in bicicletta.' *Cinema nuovo* 28 (1 February 1954), 38–9.

Masi, Stefano. *De Santis*. Florence: La Nuova Italia, 1982

– 'Il cinema regionale della sceneggiata.' *Cineforum* 184 (May 1979), 266–81.

Matarazzo, Raffaello. '37 milioni di spettatori hanno visto i miei film.' *L'Unità*, 18 December 1955, 10.

Menon, Gianni. 'Renato Castellani in periodo neorealista.' In *Il neorealismo cinematografico italiano*, ed. Lino Miccichè, 318–27. Venice: Marsilio Editori, 1975.

Metz, Christian. *La significazione nel cinema*. Milan: Bompiani, 1975.

Miccichè, Lino. 'De Santis e la trilogia della terra.' In *Il cinema di Giuseppe De Santis*, ed. Vincenzo Camerino, 149–56. Lecce: Elle Edizioni, 1982.

– *Il cinema italiano degle anni '6o*. Venice: Marsilio Editori, 1975.

– *Il neorealismo cinematografico italiano*. Venice: Marsilio Editori, 1975.

– 'Per una verifica del neorealismo.' In *Il neorealismo cinematografico italiano*, ed. Lino Miccichè, 7–28. Venice: Marsilio Editori, 1975.

– 'Quando una nave è un desiderio.' *Avanti*, 20 October 1977, 9.

– 'Un'alternativa epica al neorealismo.' *Aut*, May 1975, 307–17.

– *Visconti e il neorealismo*. Venice: Marsilio Editori, 1990.

Michalczyk, John. *The Italian Political Filmmakers*. Rutherford, NJ: Fairleigh Dickinson University Press, 1986.

Mida, Massimo. 'Cinema e antifascismo: Testimonianza su una genesi.' In *Dai telefoni bianchi al neorealismo*, eds. Massimo Mida and Lorenzo Quaglietti, 275–85. Rome–Bari: Laterza, 1980.

Mida, Massimo, and Lorenzo Quaglietti, eds. *Dai telefoni bianchi al neorealismo*. Rome–Bari: Laterza, 1980.

Mignone, Mario B., ed. *Columbus: Meeting of Cultures*. Proceedings of the Symposium held at the State University of New York at Stony Brook, 16–17 October 1992. New York: Forum Italicum, 1993.

Montesanti, Fausto. 'Della ispirazione cinematografica.' *Cinema* 129 (10 November 1941), 280–1.

Moravia, Alberto. 'Neodannunzianesimo tra i Ciociari.' *Vie nuove*, 8 October 1950, 12.

Morin, Edgar. *Le cinéma ou l'homme imaginaire*. Paris: Ed. de Minuit, 1958; *Il cinema o dell'immaginario*. Milan: Silva Editore 1962.

– *L'ésprit du temps*. Paris. Ed. de Minuit, 1962; *L'industria culturale*. Bologna: Il Mulino, 1963.

– *Les stars*. Paris. Editions du Seuil, 1957; *I divi*. Milan: Garzanti, 1977.

Murgia, Pier Giuseppe. *Il vento del nord*. Milan: SugarCo Edizioni, 1978.

Muscio, Giuliana. *Hollywood/Washington. L'industria cinematografica americana nella guerra fredda*. Padua: CLEUP, 1977.

Muzii, Enzo. 'La strada di De Santis.' *L'Unità*, 6 February 1960, 3.

Napoli, Gregorio. 'Il sacrificio del prete.' Review of *Un apprezzato professionista di sicuro avvenire*. *Il giornale di Sicilia*, 29 April 1972, 15.

Oms, Marcel. 'Giuseppe De Santis.' *Positif*, 23 April 1957, 13–23.

Overby, David, ed. *Springtime in Italy: A Reader in Neorealism*. Hamden, CT: Archon Books, 1979.

Parisi, Antonio. *Il cinema di Giuseppe De Santis: Tra passione e ideologia*. Roma: Cadmo Editore, 1983.

Patat, Piera. 'Il cinema di Giuseppe De Santis.' Thesis, University of Trieste, 1976–7.

Pavolini, Alessandro. 'Il rapporto della cinematografia italiana.' In *Dai telefoni bianchi al neorealismo*, eds. Massimo Mida and Lorenzo Quaglietti, 34–8. Rome–Bari: Laterza, 1980.

Pellizzari, Lorenzo, ed. *Cineromanzo: Il cinema italiano, 1945–1953*. Milan: Longanesi, 1978.

– Review of *Italiani brava gente*. *Cinema nuovo* 172 (April 1964), 134–6.

Petri, Elio. *'Roma, Ore 11.'* Milan-Rome: Edizioni Avantii, 1956.

Placido, Beniamino. 'Maciste in lotta con la critica.' *La repubblica*, 16 October 1977, 14.

– 'Mille lire al mese: Una risposta a milioni di baionette.' *La repubblica*, 29 October 1976. Reprinted in *Cinema italiano sotto il fascismo*, ed. Riccardo Redi, 264–6. Venice: Marsilio Editori, 1979.

– 'Proibito giocare: L'ha detto il professore.' ·*La repubblica*, 25 October 1977, 15.

Ponte, Luca. 'Un pittore cineasta riscopre la sua Ciociaria.' *Cinema* 12/135 (10 June 1954), 327–32.

Procacci, Giuliano. *History of the Italian People*. Trans. Anthony Paul. New York: Harper and Row, 1970.

Puccini, Gianni. 'Il venticinque luglio del cinema italiano.' *Filmcritica* 24 (December 1953), 340–1.

– 'I tempi di *Cinema*.' *Filmcritica* 5 (May 1951), 151–5.

Puccini, Massimo Mida. 'Le quercie.' *L'Unità*, 1 December 1949, 6.

Purificato, Domenico. 'Pittura e cinema. L'avventura del colore.' *Cinema* 3 (April 1940), 93–106.

– 'Spettacolo e realtà.' *Cinema* 75 (25 January 1956), 36.

Quaglietti, Lorenzo.. *Il cinema italiano del dopoguerra. Leggi, produzione, distribuzione, esercizio*, quad. inf. 58. Pesaro: Mostra Intern. del Cinema nuova, 1974.

- 'Situazione del cinema realistico.' *Rassegne*, Fall 1954, 338–52.
- *Storia economico-politica del cinema italiano*. Rome: Editori Riuniti, 1980.
Renzi, Renzo. '"Riso amaro".' *Cinema* 24 (15 December 1949), 318.
Rondi, Gian Luigi. 'Validità del neorealismo italiano.' *Teatro scenario*, 15 July 1952, 21–2.
Rondolini, Gianni. *Dizionario del cinema italiano: 1945–1969*. Turin: Einaudi, 1969.
Rondolini, Gianni, ed. *Catalogo Bolaffi del cinema italiano, primo volume: Tutti i film dal 1945 al 1955*. Turin: Bolaffi, 1967, 1977.
Rossi, Umberto. 'Ha dovuto o lo hanno fatto tacere?' In *Il cinema di Giuseppe De Santis*, ed. Vincenzo Camerino, 65–81. Lecce: Elle Edizione, 1982.
Sadoul, Georges. *Dictionary of Filmmakers*. Trans., ed., and updated by Peter Morris. Berkeley and Los Angeles: University of California Press, 1972.
Savio, Francesco. *Ma l'amore no. Realismo, formalismo, propaganda e telefoni bianchi nel cinema italiano di regime (1930–1943)*. Milan: Sonzogno, 1975.
Scagnetti, Aldo. 'De Santis sette anni dopo: "Non cambio idea".' *Paese sera*, 27 April 1971, 16.
Seguin, Louis. 'Hommes et loups. Le loups sans le miracle.' *Positif* 24 (November 1957), 40–1.
Silvestri, Roberto. 'Il cinema italiano dal 1929 al 1943.' *Il manifesto*, 23 October 1976, 10.
Solmi, Angelo. '"Caccia tragica" non ha portato voti al fronte, il film di Giuseppe De Santis doveva essere l'antidoto di "Ninotchka".' *Oggi*, May 1948, 21.
- 'Non sparate sul regista.' *Oggi illustrato* 28/24 (6 October 1972), 122, 124.
Sparti, Pepa, ed. *Cinema e mondo contadino due esperienze a confronto: Italia e Francia*. Venice: Marsilio Editori, 1982.
Spinazzola, Vittorio. *Cinema e pubblico: Lo spettacolo filmico in Italia, 1945–1965*. Milan: Bompiani, 1974.
- 'Giuseppe De Santis.' *Cinema nuovo* 64 (10 August 1955), 108–10.
- 'Narrativa verista e cinema neorealista.' *Cinema nuovo* 134 (July/August 1958), 11.
- 'Neorealismo e narrativa popolare.' *Cinema nuovo* 62 (February 1955), 27–9.
Tinazzi, Giorgio, ed. *Il cinema italiano degli anni '50*. Venice: Marsilio Editori, 1979.
Tinazzi, Giorgio, and Marina Zancan, eds. *Cinema e letteratura del neorealismo*. Venice: Marsilio Editori, 1990.
Torri, Bruno. *Cinema italiano: Dalla realtà alle metafore*. Palermo: Palumbo, 1973.
Trombadori, Antonello. 'La strada lunga un anno e alcuni problemi del realis-

mo nel cinema.' In *Il cinema di Giuseppe De Santis*, ed. Vincenzo Camerino, 157–77. Lecce: Elle Edizioni, 1982.

Truchtenberg, Peter. *The Casanova Complex*. New York: Poseidon Press, 1981.

Tyler, Parker. *Magic and Myth of the Movies*. London: Secker and Warburg, 1971.

Vaccari, Luigi. '"Riso amaro".' *Il messaggero*, 9 March 1977, 20.

Vargas Llosa, Mario. '"The Children of Columbus": From Violent Conquest to Common Culture.' *Reason*, January 1995, 30–4.

Vento, Giovanni, and Massimo Mida, eds. *Cinema e resistenza*. San Giovanni Valdarno: Luciano Landi Editore, 1959.

Verdone, Mario. *Il cinema neorealista*. Palermo: Celebes, 1977.

Vergano, Aldo. 'L'ANPI presenta.' In *L'avventurosa storia del cinema italiano raccontata dai suoi protagonisti, 1935–1959*, eds. Franca Faldini and Goffredo Fofi, 71–3. Milan: Feltrinelli, 1979.

Vice. 'Pro e contro De Santis.' *Mondo operaio*, 5 January 1954, 23.

Visconti, Luchino. 'Cadaveri.' In *Dai telefoni bianchi al neorealismo*, eds. Massimo Mida and Lorenzo Quaglietti, 147–9. Rome–Bari: Laterza, 1980.

Vitti, Antonio. 'The Influence of Hollywood on De Santis's Earth Trilogy.' In *Italian Americans Celebrate Life: The Arts and Popular Culture*. Selected Proceedings of the 22nd Annual Conference of the American Italian Historical Association, ed. Paola Sensi Isolani and Anthony J. Tamburri, 47–58. Published by the American Italian Historical Association, 1990.

Wagner, Jean. 'Giuseppe De Santis. Dossiers du cinéma.' In *Cinéastes II*, 45–8. Bruxelles: Casterman, 1971.

Wood, Robin. 'Ideology, Genre, Auteur.' *Film Comment*, January/February 1977, 46–51.

Zangrandi, Ruggero. *Il lungo viaggio attraverso il fascismo*, 2d ed. Milan: Feltrinelli, 1962.

Zavattini, Cesare. *Diario cinematografico*. Ed. Valentina Fortichiari. Milan: Bompiani, 1979.

– 'Il neorealismo.' *Il contemporaneo* 2 (July 1955), 6, 27.

– *Neorealismo ecc.* Ed. Mino Argenti. Milan: Bompiani, 1979.

– *Sequences from a Cinematic Life*. Trans. William Weaver. Englewood Cliffs, NJ: Prentice-Hall, 1970.

– 'Una grossa botta in testa al neorealismo.' In *Antologia di 'Cinema nuovo,'* ed. Guido Aristarco, 888–92. Rimini–Florence: Guaraldi Editori, 1975.

Zhdanov, A.A. *Politica e ideologia*. Rome: Editori Riuniti, 1949.

Filmography
Giuseppe De Santis
Born in Fondi, on 11 February 1917

ASSISTANT DIRECTOR

1942 *Ossessione.* Directed by Luchino Visconti
1943 *Scalo merci* (Freight Yard). Started by Roberto Rossellini. Finished by Marcello Paglieri, with the new title *Desiderio* (Desire)
1946 *Il sole sorge ancora* (The Sun Rises Again). Directed by Aldo Vergano

DIRECTOR

1942 *La gatta* (The Cat; no English version)
    Production: Il Centro Sperimentale. Screenplay by Giuseppe De Santis from his original story. The film was made while he was a student at the Centro. Vittorio Duse played the protagonist.
1947 *Caccia tragica* (Tragic Pursuit).
    Production: ANPI Film. Producer: G. Giorgio Agliani. Screenplay by Michelangelo Antonioni, Umberto Barbaro, Giuseppe De Santis, Carlo Lizzani, and Cesare Zavattini, from a story by Giuseppe De Santis, Carlo Lizzani, and Lamberto Rem-Picci. Photographed by Otello Martelli. Camera operators: Carlo Carlini and Gianni Di Venanzo. Scenography and sets by Carlo Egidi. Costumes by Anna Gobbi. Make-up by Guglielmo Bonotti. Music by Giuseppe Rosati, performed by the RAI Orchestra under the direction of Maestro Ferdinando Previtali. Assistant directors: Sergio Grieco and Carlo Lizzani. Director of production: Marcello Caccialupi. Editor: Mario Serandrei. Secretary of production:

Anna Davini. Production: Giovanna Valeri. Shot in the Po Valley. First shown at Ravenna on 11 April 1947. Premiere in Milan, April 1948. Running time: 80 minutes. With: Vivi Gioi (Daniela), Andrea Checchi (Alberto), Carla Del Poggio (Giovanna), Vittorio Duse (Giuseppe), Massimo Girotti (Michele), Checco Rissone (Mimì), Umberto Sacripante (lo Zoppo/lame man), Alfredo Salvadori and Folco Lulli (farm owners), Michele Riccardini (police inspector), Guido della Valle (the German), Ermanno Randi (Andrea), Massimo Rossini (il Camoscio), and Enrico Tachetti (the accountant). Distributor: Libertas Film (1947–8).

The film grossed 80,000,000 lire and placed twenty-eighth for the year 1948. It received The Prize of the Presidency of the Council of Ministers for the best Italian film at the 1947 Venice Film Festival. It also won the Silver Ribbon (ex-aequo, with Lattuada's *Giovanni Episcopo*) for best director (Vivi Gioi received a Silver Ribbon for starring actress); Best Director at the Marianske Lazne Festival on August 1948; and special mention at The Karlovy Vary Festival in 1948.

1948 *Riso amaro* (Bitter Rice)
Production: Lux Film. Producer: Dino De Laurentiis. Screenplay by Giuseppe De Santis, Carlo Lizzani, Gianni Puccini, Corrado Alvaro, Carlo Musso, and Ivo Perilli, from a story by Giuseppe De Santis, Carlo Lizzani, and Gianni Puccini. Photographed by Otello Martelli, assisted by Roberto Gerardi and Luciano Trasatti. Costumes by Anna Gobbi. Make-up by Amato Garbini. Music by Goffredo Petrassi, directed by Maestro Ferdinando Previtali. The song 'Il baion' was composed by Roman Batrov (Armando Trovajoli). Assistant director: Piero Nelli, assisted by Gianni Puccini and Basilio Franchina. Director of production: Luigi De Laurentiis. Editor: Gabriele Varriale. Shot in the rice field of Vercelli. First shown in Florence 21 September 1949. Running time: 100 minutes. With: Vittorio Gassman (Walter), Doris Dowling (Francesca), Silvana Mangano (Silvana Melega), Raf Vallone (Sergeant Marco Galli), Maria Grazia Francia (Gabriella), and Carlo Mazzarella (The vendor). Distributor: Lux Film (1949).

The film grossed 445,000,000 lire and placed fifth for the year. It was nominated for an Oscar for best original story in 1950.

1949 *Non c'è pace tra gli ulivi* (No Peace under the Olives)
Production: Lux Film. Producer: Domenico Forges Davanzati.

Screenplay by Libero De Libero, Carlo Lizzani, Giuseppe De Santis, and Gianni Puccini, from a story by Giuseppe De Santis and Gianni Puccini. Photographed by Piero Portalupi. Camera operated by Marco Scarpelli, assisted by Idelmo Simonelli and Pasqualino De Santis. Costumes by Anna Gobbi. Make-up by Libero Politi. Music by Goffredo Petrassi, directed by Maestro Antonio Pedrotti with the Symphonic Orchestra DISCO. Director of production: Vittorio Glori. Editor: Gabriele Varriale. Shot in the mountains of Ciociaria. First shown in Alassi 10 September 1950. Premiere in Milan 12 November 1950. Running time: 100 minutes. With: Raf Vallone (Francesco Dominici), Lucia Bosè (Lucia Silvestri), Folco Lulli (Agostino Bonfiglio), Maria Grazia Francia (Maria Grazia Dominici), Dante Maggio (Salvatore Capuano), Michele Riccardini (Police inspector), Vincenzo Talarico, Pietro Tordi, Attilio Torelli, Giacomo Sticca, Maddalena Di Trocchio, Giuseppina Corona, Angelina Chiusano, Tommaso Di Gregorio, Giovanni Paparella, Vincenzo Jannone, and Vincenzo Vaticone (all shepherds from Quercie, a district of Fondi). Distributor: Lux Film (1950).

The film grossed 405,000,000 lire and placed fifteenth for the year. It was recognized with various awards in Eastern Europe and a special mention at the Karlovy Vary Festival in 1950.

1952 *Roma, Ore 11* (Rome, 11 O'Clock)
Production: Transcontinental Film Rome–Paris, in association with Titanus Rome. Producer: Paul Graetz. Screenplay by Cesare Zavattini, Basilio Franchina, Giuseppe De Santis, Rodolfo Sonego, Gianni Puccini, and Elio Petri, from the news item of a staircase crash in Rome on Savoia Street, 15 January 1951. Photographed by Otello Martelli. Sets by Léon Barsacq (also artistic director). Costumes by Elio Costanzi. Make-up by Eligio Trani. Music by Mario Nascimbene. Orchestra directed by Ugo Giacomozzi. Assistant director: Elio Petri. Director of production: Giorgio Adriani and Louis Wipf. Shot at Titanus Studios in Farnesina. First shown in Catania 2 February 1952. Running time: 105 minutes. With: Lucia Bosè (Simona), Carla Del Poggio (Luciana), Maria Grazia Francia (Cornelia), Lea Padovani (Caterina), Delia Scala (Angelina), Elena Varzi (Adriana), Raf Vallone (Carlo), Massimo Girotti (Nando), Paolo Stoppa (Father of one of the girls), Armando Francioli (Romoletto), Paola Borboni (Simona's mother), Checco Durante (Adriana's father), Alberto Farnese

(Augusto), Irene Galter (Clara), and Loretta Paoli (Loretta). Distributors: Titanus in Italy and RKO Radio Pictures Inc., for the rest of the world.

The film grossed 270,000,000 lire and placed twenty-second for the year. Mario Nascimbene received The Silver Ribbon for best music. The film was awarded various prizes in South America.

1953 *Un marito per Anna Zaccheo* (A Husband for Anna Zaccheo) Production: The Production Society Domenico Forges Davanzati. Producer: Domenico Forges Davanzati. Screenplay by Giuseppe De Santis, Alfredo Giannetti, Salvatore Laurani, Elio Petri, Gianni Puccini, and Cesare Zavattini, from a story by Giuseppe De Santis, Alfredo Giannetti, and Salvatore Laurani. Photographed by Otello Martelli. Camera operator: Roberto Gerardi, assisted by Arturo Zavattini. Costumes by Paolo Ricci. Make-up by Duilio Giustini. Hairdresser: Gustavo Sisi. Music by Rino Da Positano and Alberto Continisio. Singer: Rino Da Positano (the song 'E cummarelle' is sung by Eduardo Caliendo). Editing secretary: Spartaco Conversi. Assistant directors: Elio Petri and Cesare Aldo Trionfo. Director of production: Vittorio Glori. Edited by Gabriele Varriale. First shown in Cortina d'Ampezzo 22 August 1953. Running time: 95 minutes. With: Silvana Pampanini (Anna Zaccheo), Amedeo Nazzari (Dottor Illuminato), Massimo Girotti (Andrea), Umberto Spadaro (Don Antonio Percuoco), Monica Clay, Anna Galasso, Dora Scarpetta, Agostino Salvietti, Edoardo Imperatrice, Franco Bologna, Giovanni Berardi, Enrico Glori, Enzo Maggio, Nando di Claudio, Nello Ascoli, Renato Terra, and Carletto Sposito. Distributor: Diana Cinematografica.

The film grossed 349,500,000 lire and placed twenty-ninth for the year. Silvana Pampanini was awarded a Silver Medal for acting by the Mexican Film Journalists.

1953 *Giorni d'amore* (Days of Love) Production: Excelsa-Minerva Film. Screenplay by Libero De Libero, Giuseppe De Santis, Elio Petri, and Gianni Puccini. Photographed by Otello Martelli. Camera operator: Roberto Gerardi. Costumes and Art Direction by Domenico Purificato. Sets by Carlo Egidio. Editor: Gabriele Varriale. Music by Mario Nascimbene. Assistant director: Elio Petri. Second Unit assistant director: Paolo Russo. Editing assistants: Maria Sterbini and Ruggero Mastroianni. Hairdresser: Maria Miccinilli. Make-up:

Libero Politi. Director of the production: Nello Meniconi. Editing secretary: Giovanna Valeri. Shot in and around Fondi. First shown in Perugia 10 January 1954. Running time: 109 minutes. With: Marcello Mastroianni (Pasquale Trocchio), Marina Vlady (Angela Cafalla), Angelina Longobardi (Concetta), Dora Scarpetta (Nunziata), Giulio Cali (Grandpa Pietro), Fernando Jacovolta (Adolfo), Renato Chiantoni (Francesco), Pina Galliani (Grandma Filomena), Angelina Chiusano (Loreta), Lucien Gallas (Oreste), Franco Avallone (Leopoldo) Cosimo Poerio (Grandpa Onorato), and Santina Tucci (Teresa). Distributor: Minerva Film (1954).

The film grossed 339,600,000 lire and was thirtieth for the year. Marcello Mastroianni was awarded the Silver Ribbon as best actor. At the 1954–5 San Sebatian Festival, the film was awarded first prize for colour.

1955 *Uomini e lupi* (Men and Wolves)
Production: Trionfalcine and Titanus. Producer: Giovanni Addessi. Screenplay by Giuseppe De Santis, Tonino Guerra, Elio Petri, Ugo Pirro, and Gianni Puccini, with the collaboration of Ivo Perilli, from a story by Giuseppe De Santis, Tonino Guerra, and Elio Petri. Photographed by Piero Portalupi in Eastmanocolor-cinemascope. Camera operator: Idelmo Simonelli, assisted by Pasqualino De Santis. Sets by Ottavio Scotti. Costumes by Graziella Ubinati. Editing by Gabriele Varriale. Music by Mario Nascimbene. Sound by Guido Nardone. Assistant directors: Paolo Russo and Franco Giraldi. Production secretary: Franco Giraldi. Director of production: Alfredo De Laurentiis. The outside scenes were shot at the National Park of Abruzzo, and the interior scenes were filmed at Titanus Studios in Rome. First shown 3 March 1957. Running time: 105 minutes. With: Silvana Mangano (Teresa), Yves Montand (Ricuccio), Pedro Armendariz (Giovanni), Irene Cefaro (Bianca), Giulio Calì (Nazareno), Euro Teodori (Amerigo), Giovanni Matta (Pasqualino), and Guido Celano (Don Pietro). The original length of the film was 3,300 metres, the released version is 2,800 metres. Distributor: Titanus and Trionfalcine.

The film grossed 382,685,000 lire and placed twenty-eighth for the year 1957.

1958 *Cesta Duga Godinu Dana* [*La strada lunga un anno*] (The One-Year-Long Road)
Production: Jadran Film of Zagreb. Producer: Ivo Vrhovec.

Screenplay by Giuseppe De Santis, Maurizio Ferrara, Tonino Guerra, Elio Petri, Gianni Puccini, and Mario Socrate, from a story by Giuseppe De Santis, Elio Petri, and Gianni Puccini. Photographed by Marco Scarpelli in Ultrascope. Camera operators: Pasquale De Santis and Branko Blazina, assisted by Kreso Grcevic and Antun Markic. Assistant director: Franco Giraldi, assisted by Ksto Petanjek and Stipe Delic. Sets by Zrlimir Zagota. Costumes by Oto Reisinger and Jagoda Buic-Bonetti. Production secretary: Dana Loncar. Make-up by Euclide Santoli, Duje Duplancic, and Lojizika Gal. Music by Vladimir Kraus-Rajteric, directed by Maestro Mladen Basic and performed by The Philharmonic Orchestra of Zagreb. Running time: 130 minutes. With: Silvana Pampanini (Giuseppina Pancrazi), Eleonora Rossi Drago (Susanna), Massimo Girotti (Chiacchiera), Bert Sotlar (Guglielmo Cosma), Milivoje Zivanovic (Davide), Gordana Miletic (Angela), Niksa Stefani, Hermina Pipinic, Lya Rho-Barbieri, Antun Vrdoliak, Branko Tatic, Radoiko Jezic, Nada Skrinjar, Rikard Brzeska, Peter Spajic Suljo, Dragica Mezmaric, Augusto Tilic, Aca Stojkoric, Ljubo Dijan, Milan Lentic, Tihomil Polanec, Zdeavko Smovrev, Milan Ramljak, Ljudovit Galic, Marko Soljacic, Alexandar Andrijic, Zeliko Ringl, Moric Danon, Dragan Knapic, and Ivo Pajer. Distributor: Cino Del Duca. First shown in summer 1958 in Pola at the Yugoslav International Film Festival where it was awarded a prize. The film was never well distributed in Italy and was mostly shown at private screenings. The Italian version was first shown 14 May 1959, in Modena.

De Santis was awarded first prize for Best Director at the 1958 Pola festival. The film was nominated for an Oscar for best foreign film in 1958. It received the Golden Globe in 1949 for best foreign film, and Massimo Girotti was awarded first prize for best actor at the San Francisco Film Festival in 1959.

1960 *La Garçonnière* (The Love-Nest; no English version) Production: Roberto Amoroso. Screenplay by Giuseppe De Santis, Franco Giraldi, Tonino Guerra, and Elio Petri, from a story by Giuseppe De Santis, Tonino Guerra, and Elio Petri. Assistant director: Franco Giraldi, assisted by Mario Tota. Photographed by Roberto Gerardi. Camera operator: Pasqualino De Santis. Assistant camera operators: Ennio Guarnieri and Luciano Graffigna. Sets by Ottavio Scotti. Choreography by Alba Arnova. Editing secretary: Rometta Pietrostefani. Edited by Otello Colangeli.

Music by Mario Nascimbene, directed by Gianni Ferrio; trumpet played by Nini Rosso. Songs: 'Notte lunga notte,' composed by Migliacci-Polito, sung by Domenico Modugno on a Fonit record by Ester Music; 'Nun è peccato' composed by Calise-Rossi, sung by Peppino di Capri on a Carish record; 'Quando vien la sera,' composed by Testa-Rossi sung by Joe Sentieri on a Juke-Box record; 'Favole,' composed by Vinci-Fange-Tassone, sung by Marino Barreto Jr. on a Philips record; 'Sei proprio tu,' composed by Bulzonar-Lucarelli-Tassone, sung by Corrado Loiacono on a Fontana record; 'Ch'aggia fa,' composed by Faiella-Cenci, sung by Peppino di Capri on a Carish record; 'Vivrò per sognare,' composed by Tassone-Danell, sung by Carol Danel on a Fonit record; 'Bamble,' a mambo composed by Tassone-De Martino on a Fonit record; 'Eso es el amor,' composed and sung by Iglesias on a Carish record. Director of production: Giorgio Adriani. Shot at Titanus Studios, Cinecittà, in Rome. First shown 10 October 1960, in Bologna. Running time: 90 minutes. With: Raf Vallone (Alberto Fiorini), Eleonora Rossi Drago (Giulia Fiorini), Marisa Merlini (Pupa), Gordana Miletic (Laura), Nino Castelnuovo (Vincenzo), Maria Fiore (Clementina), Clelia Matania (Angelina), Ennio Girolami (Alvaro), Renato Baldini (Father of the child), Franca Marzi (Mother of the child), Nando Di Claudio, Miranda Campa, Franco Balducci, Luigi Borghese, Piero Bugli, Marrico Melchiorre, Mauro Del Vecchio, M. Antonietta Leoni, Fabio Altamura, and Gabriella Pagani. Distributor: Roberto Amoroso.

    The film grossed 124,436,000 lire. The original length was 3,100 metres. After being cut by the censors, it was released 27 September 1960 at a length of 2,598 metres.

1964 *Italiani brava gente* [*Italiano brava gente*] (Attack or Retreat). Production: Mosfilm and Galatea. Producer: Lionello Santi. Screenplay by Serghei Smirnov, Ennio De Concini, Giuseppe De Santis, Augusto Frassinetti, and Gian Domenico Giagni, from a story by Ennio De Concini and Giuseppe De Santis. Photographed by Tony Secchi. Camera operator: Gino Santini. Assistant director: Luciana Marinucci. Second Unit director: Dimitri Vassiliev. Scenography by Ermanno Manco. Costumes by Luciana Marinucci. Edited by Mario Serandrei and Claudia Moskvina, assisted by Lina Caterini. Directors of production: Alexander But and Luigi Millozza. Music by Armando Trovajoli. The external episodes were shot on the Bessarabia Front on the River Bug-Kniepro-Petrovsk and on the Don-Front, where the 1941–3 Italian–Russian campaign took place. First shown in Italy on 9 April 1964, in Rome. Running time: 104 minutes. With: Arthur Kennedy (Major Ferro Maria Ferri), Tatiana Samojlova (Sonia), Gianna Prokhorenko (Katja), Raffaele Pisu (Libero Gabrielli), Andrea Checchi (Colonel Sermonti), Riccardo Cucciolla (Giuseppe Sanna), Nino Vingelli (Sergeant Manfredonia), Lev Prygunov (Loris Bazzocchi), Peter Falk (Dr Mario Salvioni), Grigorij Mikhailov (Partisan) Valerij Somov (Giuliani), Gino Pernice (Collodi), Boris Kozhukhov (Major), S. Lukyanov (Partisan leader), Yu Kaberdaze (Russian prisoner), I. Paramanov (German), E. Knausmuller (German general), Ya. Yanakiev (Doctor), Vincenzo Polizzi (The Sicilian), Franco Morici, Pasqualino Ferri, Mario Annibali, Alvaro Caccarelli, Livia Contardi. Distributor: Titanus.

The film grossed 573,351,000 lire.

1972 *Un apprezzato professionista di sicuro avvenire* (An Esteemed Professional with a Secure Future; no English version)
Production: Film-Nova (Giuseppe De Santis and Giorgio Salvioni). Screenplay and story by Giuseppe De Santis and Giorgio Salvioni. Photographed by Carlo Carlini. Camera operator: Sergio Martinelli. Sets, scenography, and costumes by Giuseppe Selmo and Enrico Checchi. Music by Maurizio Vandelli directed by Natale Massara. 'Quis, quid, Burana' is based on Vandelli's personal adaptation of *Carmina Burana*. Edited by Adriano Tagliavia. Assistant to the director: Ferruccio Castronuovo. Editing secretary: Flavia Vanin. Artistic director: Giuseppe De Santis. First shown in Rimini 4 July 1972. Running time: 100 minutes. With Lino Capolicchio (Vincenzo Arduni), Riccardo Cucciolla (Nicola Parella), Fermi Benussi (Lucietta Arduni), Robert Hoffmann (Don Marco), Andrea Checchi (Vincenzo's father), Ivo Garrani (Lucietta's father), Yvonne Sanson (Lucietta's mother), Nino Vingelli (Police inspector), Massimo Serato (Monsignor), Luisa De Santis (Maria), Vittorio Duse, Annamaria Dossena, Pietro Zardini, Giulio Massimini, Ugo Carboni, Sergio Serafini, Winni Riva, Bianca Mallerini Zardini, Giovanni Sabbatini, Luigi Daniela De Simon, Cesare De Vita, Stefania Fassio, Eugenio Galadini, Claudio Giorgiutti, Letizia Lehir, Enrico Papa, Giancarlo Piacentini and Toni Ventura. Distributor: CIDIF.

Gross-receipt figure not available.

SCREENWRITER

1940 *Don Pasquale*, in collaboration with Gianni Puccini. Directed by Camillo Mastrocinque.

1942 *Ossessione*, in collaboration with Gianni Puccini, Mario Alicata, and Luchino Visconti. Directed by Luchino Visconti.

1943 *Desiderio*, in collaboration with Roberto Rossellini. Started by Roberto Rossellini and finished by Marcello Pagliero in 1945.

1946 *Il sole sorge ancora*, in collaboration with Guido Aristarco, Carlo Lizzani, and Aldo Vergano. Directed by Aldo Vergano.
Ultimo amore, in collaboration with Luigi Chiarini. Directed by Luigi Chiarini.

1951 *Il capitano di Venezia*, in collaboration with Gianni Puccini. Directed by Gianni Puccini. In *Filmlexicon degli autori e delle opere*, edited by Filippo Maria De Sanctis, Giuseppe De Santis is listed as collaborating on the screenplay, which he denies.

1953 *Donne proibite*, in collaboration with Giuseppe Amato. Directed by Giuseppe Amato.

1964 *La visita*. De Santis wrote the subject. Directed by Antonio Pietrangeli.

Index